. . .

EDGAR ALLAN POE

EDGAR ALLAN POE READER

COURAGE
BOOKS

an imprint of
RUNNING PRESS
Philadelphia, Pennsylvania

Canadian representatives: General Publishing Co., Ltd.,
30 Lesmill Road, Don Mills, Ontario M3B 2T6.

International representatives: Worldwide Media Services, Inc.,
30 Montgomery Street, Jersey City, New Jersey 07302.

9 8 7 6 5 4 3 2 1
Digit on the right indicates the number of this printing.

Library of Congress Cataloging-in-Publication Number 92−54932

ISBN 1−56138−277−9

Editor: Ashley Stoudt
Portrait of Edgar Allan Poe provided by The Granger Collection, New York
Cover design by Toby Schmidt
Interior design by Elizabeth Schwartz
Typography: ITC Berkeley Oldstyle, by Deborah Lugar

Published by Courage Books, an imprint of
Running Press Book Publishers
125 South Twenty-second Street
Philadelphia, Pennsylvania 19103

. . .

INTRODUCTION

ALTHOUGH EDGAR ALLAN POE is recognized as the originator of the mystery story genre and as a master of the short story, literary critics and the general public have debated the extent of both his genius and his madness since his death in 1849.

Poe rose from destitute beginnings to a childhood of relative comfort, only to descend through poverty and mental illness to an early death at the age of forty. In his short career, he produced dozens of poems, stories, and critical essays that reflect his brilliant, creative intellect.

Born in 1809 into a family of traveling actors, Poe was orphaned by the time he was four. He was taken into the home of a prosperous businessman in Richmond, Virginia, but he was never formally adopted – a situation that undoubtedly reinforced the instability of his early life. At the encouragement of his new family, Poe enrolled at the University of Virginia, but he neglected his studies for a wild crowd of friends and was eventually expelled. This provoked a fallout with his father, and Poe moved to Boston. There he published his first collection of poems, *Tamerlane and Other Poems*, in 1827; it received little attention.

After a few years in the Army as an enlisted man, Poe reconciled with his adoptive father, who secured him a place at West Point. But Poe was expelled from there too, precipitating a final break with his family. During his time at West Point, he published a second volume of poems, although these did not earn him much acclaim.

Poe eventually moved to Baltimore to live with his impoverished aunt and her daughter, Virginia. Although Virginia was only fourteen years old, they married. Poe was obviously devoted to his young wife, and idealized images of her appear in many of his female characters. It is difficult to suppose, however, that they shared a marriage of equanimity, since she was many years younger and chronically ill with tuberculosis.

Poe wrote for various newspapers and magazines during this time, making great strides in literary criticism and developing his short-story style, but he achieved no monetary success. His sensitive personality and a hereditary tendency to neurosis contributed to a tragic mental decline; however, this only seems to have reinforced the brilliant imagery and fascinating morbidity that he achieved in his tales. Many critics speculate that Poe also suffered from alcoholism and opium addiction. The fantastical quality of his work earned him a devoted posthumous following in France, but he was generally disparaged by his American contemporaries.

Poe's stunning imagination and macabre style continue to provoke strong reactions from readers. This collection gathers the most representative of his poems and tales, revealing both the terrible sense of horror and the romantic beauty produced by Poe's troubled genius.

. . .

CONTENTS

INTRODUCTION

A DREAM

A WILDER'D BEING from my birth
   My spirit spurn'd control,
But now, abroad on the wide earth,
   Where wand'rest thou my soul?

In visions of the dark night
   I have dreamed of joy departed—
But a waking dream of life and light
   Hath left me broken-hearted.

And what is not a dream by day
   To him whose eyes are cast
On things around him with a ray
   Turned back upon the past?

That holy dream—that holy dream,
   While all the world were chiding,
Hath cheered me as a lovely beam
   A lonely spirit guiding.

What though that light, thro' misty night,
   So dimly shone afar—
What could there be more purely bright
   In Truth's day-star?

[1827]

S ONG :   T O ____

I SAW THEE on thy bridal day—
    When a burning blush came o'er thee,
Though happiness around thee lay,
    The world all love before thee:

And in thine eye the kindling light
    Of young passion free
Was all on Earth my chain'd sight
    Of Loveliness might see.

That blush, I ween, was maiden shame—
    As such it well may pass—
Though its glow hath raised a fiercer flame
    In the breast of him, alas!

Who saw thee on that bridal day,
    When that deep blush *would* come o'er thee,
Though happiness around thee lay,
    The world all love before thee.

[1827]

THE LAKE

IN YOUTH'S SPRING, it was my lot
To haunt of the wide earth a spot
The which I could not love the less;
So lovely was the loneliness
Of a wild lake, with black rock bound,
And the tall trees that tower'd around.
But when the night had thrown her pall
Upon that spot—as upon all,
And the wind would pass me by
In its stilly melody,
My infant spirit would awake
To the terror of the lone lake.
Yet that terror was not fright—
But a tremulous delight,
And a feeling undefin'd,
Springing from a darken'd mind.
Death was in that poison'd wave
And in its gulf a fitting grave
For him who thence could solace bring
To his dark imagining;
Whose wild'ring thought could even make
An Eden of that dim lake.

[1827]

TAMERLANE

(Poe's original footnotes appear throughout the poem.)

I.

I HAVE SENT for thee, holy friar;[1]
But 'twas not with the drunken hope,
Which is but agony of desire
To shun the fate, with which to cope
Is more than crime may dare to dream,
That I have call'd thee at this hour:
Such father is not my theme—
Nor am I mad, to deem that power
Of earth may shrive me of the sin
Unearthly pride hath revell'd in—
I would not call thee fool, old man,
But hope is not a gift of thine;
If I *can* hope (O God! I can)
It falls from an eternal shrine.

II.

The gay wall of this gaudy tower
Grows dim around me—death is near.
I had not thought, until this hour
When passing from the earth, that ear
Of any, were it not the shade
Of one whom in life I made

---

1. Of the history of Tamerlane little is known; and with that little, I have taken the full liberty of a poet.—That he was descended from the family of Zinghis Khan is more than probable—but he is vulgarly supposed to have been the son of a shepherd, and to have raised himself to the throne by his own address. He died in the year 1405, in the time of Pope Innocent VII.

How I shall account for giving him "a friar," as a death-bed confessor—I cannot exactly determine. He wanted some one to listen to his tale—and why not a friar? It does not pass the bounds of possibility—quite sufficient for my purposes—and I have at least good authority on my side for such innovations.

All mystery but a simple name,
Might know the secret of a spirit
Bow'd down in sorrow, and in shame.–
Shame said'st thou?
　　Aye I did inherit
That hated portion, with the fame,
The worldly glory, which has shown
A demon-light around my throne,
Scorching my sear'd heart with a pain
Not Hell shall make me fear again.

III.

　　I have not always been as now–
The fever'd diadem on my brow
I claim'd and won usurpingly–
Aye–the same heritage hath giv'n
Rome to the Caesar–this to me;
The heirdom of a kingly mind–
And a proud spirit, which hath striv'n
Triumphantly with human kind.
　　In mountain air I first drew life;
The mists of the Taglay have shed[2]
Nightly their dews on my young head;
And my brain drank their venom then,
When after day of perilous strife
With chamois, I would seize his den
And slumber, in my pride of power,
The infant monarch of the hour–
For, with the mountain dew by night,
My soul imbib'd unhallow'd feeling;

---

2. The mountains of Belur Taglay are a branch of the Immaus, in the southern part of Independent Tartary. They are celebrated for the singular wildness, and beauty of their vallies.

And I would feel its essence stealing
In dreams upon me—while the light
Flashing from cloud that hover'd o'er,
Would seem to my half closing eye
The pageantry of monarchy!
And the deep thunder's echoing roar
Came hurriedly upon me, telling
Of war, and tumult, where my voice
My *own* voice, silly child! was swelling
(O how would my wild heart rejoice
And leap within me at the cry)
The battle-cry of victory!

IV.

    The rain came down upon my head
But barely shelter'd—and the wind
Pass'd quickly o'er me—but my mind
Was mad'ning—for 'twas man that shed
Laurels upon me—and the rush,
The torrent of the chilly air
Gurgled in my pleas'd ear the crush
Of empires, with the captive's prayer,
The hum of suitors, the mix'd tone
Of flatt'ry round a sov'reign's throne.

    The storm had ceas'd—and I awoke—
Its spirit cradled me to sleep,
And as it pass'd me by, there broke
Strange light upon me, tho' it were
My soul in mystery to steep:
For I was not as I had been;
The child of Nature, without care,
Or thought, save of the passing scene.—

V.

My passions, from that hapless hour,
Usurp'd a tyranny, which men
Have deem'd, since I have reach'd to power
My innate nature—be it so:
But, father, there liv'd one who, then—
Then, in my boyhood, when their fire
Burn'd with a still intenser glow;
(For passion must with youth expire)
Ev'n *then*, who deem'd this iron heart
In woman's weakness had a part.

I have no words, alas! to tell
The loveliness of loving well!
Nor would I dare attempt to trace
The breathing beauty of a face,
Which ev'n to *my* impassion'd mind,
Leaves not its memory behind.
In spring of life have ye ne'er dwelt
Some object of delight upon,
With steadfast eye, tell ye have felt
The earth reel—and the vision gone?
And I have held to mem'ry's eye
One object—and but one—until
Its very form hath pass'd me by,
But left its influence with me still.

VI.

'Tis not to thee that I should name—
Thou can'st not—would'st not dare to think
The magic empire of a flame
Which ev'n upon this perilous brink
Hath fix'd my soul, tho' unforgiv'n
By what it lost for passion—Heav'n.

I lov'd—and O, how tenderly!
Yes! she [was] worthy of all love!
Such as in infancy was mine
Tho' then its *passion* could not be:
'Twas such as angel minds above
Might envy—her young heart the shrine
On which my ev'ry hope and thought
Were incense—then a goodly gift—
For they were childish, without sin,
Pure as her young examples taught;
Why did I leave it and adrift,
Trust to the fickle star within?

VII.

We grew in age, and love together,
Roaming the forest and the wild;
My breast her shield in wintry weather,
And when the friendly sunshine smil'd
And she would mark the op'ning skies,
I saw no Heav'n, but in her eyes—
Ev'n childhood knows the human heart;
For when, in sunshine and in smiles,
From all our little cares apart,
Laughing at her half silly wiles,
I'd throw me on her throbbing breast,
And pour my spirit out in tears,
She'd look up in my wilder'd eye—
There was not need to speak the rest—
No need to quiet her kind fears—
She did not ask the reason why.
The hallow'd mem'ry of those years
Comes o'er me in these lonely hours,
And, with sweet loveliness, appears
As perfume of strange summer flow'rs;

Of flow'rs which we have known before
In infancy, which seen, recall
To mind – not flow'rs alone – but more
Our earthly love – and all.

VIII.

Yes! she was worthy of all love!
Ev'n such as from th' accursed time
My spirit with tempest strove,
When on the mountain peak alone,
Ambition lent it a new tone,
And bade it first to dream of crime,
My phrenzy to her bosom taught:
We still were young: no purer thought
Dwelt in a seraph's breast than *thine;*[3]
For passionate love is still divine:
I lov'd her as an angel might
With ray of the all living light
Which blazes upon Edis' shrine.[4]
It is not surely sin to name,
With such as mine – that mystic flame,
I had no being but in thee!
The world with all its train of bright
And happy beauty (for to me
All was an undefin'd delight)
The world – its joy – its share of pain
Which I felt not – its bodied forms
Of varied being, which contain
The bodiless spirits of the storms,

3. I must beg the reader's pardon for making Tamerlane, a Tartar of the fourteenth century, speak in the same language as a Boston gentleman of the nineteenth: but of the Tartar mythology we have little information.
    4. A deity presiding over virtuous love, upon whose imaginary altar, a sacred fire was continually blazing.

The sunshine, and the calm—the ideal
And fleeting vanities of dreams,
Fearfully beautiful! the real
Nothings of mid-day waking life—
Of an enchanted life, which seems,
Now as I look back, the strife
Of some ill demon, with a power
Which left me in an evil hour,
All that I felt, or saw, or thought,
Crowding, confused became
(With thine unearthly beauty fraught)
Thou—and the nothing of a name.

IX.

The passionate spirit which hath known,
And deeply felt the silent tone
Of its own self supremacy,—
(I speak thus openly to thee,
'Twere folly *now* to veil a thought
With which this aching breast is fraught)
The soul which feels its innate right—
The mystic empire and high power
Giv'n by the energetic might
Of Genius, at its natal hour;
Which knows (believe me at this time,
When falsehood were a ten-fold crime,
There *is* a power in the high spirit
To *know* the fate it will inherit)
The soul, which knows such power, will still
Find *Pride* the ruler of its will.
Yes! I was proud—and ye who know
The magic of that meaning word,
So oft perverted, will bestow
Your scorn, perhaps, when ye have heard

That the proud spirit had been broken,
The proud heart burst in agony
At one upbraiding word or token
Of her that heart's idolatry—
I was ambitious—have ye known
Its fiery passion?—ye have not—
A cottager, I mark'd a throne
Of half the world, as all my own,
And murmur'd at such lowly lot!
But it had pass'd me as a dream
Which, of light step, flies with the dew,
That kindling thought—did not the beam
Of Beauty, which did guide it through
The livelong summer day, oppress
My mind with double loveliness—

X.

We walk'd together on the crown
Of a high mountain, which look'd down
Afar from its proud natural towers
Of rock and forest, on the hills—
The dwindled hills, whence amid bowers
Her own fair hand had rear'd around,
Gush'd shoutingly a thousand rills,
Which as it were, in fairy bound
Embrac'd two hamlets—those our own—
Peacefully happy—yet alone—

I spoke to her of power and pride—
But mystically, in such guise,
That she might deem it naught beside
The moment's converse, in her eyes

I read (perhaps too carelessly)
A mingled feeling with my own;
The flush on her bright cheek, to me,
Seem'd to become a queenly throne
Too well, that I should let it be
A light in the dark wild, alone.

XI.

There–in that hour–a thought came o'er
My mind, it had not known before–
To leave her while we both were young,–
To follow my high fate among
The strife of nations, and redeem
The idle words, which, as a dream
Now sounded to her heedless ear–
I held no doubt–I knew no fear
Of peril in my wild career;
To gain an empire, and throw down
As nuptial dowry–a queen's crown,
The only feeling which possest,
With her own image, my fond breast–
Who, that had known the secret thought
Of a young peasant's bosom then,
Had deem'd him, in compassion, aught
But one, whom phantasy had led
Astray from reason–Among men
Ambition is chain'd down–nor fed
(As in the desert, where the grand,
The wild, the beautiful, conspire
With their own breath to fan its fire)
With thoughts such feeling can command;
Uncheck'd by sarcasm, and scorn
Of those, who hardly will conceive

That any should become "great," born[5]
In their own sphere–will not believe
That they shall stoop in life to one
Whom daily they are wont to see
Familiarly–whom Fortune's sun
Hath ne'er shown dazzlingly upon
Lowly–and of their own degree–

XII.

I pictur'd to my fancy's eye
Her silent, deep astonishment,
When, a few fleeting years gone by,
(For short the time my high hope lent
To its most desperate intent,)
She might recall in him, whom Fame
Had gilded with a conquerer's name,
(With glory–such as might inspire
Perforce, a passing thought of one,
Whom she had deem'd in his own fire
Wither'd and blasted; who had gone

5. Although Tamerlane speaks this, it is not the less true. It is a matter of the
greatest difficulty to make the generality of mankind believe that one, with whom they are
upon terms of intimacy, shall be called, in the world, a "great man." The reason is evident.
There are few great men. Their actions are consequently viewed by the mass of people thro'
the medium of distance.–The prominent parts of their character are alone noted; and
those properties, which are minute and common to every one, not being observed, seem to
have no connection with a great character.
    Who ever read the private memorials, correspondence, &c., which have become
so common in our time, without wondering that "great men" should act and think
"so abominably"?

A traitor, violate of the truth
So plighted in his early youth,)
Her own Alexis, who should plight [6]
The love he plighted *then* – again,
And raise his infancy's delight,
The bride and queen of Tamerlane –

XIII.

One noon of a bright summer's day
I pass'd from out the matted bow'r
Where in a deep, still slumber lay
My Ada. In that peaceful hour,
A silent gaze was my farewell.
I had no other solace – then
T' awake her, and a falsehood tell
Of a feign'd journey, were again
To trust the weakness of my heart
To her soft thrilling voice: To part
Thus, haply, while in sleep she dream'd
Of long delight, not yet had deem'd
Awake, that I had held a thought
Of parting, were with madness fraught;
I knew not woman's heart, alas!
Tho' lov'd, and loving – let it pass. –

XIV.

I went from out the matted bow'r,
And hurried madly on my way:
And felt, with ev'ry flying hour,
That bore me from my home, more gay;

---

6. That Tamerlane acquir'd his renown under a feigned name is not entirely a fiction.

There is of earth an agony
Which, ideal, still may be
The worst ill of mortality,
'Tis bliss, in its own reality,
Too real, to *his* breast who lives
Not within himself but gives
A portion of his willing soul
To God, and to the great whole –
To him, whose loving spirit will dwell
With Nature, in her wild paths; tell
Of her wond'rous ways, and telling bless
Her overpow'ring loveliness!
A more than agony to him
Whose failing sight will grow dim
With its own living gaze upon
That loveliness around: the sun –
The blue sky – the misty light
Of the pale cloud therein, whose hue
Is grace to its heav'nly bed of blue;
Dim! tho' looking on all bright!
O God! when the thoughts that may not pass
Will burst upon him, and alas!
For the flight on Earth to Fancy giv'n,
There are no words – unless of Heav'n.

XV.

Look 'round thee now on Samarcand,[7]
Is she not queen of earth? her pride
Above all cities? in her hand
Their destinies? with all beside
Of glory, which the world hath known?
Stands she not proudly and alone?

7. I believe it was after the battle of Angoria that Tamerlane made Samarcand his
residence. It became for a time the seat of learning and the arts.

And who her sov'reign? Timur he[8]
Whom th' astonish'd earth hath seen,
With victory, on victory,
Redoubling age! and more, I ween,
The Zinghis' yet re-echoing fame[9]
And now what has he? what! a name.
The sound of revelry by night
Comes o'er me, with the mingled voice
Of many with a breast as light,
As if 'twere not the dying hour
Of one, in whom they did rejoice –
As in a leader, haply – Power
Its venom secretly imparts;
Nothing have I with human hearts.

XVI.

When Fortune mark'd me for her own,
And my proud hopes had reach'd a throne
(It boots me not, good friar, to tell
A tale the world but knows too well,
How by what hidden deeds of might,
I clamber'd to the tottering height,)
I still was young; and well I ween
My spirit what it e'er had been.
My eyes were still on pomp and power,
My wilder'd heart was far away,
In vallies of the wild Taglay,
In mine own Ada's matted bow'r.

8. He was called Timur Bek as well as Tamerlane.
9. The conquests of Tamerlane far exceeded those of Zinghis Khan. He boasted to
have two thirds of the world at his command.

I dwelt not long in Samarcand
Ere, in a peasant's lowly guise,
I sought my long-abandon'd land,
By sunset did its mountains rise
In dusky grandeur to my eyes:
But as I wander'd on the way
My heart sunk with the sun's ray.
To him, who still would gaze upon
The glory of the summer sun,
There comes, when that sun will from him part,
A sullen hopelessness of heart.
That soul will hate the ev'ning mist
So often lovely, and will list
To the sound of the coming darkness (known
To those whose spirits hark'n)[10] as one
Who in a dream of night *would* fly
But cannot from a danger nigh.
What though the moon—the silvery moon
Shine on his path, in her high noon;
Her smile is chilly, and *her* beam
In that time of dreariness will seem
As the portrait of one after death;
A likeness taken when the breath
Of young life, and the fire o' the eye
Had lately been but had passed by.
'Tis thus when the lovely summer sun
Of our boyhood, his course hath run:
For all we live to know—is known;
And all we seek to keep—hath flown;

10. I have often fancied that I could distinctly hear the sound of the darkness, as it
steals over the horizon—a foolish fancy perhaps, but not more unintelligible than to
see music—
     "The mind the music breathing from her face."

With the noon-day beauty, which is all.
Let life, then, as the day-flow'r fall –
The transient, passionate day-flow'r,[11]
Withering at the ev'ning hour.

XVII.

I reach'd my home – my home no more –
For all was flown that made it so –
I pass'd from out its mossy door,
In vacant idleness of woe.
There met me on its threshold stone
A mountain hunter, I had known
In childhood but he knew me not.
Something he spoke of the old cot:
It had seen better days, he said;
There rose a fountain once, and *there*
Full many a fair flow'r raised its head:
But she who rear'd them was long dead,
And in such follies had no part,
What was there left me *now?* despair –
A kingdom for a broken – heart.

[1827]

11. There is a flow'r, (I have never known its botanic name,) vulgarly called the day flower. It blooms beautifully in the day-light, but withers toward evening, and by night its leaves appear totally shrivelled and dead. I have forgotten, however, to mention in the text, that it lives again in the morning. If it will not flourish in Tartary, I must be forgiven for carrying it thither.

To the River –

FAIR RIVER! IN thy bright, clear flow
   Of labyrinth-like water,
Thou art an emblem of the glow
     Of beauty – the unhidden heart –
     The playful maziness of art
   In old Alberto's daughter;
But when within thy wave she looks –
   Which glistens then, and trembles –
Why, then the prettiest of brooks
   My pretty self resembles;
For in his heart, as in thy stream,
   Her image deeply lies –
His heart which trembles at the beam
   Of her soul-searching eyes.

[1829]

A L A A R A A F

(Among the Arabians, Al Aaraaf, a medium between Heaven and Hell, is supposed to be
located in the celebrated star discovered by Tycho Brahe, which burst forth in one night
upon the eyes of the world, and disappeared as suddenly. – Michael Angelo is represented
as transferred to this star, and speaking to the "lady of his unearthly love" of the
regions he had left. Poe's original footnotes appear throughout the poem.)

PART I

O! NOTHING EARTHLY save the ray
(Thrown back from flowers) of Beauty's eye,
As in those gardens where the day
Springs from the gems of Circassy –
O! nothing earthly save the thrill
Of melody in woodland rill –
Or (music of the passion-hearted)
Joy's voice so peacefully departed
That like the murmur in the shell,
Its echo dwelleth and will dwell –
With nothing of the dross of ours –
Yet all the beauty – all the flowers
That list our Love, and deck our bowers –
Adorn yon world afar, afar –
The wandering star.

'Twas a sweet time for Nesace – for there
Her world lay lolling on the golden air,
Near four bright suns – a temporary rest –
A garden-spot in desert of the blest.
Away – away –'mid seas of rays that roll
Empyrean splendor o'er th' unchained soul –
The soul that scarce (the billows are so dense)
Can struggle to its destin'd eminence –
To distant spheres, from time to time, she rode,
And late to ours, the favour'd one of God –

But, now, the ruler of an anchor'd realm,
She throws aside the sceptre – leaves the helm,
And, amid incense and high spiritual hymns,
Laves in quadruple light her angel limbs.

  Now happiest, loveliest in yon lovely Earth,
Whence sprang the "Idea of Beauty" into birth,
(Falling in wreaths thro' many a startled star,
Like woman's hair 'mid pearls, until, afar,
It lit on hills Achaian, and there dwelt)
She look'd into Infinity – and knelt.
Rich clouds, for canopies, about her curled –
Fit emblems of the model of her world –
Seen but in beauty – not impeding sight
Of other beauty glittering thro' the light –
A wreath that twined each starry form around,
And all the opal'd air in color bound.

  All hurriedly she knelt upon a bed
Of flowers: of lilies such as rear'd the head
On the fair Capo Deucato, and sprang[1]
So eagerly around about to hang
Upon the flying footsteps of ____ – deep pride –
Of her who lov'd a mortal – and so died.[2]
The Sephalica, budding with young bees,
Uprear'd its purple stem around her knees:
And gemmy flower, of Trebizond misnamed –[3]
Inmate of highest stars, where erst it sham'd
All other loveliness: its honied dew
(The fabled nectar that the heathen knew)

1. On Santo Maura – olim Deucadia.
2. Sappho.
3. This flower is much noticed by Lewenhoeck and Tournefort. The bee, feeding
upon its blossom, becomes intoxicated.

Deliriously sweet, was dropp'd from Heaven,
And fell on gardens of the unforgiven
In Trebizond – and on a sunny flower
So like its own above that, to this hour,
It still remaineth, torturing the bee
With madness, and unwonted reverie:
In Heaven, and all its environs, the leaf
And blossom of the fairy plant, in grief
Disconsolate linger – grief that hangs her head,
Repenting follies that full long have fled,
Heaving her white breast to the balmy air,
Like guilty beauty, chasten'd, and more fair:
Nyctanthes too, as sacred as the light
She fears to perfume, perfuming the night:
And Clytia pondering between many a sun,[4]
While pettish tears adown her petals run:
And that aspiring flower that sprang on Earth –[5]
And died, ere scarce exalted into birth,
Bursting its odorous heart in spirit to wing
Its way to Heaven, from garden of a king:
And Valisnerian lotus thither flown[6]
From struggling with the waters of the Rhone:

4. Clytia – The *Chrysanthemum peruvianum*, or, to employ a better-known term, the turnsol – which turns continually towards the sun, covers itself, like Peru, the country from which it comes, with dewy clouds which cool and refresh its flowers during the most violent heat of the day. – *B. de St. Pierre.*

5. There is cultivated in the king's garden at Paris, a species of serpentine aloes without prickles, whose large and beautiful flower exhales a strong odour of the vanilla, during the time of its expansion, which is very short. It does not blow till towards the month of July – you then perceive it gradually open its petals – expand them – fade and die. – *St. Pierre.*

6. There is found, in the Rhone, a beautiful lily of the Valisnerian kind. Its stem will stretch to the length of three or four feet – thus preserving its head above water in the swellings of the river.

And thy most lovely purple perfume, Zante![7]
Isola d'oro!–Fior di Levante!
And the Nelumbo bud that floats for ever [8]
With Indian Cupid down the holy river–
Fair flowers, and fairy! to whose care is given
To bear the Goddess' song, in odors, up to Heaven:[9]
"Spirit! that dwellest where,
      In the deep sky,
The terrible and fair,
      In beauty vie!
Beyond the line of blue–
      The boundary of the star
Which turneth at the view
      Of thy barrier and thy bar–
Of the barrier overgone
      By the comets who were cast
From their pride, and from their throne
      To be drudges till the last–
To be carriers of fire
      (The red fire of their heart)
With speed that may not tire
      And with pain that shall not part–
Who livest–*that* we know–
      In Eternity–we feel–
But the shadow of whose brow
      What spirit shall reveal?
Tho' the beings whom thy Nesace,
Thy messenger hath known

---

7. The Hyacinth.
    8. It is a fiction of the Indians, that Cupid was first seen floating in one of these down the river Ganges–and that he still loves the cradle of his childhood.
    9. And golden vials full of odors which are the prayers of the saints.–*Rev. St. John.*

Have dream'd for thy Infinity
A model of their own – [10]
Thy will is done, Oh, God!
The star hath ridden high
Thro' many a tempest, but she rode
Beneath thy burning eye;
And here, in thought, to thee –
In thought that can alone
Ascend thy empire and so be
A partner of thy throne –
By wingèd Fantasy, [11]
My embassy is given,
Till secrecy shall knowledge be
In the environs of Heaven."

10. The Humanitarians held that God was to be understood as having really a human form. – *Vide Clarke's Sermons*, vol. 1, page 26, fol. edit.

The drift of Milton's argument, leads him to employ language which would appear, at first sight, to verge upon their doctrine, but it will be seen immediately, that he guards himself against the charge of having adopted one of the most ignorant errors of the dark ages of the church. – Dr. *Sumner's Notes on Milton's Christian Doctrine.*

This opinion, in spite of many testimonies to the contrary, could never have been very general. Audeus, a Syrian of Mesopotamia, was condemned for the opinion, as heretical. He lived in the beginning of the fourth century. His disciples were called Anthropomorphites – *Vide Du Pin.*

Among Milton's minor poems are these lines: –
   Dicite sacrorum præsides nemorum Deæ, &c.
   Quis ille primus cujus ex imagine
   Natura solers finxit humanum genus?
   Eternus, incorruptus, æquævus polo,
   Unusque et universus exemplar Dei. – And afterwards,
   Non cui profundum Cæcitas lumen dedit
   Dircæus augur vidit hunc alto sinu, &c.
   [Speak ye goddesses who rule over the sacred groves, etc.
   Who was the first one in whose image
   Skillful nature formed the human race?
   Eternal, untainted, as old as the heavens,
   He was the one, universal pattern [used by] God.
   The Theban soothsayer, to whom Blindness gave vast light,
   Did not see this deep in his bosom, etc.]
11. Seltsamen Tochter Jovis
   Seinem Schosskinde
   Der Phantasie. – *Goethe*

She ceas'd–and buried then her burning cheek
Abash'd, amid the lilies there, to seek
A shelter from the fervour of His eye;
For the stars trembled at the Deity.
She stirr'd not–breath'd not–for a voice was there
How solemnly pervading the calm air!
A sound of silence on the startled ear
Which dreamy poets name "the music of the sphere."
Silence is the voice of God–
Ours is a world of words: Quiet we call
"Silence"–which is the merest word of all.
Here Nature speaks, and ev'n ideal things
Flap shadowy sounds from visionary wings–
But ah! not so when, in the realms on high
The eternal voice of God is moving by,
And the red winds are withering in the sky!

"What tho' in worlds which sightless cycles run,[12]
Link'd to a little system, and one sun–
Where all my love is folly and the crowd
Still think my terrors but the thunder cloud,
The storm, the earthquake, and the ocean-wrath–
(Ah! will they cross me in my angrier path?)
What tho' in worlds which own a single sun
The sands of Time grow dimmer as they run,
Yet thine is my resplendency, so given
To bear my secrets thro' the upper Heaven.
Leave tenantless thy crystal home, and fly,
With all thy train, athwart the moony sky–
Apart–like fire-flies in Sicilian night,[13]
And wing to other worlds another light!

12. Sightless–too small to be seen–*Legge.*
13. I have often noticed a peculiar movement of the fire-flies:–they will collect in a body and fly off, from a common centre, into innumerable radii.

Divulge the secrets of thy embassy
To the proud orbs that twinkle – and so be
To ev'ry heart a barrier and a ban
Lest the stars totter in the guilt of man!"

Up rose the maiden in the yellow night,
The single-mooned eve! – on Earth we plight
Our faith to one love – and one moon adore –
The birth-place of young Beauty had no more.
As sprang that yellow star from downy hours
Up rose the maiden from her shrine of flowers,
And bent o'er sheeny mountain and dim plain
Her way – but left not yet her Therasæn reign.[14]

PART II

High on a mountain of enamell'd head –
Such as the drowsy shepherd on his bed
Of giant pasturage lying at his ease,
Raising his heavy eyelid, starts and sees,
With many a mutter'd "hope to be forgiven"
What time the moon is quadrated in Heaven –
Of rosy head, that towering far away
Into the sunlit ether, caught the ray
Of sunken suns at eve – at noon of night,
While the moon danc'd with the fair stranger light –
Uprear'd upon such height arose a pile
Of gorgeous columns on th' unburthened air,
Flashing from Parian marble that twin smile
Far down upon the wave that sparkled there,
And nursled the young mountain in its lair.
Of molten stars their pavement, such as fall[15]

14. Therasæa, or Therasea, the island mentioned by Seneca, which, in a moment, arose from the sea to the eyes of astonished mariners.
15. Some star which from the ruin'd roof
    Of shak'd Olympus, by mischance, did fall. – *Milton.*

Thro' the ebon air, besilvering the pall
Of their own dissolution, while they die –
Adorning then the dwellings of the sky.
A dome, by linkèd light from Heaven let down,
Sat gently on these columns as a crown –
A window of one circular diamond, there,
Look'd out above into the purple air,
And rays from God shot down that meteor chain
And hallow'd all the beauty twice again,
Save when, between th' Empyrean and that ring,
Some eager spirit flapp'd a dusky wing.
But on the pillars Seraph eyes have seen
The dimness of this world: that greyish green
That Nature loves the best for Beauty's grave
Lurked in each cornice, round each architrave –
And every sculptur'd cherub thereabout
That from his marble dwelling ventured out,
Seem'd earthly in the shadow of his niche –
Achaian statues in a world so rich?
Friezes from Tadmor and Persepolis – [16]
From Balbec, and the stilly, clear abyss
Of beautiful Gomorrah! – O! the wave[17]
Is now upon thee – but too late to save!

16. Voltaire, in speaking of Persepolis, says, "Je connois bien l'admiration qu'inspirent
ces ruines – mais un palais erigé au pied d'une chaine des rochers sterils – peut il être un
chef d'œuvre des arts! [I know well the admiration that these ruins inspire, but a palace
erected at the foot of a chain of sterile rocks can be a masterpiece of all the arts!]"

17. "Oh! the wave" – Ula Deguisi is the Turkish appellation; but, on its own shores, it is
called Bahar Loth, or Almotanah. There were undoubtedly more than two cities engulphed
in the "dead sea." In the valley of Siddim were five – Adrah, Zeboin, Zoar, Sodom and
Gomorrah. Stephen of Byzantium mentions eight, and Strabo thirteen, (engulphed) – but
the last is out of all reason.

It is said, (Tracitus, Strabo, Josephus, Daniel of St. Saba, Nau, Maundrell, Troilo,
D'Arvieux) that after an excessive drought, the vestiges of columns, walls, &c. are seen
above the surface. At any season, such remains may be discovered by looking down into
the transparent lake, at such distances as would argue the existence of many settlements in
the space now usurped by the 'Asphaltites.'

Far down within the crystal of the lake
Thy swollen pillars tremble – and so quake
The hearts of many wanderers who look in
Thy luridness of beauty – and of sin.

Sound loves to revel in a summer night:
Witness the murmur of the grey twilight
That stole upon the ear, in Eyraco,[18]
Of many a wild star-gazer long ago –
That stealeth ever on the ear of him
Who, musing, gazeth on the distance dim.
And sees the darkness coming as a cloud –
Is not its form – its voice – most palpable and loud?[19]

But what is this? – it cometh – and it brings
A music with it –'tis the rush of wings –
A pause – and then a sweeping, falling strain
And Nesace is in her halls again.
From the wild energy of wanton haste
    Her cheek was flushing, and her lips apart;
And zone that clung around her gentle waist
    Had burst beneath the heaving of her heart.
Within the centre of that hall to breathe
She paus'd and panted, Zanthe! all beneath,
The fairy light that kiss'd her golden hair
And long'd to rest, yet could but sparkle there!

Young flowers were whispering in melody[20]
To happy flowers that night – and tree to tree;

18. Eyraco – Chaldea.
19. I have often thought I could distinctly hear the sound of the darkness as it stole over the horizon.
20. Fairies use flowers for their charactery. – *Merry Wives of Windsor.*

Fountains were gushing music as they fell
In many a star-lit grove, or moon-lit dell;
Yet silence came upon material things—
Fair flowers, bright waterfalls and angel wings—
And sound alone that from the spirit sprang
Bore burthen to the charm the maiden sang:
" 'Neath blue-bell or streamer—
      Or tufted wild spray
That keeps, from the dreamer,
      The moonbeam away—[21]
Bright beings! that ponder,
      With half closing eyes,
On the stars which your wonder
      Hath drawn from the skies,
Till they glance thro' the shade, and
      Come down to your brow
Like—eyes of the maiden
      Who calls on you now—
Arise! from your dreaming
      In violet bowers,
To duty beseeming
      These star-litten hours—
And shake from your tresses
      Encumber'd with dew
The breath of those kisses
      That cumber them too—
(O! how, without you, Love!
      Could angels be blest?)
Those kisses of true love
      That lull'd ye to rest!

---

21. In Scripture is this passage—"The sun shall not harm thee by day, nor the moon by night." It is perhaps not generally known that the moon, in Egypt, has the effect of producing blindness to those who sleep with the face exposed to its rays, to which circumstance the passage evidently alludes.

Up!–shake from your wing
    Each hindering thing:
The dew of the night–
    It would weigh down your flight;
And true love caresses–
    O! leave them apart!
They are light on the tresses,
    But hang on the heart.
Ligeia! Ligeia!
    My beautiful one!
Whose harshest idea
    Will to melody run,
O! is it thy will
    On the breezes to toss?
Or, capriciously still,
    Like the lone Albatross,[22]
Incumbent on night
    (As she on the air)
To keep watch with delight
    On the harmony there?

Ligeia! wherever
    Thy image may be,
No magic shall sever
    Thy music from thee.
Thou hast bound many eyes
    In a dreamy sleep–
But the strains still arise
    Which *thy* vigilance keep–
The sound of the rain
    Which leaps down to the flower,
And dances again
    In the rhythm of the shower–

22. The Albatross is said to sleep on the wing.

The murmur that springs[23]
From the growing of grass
Are the music of things –
But are modell'd, alas! –
Away, then my dearest,
O! hie thee away
To springs that lie clearest
Beneath the moon-ray –
To lone lake that smiles,
In its dream of deep rest,
At the many star-isles
That enjewel its breast –
Where wild flowers, creeping,
Have mingled their shade,
On its margin is sleeping
Full many a maid –
Some have left the cool glade, and
Have slept with the bee –[24]
Arouse them my maiden,
On moorland and lea –
Go! breathe on their slumber,
All softly in ear,
The musical number
They slumber'd to hear –

23. I met with this idea in an old English tale, which I am now unable to obtain and
quote from memory: –"The verie essence and, as it were, springeheade and origine of all
musiche is the verie pleasaunte sounde which the trees of the forest do make when
they growe."
24. The wild bee will not sleep in the shade if there be moonlight.
   The rhyme in this verse, as in one about sixty lines before, has an appearance of
affectation. It is, however, imitated from Sir W. Scott, or rather from Claud Halcro – in
whose mouth I admired its effect:
      O! were there an island,
      Tho' ever so wild
      Where woman might smile, and
      No man be beguil'd, &c.

For what can awaken
An angel so soon
Whose sleep hath been taken
Beneath the cold moon,
As the spell which no slumber
Of witchery may test,
The rhythmical number
Which lull'd him to rest?"

Spirits in wing, and angels to the view,
A thousand seraphs burst th' Empyrean thro',
Young dreams still hovering on their drowsy flight –
Seraphs in all but "Knowledge," the keen light
That fell, refracted, thro' thy bounds, afar
O Death! from eye of God upon that star:
Sweet was that error – sweeter still that death –
Sweet was that error – ev'n with us the breath
Of Science dims the mirror of our joy –
To them 'twere the Simoom, and would destroy –
For what (to them) availeth it to know
That Truth is Falsehood – or that Bliss is Woe?
Sweet was their death – with them to die was rife
With the last ecstasy of satiate life –
Beyond that death no immortality
But sleep that pondereth and is not "to be" –
And there – oh! may my weary spirit dwell –
Apart from Heaven's Eternity – and yet how far from Hell![25]

25. With the Arabians there is a medium between Heaven and Hell, where men suffer
no punishment, but yet do not attain that tranquil and even happiness which they suppose
to be characteristic of heavenly enjoyment.

Un no rompido sueno –
Un dia puro – allegre – libre
Quiera –
Libre de amor – de zelo –
De odio – de esperanza – de rezelo. – *Luis Ponce de Leon.*

What guilty spirit, in what shrubbery dim,
Heard not the stirring summons of that hymn?
But two: they fell: for Heaven no grace imparts
To those who hear not for their beating hearts.
A maiden-angel and her seraph-lover –
O! where (and ye may seek the wide skies over)
Was Love, the blind, near sober Duty known?
Unguided Love hath fallen –'mid "tears of perfect moan."²⁶

He was a goodly spirit – he who fell:
A wanderer by mossy-mantled well –
A gazer on the lights that shine above –
A dreamer in the moonbeam by his love:
What wonder? for each star is eye-like there,
And looks so sweetly down on Beauty's hair –
And they, and ev'ry mossy spring were holy
To his love-haunted heart and melancholy.
The night had found (to him a night of wo)
Upon a mountain crag, young Angelo –
Beetling it bends athwart the solemn sky,
And scowls on starry worlds that down beneath it lie.
Here sate he with his love – his dark eye bent
With eagle gaze along the firmament:
Now turned it upon her – but ever then
It trembled to one constant star again.

"Ianthe, dearest, see! how dim that ray!
How lovely 'tis to look so far away!

Sorrow is not excluded from "Al Aaraaf," but it is that sorrow which the living love to cherish for the dead, and which, in some minds, resembles the delirium of opium. The passionate excitement of Love and the buoyancy of spirit attendant upon intoxication are its less holy pleasures – the price of which, to those souls who make choice of "Al Aaraaf" as their residence after life, is final death and annihilation.
    26. There be tears of perfect moan
       Wept for thee in Helicon.–*Milton.*

She seem'd not thus upon that autumn eve
I left her gorgeous halls – not mourn'd to leave.
That eve – that eve – I should remember well –
The sun-ray dropp'd, in Lemnos, with a spell
On th' Arabesque carving of a gilded hall
Wherein I sate, and on the draperied wall –
And on my eye-lids – O the heavy light!
How drowsily it weigh'd them into night!
On flowers, before, the mist, and love they ran
With Persian Saadi in his Gulistan:
But O that light! – I slumber'd – Death, the while,
Stole o'er my senses in that lovely isle
So softly that no single silken hair
Awoke that slept – or knew that it was there.
The last spot of her orb I trod upon
Was a fair temple called Parthenon – [27]
More beauty clung around her columned wall
Than even thy glowing bosom beats withal,[28]
And when old Time my wing did disenthral
Thence sprang I – as the eagle from his tower,
And years I left behind me in an hour.
What time upon her airy bounds I hung
One half the garden of her globe was flung
Unrolling as a chart unto my view –
Tenantless cities of the desert too!
Ianthe, beauty crowded on me then,
And half I wish'd to be again of men."

27. It was entire in 1687 – the most elevated building in Athens.
28. Shadowing more beauty in their airy brows
     Than have the white breasts of the Queen of Love. – Marlowe.

"My Angelo! and why of them to be?
A brighter dwelling-place is here for thee –
And greener fields than in yon world above,
And woman's loveliness – and passionate love."

"But, list, Ianthe! when the air so soft
Fail'd, as my pennon'd spirit leapt aloft,[29]
Perhaps my brain grew dizzy – but the world
I left so late was into chaos hurl'd –
Sprang from her station, on the winds apart,
And roll'd, a flame, the fiery Heaven athwart.
Methought, Ianthe, then I ceas'd to soar
And fell – not swiftly as I rose before,
But with a downward, tremulous motion thro'
Light, brazen rays, this golden star unto!
Nor long the measure of my falling hours,
For nearest of all stars was thine to ours –
Dread star! that came, amid their night of mirth,
A red Dædalion on the timid Earth."

"We came – my Angelo – but not to us
Be given our lady's bidding to discuss:
We came, my love; around, above, below,
Gay fire-fly of the night we come and go,
Nor ask a reason save the angel-nod
She gives to us as given by her God –
But truly, Angelo, grey Time unfurl'd
Never his fairy wing o'er fairier world!

29. Pennon – for pinion. – *Milton*.

Dim was its little disk, and seraph eyes
Alone could see the phantom in the skies,
when first Al Aaraaf knew her course to be
Headlong thitherward o'er the starry sea—
But when its glory swell'd upon the sky,
As glowing Beauty's bust beneath man's eye,
We paus'd before the heritage of men,
And thy star trembled—as doth Beauty then!"

Thus, in discourse, the lovers whiled away
The night that waned and waned and brought no day.
They fell: for Heaven to them no hope imparts
Who hear not for the beating of their hearts.

                                        [1829]

ISRAFEL

And the angel Israfel who has the sweetest voice of all God's creatures. – KORAN

I

IN HEAVEN A spirit doth dwell
Whose heart-strings are a lute –
None sing so wild – so well
As the angel Israfel –
And the giddy stars are mute.

II

Tottering above
In her highest noon
The enamoured moon
Blushes with love –
While, to listen, the red levin
Pauses in Heaven.

III

And they say (the starry choir
And all the listening things)
That Israfel's fire
Is owing to that lyre
With those unusual strings.

IV

But the Heavens that angel trod
Where deep thoughts are a duty –
Where Love is a grown god –
Where Houri glances are –
–Stay! turn thine eyes afar! –
Imbued with all the beauty
Which we worship in yon star.

V

Thou art not, therefore, wrong
Israfel, who despisest
An unimpassion'd song:
To thee the laurels belong
Best bard,–because the wisest.

VI

The extacies above
With thy burning measures suit–
Thy grief–if any–thy love
With the fervor of thy lute–
Well may the stars be mute!

VII

Yes, Heaven is thine: but this
Is a world of sweets and sours:
Our flowers are merely–flowers,
And the shadow of thy bliss
Is the sunshine of ours.

VIII

If I did dwell where Israfel
Hath dwelt, and he where I,
He would not sing one half as well–
One half as passionately,
And a stormier note than this would swell
From my lyre within the sky.

[1831]

THE VALLEY NIS
[THE VALLEY OF UNREST]

FAR AWAY — FAR away —
Far away — as far at least
Lies that valley as the day
Down within the golden east —
All things lovely — are not they
Far away — far away?

It is called the valley Nis.
And a Syriac tale there is
Thereabout which Time hath said
Shall not be interpreted.
Something about Satan's dart —
Something about angel wings —
Much about a broken heart —
All about unhappy things:
But "the valley Nis" at best
Means "the valley of unrest."

Once it smiled a silent dell
Where the people did not dwell,
Having gone unto the wars —
And the sly mysterious stars,
With a visage full of meaning,
O'er the unguarded flowers were leaning:
Or the sun ray dripp'd all red
Thro' the tulips overhead,
Then grew paler as it fell
On the quiet Asphodel.

Now the *unhappy* shall confess
Nothing there is motionless:
Helen, like thy human eye
There th' uneasy violets lie—
There the reedy grass doth wave
Over the old forgotten grave—
One by one from the tree top
There the eternal dews do drop—
There the vague and dreamy trees
Do roll like seas in northern breeze
Around the stormy Hebrides—
There the gorgeous clouds do fly,
Rustling everlastingly,

Through the terror-stricken sky,
Rolling like a waterfall
O'er th' horizon's fiery wall—
There the moon doth shine by night
With a most unsteady light—
There the sun doth reel by day
"Over the hills and far away."

And Helen, like thy human eye,
Low crouched on Earth, some violets lie,
And, nearer Heaven, some lilies wave
All banner-like, above *a grave*.
And one by one, from out their tops
Eternal dews come down in drops,
Ah, one by one, from off their stems
Eternal dews come down in gems!

                                   [1831]

The Doomed City
[The City in the Sea]

Lo! Death hath rear'd himself a throne
In a strange city, all alone,
Far down within the dim west—
And the good, and the bad, and the worst, and the best,
Have gone to their eternal rest.

There shrines, and palaces, and towers
Are—not like any thing of ours—
O! no—O! no—*ours* never loom
To heaven with that ungodly gloom!
Time-eaten towers that tremble not!
Around, by lifting winds forgot,
Resignedly beneath the sky
The melancholy waters lie.

A heaven that God doth not contemn
With stars is like a diadem—
We liken our ladies' eyes to them—
But there! that everlasting pall!
It would be mockery to call
Such dreariness a heaven at all.

Yet tho' no holy rays come down
On the long night-time of that town,
Light from the lurid, deep sea
Streams up the turrets silently—
Up thrones—up long-forgotten bowers
Of sculptur'd ivy and stone flowers—
Up domes—up spires—up kingly halls—
Up fanes—up Babylon-like walls—

Up many a melancholy shrine
Whose entablatures intertwine
The mast – the viol – and the vine.

There open temples – open graves
Are on a level with the waves –
But not the riches there that lie
In each idol's diamond eye,
Not the gaily-jewell'd dead
Tempt the waters from their bed:
For no ripples curl, alas!
Along that wilderness of glass –
No swellings hint that winds may be
Upon a far-off happier sea:
So blend the turrets and shadows there
That all seem pendulous in air,
While from the high towers of the town
Death looks gigantically down.

But lo! a stir is in the air!
The wave! there is a ripple there!
As if the towers had thrown aside,
In slightly sinking, the dull tide –
As if the turret-tops had given
A vacuum in the filmy heaven:
The waves have now a redder glow –
The very hours are breathing low –
And when, amid no earthly moans,
Down, down that town shall settle hence,
Hell rising from a thousand thrones
Shall do it reverence,
And Death to some more happy clime
Shall give his undivided time.

[1831]

S HADOW – A FABLE

Yea! though I walk through the valley of the shadow. . .
                    –Psalm of David

YE WHO READ are still among the living, but I who write shall
have long since gone my way into the region of shadows. For
indeed strange things shall happen, and many secret things be
known, and many centuries shall pass away, ere these
memorials be seen of men. And, when seen, there will be
some to disbelieve, and some to doubt, and yet a few who will
find much to ponder upon in the characters here graven with
a stylus of iron.

The year had been a year of terror, and of feelings more
intense than terror for which there is no name upon the earth.
For many prodigies and signs had taken place, and far and
wide, over sea and land, the black wings of the Pestilence were
spread abroad. To those, nevertheless, cunning in the stars, it
was not unknown that the heavens wore an aspect of ill; and
to me, the Greek Oinos, among others, it was evident that now
had arrived the alternation of that seven hundred and ninety-
fourth year when, at the entrance of Aries, the planet Jupiter is
conjoined with the red ring of the terrible Saturnus. The
peculiar spirit of the skies, if I mistake not greatly, made itself
manifest, not only in the physical orb of the earth, but in the
souls, imaginations, and meditations of mankind.

Over some flasks of the red Chian wine, within the walls
of a noble hall, in a dim city by the melancholy sea, we sat, at
night, a company of seven. And to our chamber there was no
entrance save by a lofty door of brass: and the door was
fashioned by the artisan Corinnos, and, being of rare
workmanship, was fastened from within. Black draperies,
likewise, in the gloomy room, shut out from our view the
moon, the lurid stars, and the peopleless streets – but the

boding and the memory of Evil, they would not be so
excluded. There were things around us and about of which I
can render no distinct account – things material and spiritual.
Heaviness in the atmosphere – a sense of suffocation –
anxiety – and, above all, that terrible state of existence which
the nervous experience when the senses are keenly living and
awake, and meanwhile the powers of thought lie dormant. A
dead weight hung upon us. It hung upon our limbs – upon the
household furniture – upon the goblets from which we drank;
and all things were depressed, and borne down thereby – all
things save only the flames of the seven iron lamps which
illumined our revel. Uprearing themselves in tall slender lines
of light, they thus remained burning all pallid and motionless;
and in the mirror which their lustre formed upon the round
table of ebony at which we sat, each of us there assembled
beheld the pallor of his own countenance, and the unquiet
glare in the downcast eyes of his companions. Yet we laughed
and were merry in our proper way – which was hysterical; and
sang the songs of Anacreon – which are madness; and drank
deeply – although the purple wine reminded us of blood. For
there was yet another tenant of our chamber in the person of
young Zoilus. Dead, and at full length he lay, enshrouded; – the
genius and the demon of the scene. Alas! he bore no portion
in our mirth, save that his countenance, distorted with the
plague, and his eyes in which Death had but half extinguished
the fire of the pestilence, seemed to take such interest in our
merriment as the dead may take in the merriment of those
who are to die. But although I, Oinos, felt that the eyes of the
departed were upon me, still I forced myself not to perceive
the bitterness of their expression, and, gazing down steadily
into the depths of the ebony mirror, sang with a loud and
sonorous voice the songs of the son of Teios. But gradually
my songs they ceased, and their echoes, rolling afar off among
the sable draperies of the chamber, became weak, and

indistinguishable, and so fainted away. And lo! from among those sable draperies where the sounds of the song departed, there came forth a dark and undefined shadow—a shadow such as the moon, when low in heaven, might fashion from the figure of a man: but it was the shadow neither of man, nor of God, nor of any familiar thing. And, quivering awhile among the draperies of the room, it at length rested in full view upon the surface of the door of brass. But the shadow was vague, and formless, and indefinitive, and was the shadow neither of man nor God—neither God of Greece, nor God of Chaldæa, nor any Egyptian God. And the shadow rested upon the brazen doorway, and under the arch of the entablature of the door, and moved not, nor spoke any word, but there became stationary and remained. And the door whereupon the shadow rested was, if I remember aright, over against the feet of the young Zoilus enshrouded. But we, the seven there assembled, having seen the shadow as it came out from among the draperies, dared not steadily behold it, but cast down our eyes, and gazed continually into the depths of the mirror of ebony. And at length I, Oinos, speaking some low words, demanded of the shadow its dwelling and its appellation. And the shadow answered, "I am SHADOW, and my dwelling is near to the Catacombs of Ptolemais, and hard by those dim plains of Helusion which border upon the foul Charonian canal." And then did we, the seven, start from our seats in horror, and stand trembling, and shuddering, and aghast: for the tones in the voice of the shadow were not the tones of any one being, but of a multitude of beings, and, varying in their cadences from syllable to syllable, fell duskily upon our ears in the well remembered and familiar accents of a thousand departed friends.

[September, 1835]

LIGEIA

And the will therein lieth, which dieth not. Who knoweth the
mysteries of the will, with its vigour? For God is but a great will
pervading all things by nature of its intentness. Man doth not yield
himself to the angels, nor unto death utterly, save only through the
weakness of his feeble will.

—JOSEPH GLANVILL.

I CANNOT, FOR my soul, remember how, when, or even precisely
where I first became acquainted with the lady Ligeia. Long
years have since elapsed, and my memory is feeble through
much suffering: or, perhaps, I cannot *now* bring these points to
mind, because, in truth, the character of my beloved, her rare
learning, her singular yet placid cast of beauty, and the
thrilling and enthralling eloquence of her low, musical
language, made their way into my heart by paces, so steadily
and stealthily progressive, that they have been unnoticed and
unknown. Yet I know that I met her most frequently in some
large, old, decaying city near the Rhine. Of her family–I have
surely heard her speak–that they are of a remotely ancient
date cannot be doubted. Ligeia! Buried in studies of a nature
more than all else adapted to deaden impressions of the
outward world, it is by that sweet word alone–by Ligeia, that I
bring before mine eyes in fancy the image of her who is no
more. And not, while I write, a recollection flashes upon me
that I have *never known* the paternal name of her who was my
friend and my betrothed, and who became the partner of my
studies, and eventually the wife of my bosom. Was it a playful
charge on the part of my Ligeia? or was it a test of my strength
of affection that I should institute no inquiries upon this
point? or was it rather a caprice of my own–a wildly romantic
offering on the shrine of the most passionate devotion? I but
indistinctly recall the fact itself–what wonder that I have
utterly forgotten the circumstances which originated or

attended it? And indeed, if ever that spirit which is entitled
Romance – if ever she, the wan and misty-winged *Ashtophet* of
idolatrous Egypt, presided, as they tell, over marriages ill-
omened then most surely she presided over mine.

There is one dear topic, however, on which my memory
faileth me not. It is the person of Ligeia. In stature she was tall,
somewhat slender, and in her latter days even emaciated. I
would in vain attempt to portray the majesty, the quiet ease of
her demeanor, or the incomprehensible lightness and elasticity
of her footfall. She came and departed like a shadow. I was
never made aware of her entrance into my closed study, save
by the dear music of her low sweet voice, as she placed her
delicate hand upon my shoulder. In beauty of face no maiden
ever equalled her. It was the radiance of an opium dream – an
airy and spirit-lifting vision more wildly divine than the
phantasies which hovered about the slumbering souls of the
daughters of Delos. Yet her features were not of that regular
mould which we have been falsely taught to worship in the
classical labors of the Heathen. "There is no exquisite beauty,"
says Verülam, Lord Bacon, speaking truly of all the forms and
genera [types] of beauty, "without some *strangeness* in the
proportions." Yet, although I saw that the features of Ligeia
were not of classic regularity, although I perceived that her
loveliness was indeed "exquisite," and felt that there was much
of "strangeness" pervading it, yet I have tried in vain to detect
the irregularity and to trace home my own perception of "the
strange." I examined the contour of the lofty and pale forehead – it was faultless – how cold indeed that word when
applied to a majesty so divine. The skin rivalling the purest
ivory, the commanding breadth and repose, the gentle
prominence of the regions above the temples, and then the
raven-black, the glossy, the luxuriant and naturally-curling
tresses, setting forth the full force of the Homeric epithet,
"hyacinthine!" I looked at the delicate outlines of the nose –

and nowhere but in the graceful medallions of the Hebrews had I beheld a similar perfection. There was the same luxurious smoothness of surface, the same scarcely perceptible tendency to the aquiline, the same harmoniously curved nostril speaking the free spirit. I regarded the sweet mouth. Here was indeed the triumph of all things heavenly – the magnificent turn of the short upper lip – the soft, voluptuous repose of the under – the dimples which sported, and the colour which spoke – the teeth glancing back with a brilliancy almost startling, every ray of the holy light which fell upon them in her serene and placid, yet most exultingly radiant of all smiles. I scrutinized the formation of the chin – and here, too, I found the gentleness of breadth, the softness and the majesty, the fullness and the spirituality, of the Greek, the contour which the god Apollo revealed but in a dream to Cleomenes, the son of the Athenian. And then I peered into the large eyes of Ligeia.

For eyes we have no models in the remotely antique. It might have been, too, that in these eyes of my beloved lay the secret to which Lord Verülam alludes. They were, I must believe, far larger than the ordinary eyes of our race. They were even fuller than the fullest of the Gazelle eyes of the tribe of the valley of Nourjabad. Yet it was only at intervals – in moments of intense excitement – that this peculiarity became more than slightly noticeable in Ligeia. And at such moments was her beauty – in my heated fancy thus it appeared perhaps – the beauty of beings either above or apart from the earth – the beauty of the fabulous Houri of the Turk. The colour of the orbs was the most brilliant of black, and far over them hung jetty lashes of great length. The brows, slightly irregular in outline, had the same hue. The "strangeness," however, which I have found in the eyes of my Ligeia was of a nature distinct from the formation, or the colour, or the brilliancy of the features, and must, after all, be referred to the *expression*.

Ah, word of no meaning! behind whose vast latitude of mere
sound we intrench our ignorance of so much of the spiritual.
The expression of the eyes of Ligeia! How for long hours have I
pondered upon it! How have I, through the whole of a midsummer night, struggled to fathom it! What was it–that
something more profound than the well of Democritus–which
lay far within the pupils of my beloved? What *was* it? I was
possessed with a passion to discover. Those eyes! those large,
those shining, those divine orbs! they became to me twin stars
of Leda, and I to them devoutest of astrologers. Not for a
moment was the unfathomable meaning of their glance, by day
or by night, absent from my soul.

There is no point, among the many incomprehensible
anomalies of the science of mind, more thrillingly exciting
than the fact–never, I believe, noticed in the schools–that in
our endeavours to recall to memory something long forgotten
we often find ourselves *upon the very verge* of remembrance
without being able, in the end, to remember. And thus, how
frequently, in my intense scrutiny of Ligeia's eyes, have I felt
approaching the full knowledge of the secret of their
expression–felt it approaching–yet not quite be mine–and so
at length utterly depart. And (strange, oh strangest mystery of
all!) I found, in the commonest objects of the universe, a circle
of analogies to that expression. I mean to say that,
subsequently to the period when Ligeia's beauty passed into
my spirit, there dwelling as in a shrine, I derived from many
existences in the material world, a sentiment such as I felt
always aroused within me by her large and luminous orbs. Yet
not the more could I define that sentiment, or analyze, or even
steadily view it. I recognized it, let me repeat, sometimes in the
commonest objects of the universe. It has flashed upon me in
the survey of a rapidly-growing vine–in the contemplation of
a moth, a butterfly, a chrysalis, a stream of running water. I
have felt it in the ocean–in the falling of a meteor. I have felt

it in the glances of unusually aged people. And there are one
or two stars in heaven – (one especially, a star of the sixth
magnitude, double and changeable, to be found near the large
star in Lyra) in a telescopic scrutiny of which I have been
made aware of the feeling. I have been filled with it by certain
sounds from stringed instruments, and not unfrequently by
passages from books. Among innumerable other instances, I
well remember something in a volume of Joseph Glanvill,
which perhaps merely from its quaintness – who shall say?
never failed to inspire me with the sentiment, – "And the will
therein lieth, which dieth not. Who knoweth the mysteries of
the will, with its vigor? For God is but a great will pervading
all things by nature of its intentness. Man doth not yield him
to the angels, nor unto death utterly, but only through the
weakness of his feeble will."

Length of years, and subsequent reflection, have enabled
me to trace, indeed, some remote connection between this
passage in the old English moralist and a portion of the
character of Ligeia. An *intensity* in thought, action, or speech
was possibly, in her, a result, or at least an index, of that
gigantic volition which, during our long intercourse, failed to
give other and more immediate evidence of its existence. Of all
women whom I have ever known she, the outwardly calm, the
ever placid Ligeia, was the most violently a prey to the
tumultuous vultures of stern passion. And of such passion I
could form no estimate, save by the miraculous expansion of
those eyes which at once so delighted and appalled me – by the
almost magical melody, modulation, distinctness, and placidity
of her very low voice – and by the fierce energy (rendered
doubly effective by contrast with her manner of utterance) of
the words which she uttered.

I have spoken of the learning of Ligeia: it was immense –
such as I have never known in woman. In all the classical
tongues was she deeply proficient, and as far as my own

acquaintance extended in regard to the modern dialects of Europe, I have never known her at fault. Indeed upon any theme of the most admired, because simply the most abstruse of the boasted erudition of the academy, have I *ever* found Ligeia at fault? How singularly, how thrillingly, this one point in the nature of my wife has forced itself, at this late period only, upon my attention! I said her knowledge was such as I had never known in woman. Where breathes the man who, like her, has traversed, and successfully *all* the wide areas of moral, natural, and mathematical science? I saw not then what I now clearly perceive, that the acquisitions of Ligeia were gigantic, were astounding—yet I was sufficiently aware of her infinite supremacy to resign myself, with a child-like confidence, to her guidance through the chaotic world of metaphysical investigation at which I was most busily occupied during the earlier years of our marriage. With how vast a triumph—with how vivid a delight—with how much of all that is ethereal in hope—did I *feel*, as she bent over me in studies but little sought for—but less known, that delicious vista by slow but very perceptible degrees expanding before me, down whose long, gorgeous, and all untrodden path I might at length pass onward to the goal of a wisdom too divinely precious not to be forbidden!

How poignant, then, must have been the grief with which, after some years, I beheld my well-grounded expectations take wings to themselves and flee away! Without Ligeia I was but as a child groping benighted. Her presence, her readings alone, rendered vividly luminous the many mysteries of the transcendentalism in which we were immersed. Letters, lambent and golden, grew duller than Saturnian lead, wanting the radiant lustre of her eyes. And now those eyes shone less and less frequently upon the pages over which I pored. Ligeia grew ill. The wild eyes blazed with a too—too glorious effulgence; the pale fingers became of the transparent waxen

hue of the grave – and the blue veins upon the lofty forehead
swelled and sunk impetuously with the tides of the most
gentle emotion. I saw that she must die, and I struggled
desperately in spirit with the grim Azrael. And the struggles of
the passionate Ligeia were, to my astonishment, even more
energetic than my own. There had been much in her stern
nature to impress me with the belief that, to her, death would
have come without its terrors – but not so. Words are impotent
to convey any just idea of the fierceness of resistance with
which Ligeia wrestled with the dark shadow. I groaned in
anguish at the pitiable spectacle. I would have soothed – I
would have reasoned; but in the intensity of her wild desire
for life – for life – *but* for life, solace and reason were alike the
uttermost of folly. Yet not for an instant, amid the most con-
vulsive writhings of her fierce spirit, was shaken the external
placidity of her demeanor. Her voice grew more gentle – grew
more low – yet I would not wish to dwell upon the wild meaning
of the quietly-uttered words. My brain reeled as I hearkened,
entranced, to a melody more than mortal – to assumptions and
aspirations which morality had never before known.

That Ligeia loved me, I should not have doubted; and I
might have been easily aware that, in a bosom such as hers,
love would have reigned no ordinary passion. But in death
only, was I fully impressed with the intensity of her affection.
For long hours, detaining my hand, would she pour out before
me the overflowings of a heart whose more than passionate
devotion amounted to idolatry. How had I deserved to be so
blessed by such confessions? – How had I deserved to be so
cursed with the removal of my beloved in the hour of her
making them? But upon this subject I cannot bear to dilate.
Let me say only, that in Ligeia's more than womanly
abandonment to a love, alas, all unmerited, all unworthily
bestowed; I at length recognized the principle of her longing
with so wildly earnest a desire for the life which was now

fleeing so rapidly away. It is this wild longing–it is this eager intensity of desire for life–*but* for life–that I have no power to portray–no utterance capable of expressing.

At high noon of the night in which she departed, beckoning me, peremptorily, to her side, she bade me repeat certain verses composed by herself not many days before. I obeyed her. They were these:

[THE CONQUEROR WORM]

Lo! 'tis a gala night
    Within the lonesome latter years!
A mystic throng, bewinged, bedight
    In veils, and drowned in tears,
Sit in a theatre, to see
    A play of hopes and fears,
While the orchestra breathes fitfully
    The music of the spheres.

Mimes, in the form of God on high,
    Mutter and mumble low,
And hither and thither fly–
    Mere puppets they, who come and go
At bidding of vast shadowy things
    That shift the scenery to and fro,
Flapping from out their Condor wings
    Invisible Woe!

That motley drama–oh, be sure
    It shall not be forgot!
With its Phantom chased for evermore,
    By a crowd that seize it not,
Through a circle that ever returneth in
    To the self-same spot,

And much of Madness, and more of Sin,
    And Horror the soul of the plot.

But see, amid the mimic rout
    A crawling shape intrude!
A blood-red thing that writhes from out
    The scenic solitude!
It writhes!–it writhes!–with mortal pangs
    The mimes become its food,
And the angels sob at vermin fangs
    In human gore imbued.

Out–out are the lights–out all!
    And, over each dying form,
The curtain, a funeral pall,
    Comes down with the rush of a storm,
And the seraphs, all haggard and wan,
    Uprising, unveiling, affirm
That the play is the tragedy, "Man,"
    And its hero the Conqueror Worm.

"O God!" half shrieked Ligeia, leaping to her feet and
extending her arms aloft with a spasmodic movement, as I
made an end of these lines–"O God! O Divine Father!–shall
these things be undeviatingly so?–shall this Conqueror be not
once conquered? Are we not part and parcel in Thee? Who–
who knoweth the mysteries of the will with its vigor? Man
doth not yield him to the angels, *nor unto death utterly*, save
only through the weakness of his feeble will."

And now, as if exhausted with emotion, she suffered her
white arms to fall, and returned solemnly to her bed of Death.
And as she breathed her last sighs, there came mingled with
them a low murmur from her lips. I bent to them my ear and
distinguished, again, the concluding words of the passage in

Glanvill—*"Man doth not yield him to the angels, nor unto death utterly, save only through the weakness of his feeble will."*

She died—and I, crushed into the very dust with sorrow, could no longer endure the lonely desolation of my dwelling in the dim and decaying city by the Rhine. I had no lack of what the world terms wealth—Ligeia had brought me far more, very far more, than falls ordinarily to the lot of mortals. After a few months, therefore, of weary and aimless wandering, I purchased, and put in some repair, an abbey, which I shall not name, in one of the wildest and least frequented portions of fair England. The gloomy and dreary grandeur of the building, the almost savage aspect of the domain, the many melancholy and time-honored memories connected with both had much in unison with the feelings of utter abandonment which had driven me into that remote and musical region of the country. Yet, although the external abbey, with its verdant decay hanging about it, suffered but little alteration, I gave way with a child-like perversity, and perchance with a faint hope of alleviating my sorrows, to a display of more than regal magnificence within. For such follies even in childhood I had imbibed a taste, and now they came back to me as if in the dotage of grief. Alas, I now feel how much even of incipient madness might have been discovered in the gorgeous and fantastic draperies, in the solemn carvings of Egypt, in the wild cornices and furniture of Arabesque, in the bedlam patterns of the carpets of tufted gold! I had became a bounden slave in the trammels of opium, and my labors and my orders had taken a colouring from my dreams. But these absurdities I must not pause to detail. Let me speak only of that one chamber, ever accursed, whither in a moment of mental alienation, I led from the altar as my bride—as the successor of the unforgotten Ligeia—the fair-haired and blue-eyed lady Rowena Trevanion, of Tremaine.

There is not any individual portion of the architecture and

decoration of that bridal chamber which is not now visibly
before me. Where were the souls of the haughty family of the
bride, when, through thirst of gold, they permitted to pass the
threshold of an apartment so bedecked, a maiden and a
daughter so beloved? I have said that I minutely remember the
details of the chamber–yet I am sadly forgetful on topics of
deep moment–and here there was no system, no keeping, in
the fantastic display, to take hold upon the memory. The room
lay in a high turret of the castellated abbey, was pentagonal in
shape, and of capacious size. Occupying the whole southern
face of the pentagon was the sole window–an immense sheet
of unbroken glass from Venice–a single pane, and tinted of a
leaden hue, so that the rays of either the sun or moon, passing
through it, fell with a ghastly lustre upon the objects within.
Over the upper portion of this huge window extended the
open trellice-work of an aged vine which clambered up the
massy walls of the turret. The ceiling, of gloomy-looking oak,
was excessively lofty, vaulted, and elaborately fretted with the
wildest and most grotesque specimens of a semi-Gothic, semi-
Druidical device. From out the most central recess of this
melancholy vaulting, depended, by a single chain of gold with
long links, a huge censer of the same metal, Arabesque in
pattern, and with many perforations so contrived that there
writhed in and out of them, as if endued with a serpent
vitality, a continual succession of parti-coloured fires. Some
few ottomans and golden candelabras of Eastern figure were in
various stations about; and there was the couch, too, the bridal
couch, of an Indian model, and low, and sculptured of solid
ebony, with a canopy above. In each of the angles of the
chamber stood on end a gigantic sarcophagus of black granite,
from the tombs of the kings over against Luxor, with their aged
lids full of immemorial sculpture. But in the draping of the
apartment lay, alas! the chief phantasy of all. The lofty walls–
gigantic in height–even unproportionably so–were hung from

summit to foot, in vast folds with a heavy and massy-looking tapestry – tapestry of a material which was found alike as a carpet on the floor, as a covering for the ottomans and the ebony bed, as a canopy for the bed, and as the gorgeous volutes of the curtains which partially shaded the window. This material was the richest cloth of gold. It was spotted all over, at irregular intervals, with Arabesque figures of about a foot in diameter, and wrought upon the cloth in patterns of the most jetty black. But these figures partook of the true character of the Arabesque only when regarded from a single point of view. By a contrivance now common, and indeed traceable to a very remote period of antiquity, they were made changeable in aspect. To one entering the room they bore the appearance of ideal monstrosities; but upon a farther advance, this appearance suddenly departed; and step by step, as the visitor moved his station in the chamber, he saw himself surrounded by an endless succession of the ghastly forms which belong to the superstition of the Northman, or arise in the guilty slumbers of the monk. The phantasmagoric effect was vastly heightened by the artificial introduction of a strong continual current of wind behind the draperies – giving a hideous and uneasy vitality to the whole.

In halls such as these – in a bridal chamber such as this, I passed, with the lady of Tremaine, the unhallowed hours of the first month of our marriage – passed them with but little disquietude. That my wife dreaded the fierce moodiness of my temper – that she shunned me, and loved me but little, I could not help perceiving – but it gave me rather pleasure than otherwise. I loathed her with a hatred belonging more to demon than to man. My memory flew back, (oh, with what intensity of regret!) to Ligeia, the beloved, the beautiful, the entombed. I revelled in recollections of her purity, of her wisdom, of her lofty, her ethereal nature, of her passionate, her idolatrous love. Now, then, did my spirit fully and freely burn with more than all the fires of her own. In the excitement of my opium dreams, for I was habitually fettered in the iron shackles of the drug, I would call aloud upon her name, during the silence of the night, or among the sheltered recesses of the glens by day, as if, by the wild eagerness, the solemn passion, the consuming intensity of my longing for the departed Ligeia, I could restore her to the pathways she had abandoned upon earth.

About the commencement of the second month of the marriage, the lady Rowena was attacked with sudden illness from which her recovery was slow. The fever which consumed her, rendered her nights uneasy, and, in her perturbed state of half-slumber, she spoke of sounds, and of motions, in and about the chamber of the turret which I concluded had no origin save in the distemper of her fancy, or perhaps in the phantastic influences of the chamber itself. She became at length convalescent—finally well. Yet but a brief period elapsed, ere a second more violent disorder again threw her upon a bed of suffering—and from this attack her frame, at all times feeble, never altogether recovered. Her illnesses were, after this period, of alarming character, and of more alarming recurrence, defying alike the knowledge and the great exertions of her medical men. With the increase of the chronic disease which had thus, apparently, taken too sure hold upon her constitution to be eradicated by human means, I could not fail to observe a similar increase in the nervous irritability of her temperament, and in her excitability by trivial causes of fear. Indeed reason seemed fast tottering from her throne. She spoke again, and now more frequently and pertinaciously, of the sounds, of the slight sounds, and of the unusual motions among the tapestries, to which she had formerly alluded. It was one night, near the closing in of September, when she pressed this distressing subject with more than usual emphasis upon my attention. She had just awakened from a perturbed slumber, and I had been watching, with feelings half of anxiety, half of a vague terror, the workings of her emaciated countenance. I sat by the side of her ebony bed, upon one of the ottomans of India. She partly arose, and spoke, in an earnest low whisper, of sounds which she *then* heard, but which I could not hear, of motions which she *then* saw, but which I could not perceive. The wind was rushing hurriedly behind the tapestries, and I wished to show her (what, let me confess it, I could not *all* believe) that those faint, almost articulate breathings, and the very gentle variations of the figures upon the wall, were but the natural effects of that customary rushing of the wind. But a deadly pallor, over-spreading her face, had proved to me that my exertions to reassure her would be fruitless. She appeared to be fainting, and no attendants were within call. I remembered where was deposited a decanter of some light wine which had been ordered by her physicians, and hastened across the chamber to procure it. But, as I stepped beneath the light of the censer, two circumstances of a startling nature attracted my attention. I had felt that some palpable although invisible object had passed lightly by my person; and I saw that there lay a faint, indefinite shadow upon the golden carpet, in the very middle of the rich lustre thrown from the censer. But I was wild with the excitement of an immoderate dose of opium, and heeded these things but little, nor spoke of them to Rowena. Finding the wine, I re-crossed the chamber, and poured out a goblet-ful, which I held to the lips of the fainting lady. But she had now partially recovered, and took, herself, the vessel, while I sank upon the ottoman near me, with my eyes rivetted upon her person. It was then that I became distinctly aware of a gentle foot-fall upon the carpet, and near the couch; and, in a second thereafter, as Rowena was in the act of raising the wine to her lips, I saw, or may have dreamed that I saw, fall within the goblet, as if from some invisible spring in the atmosphere of the room, three or four large drops of a brilliant and ruby coloured fluid. If this I saw – not so Rowena. She swallowed the wine unhesitatingly, and I forbore to speak to her of a circumstance which must, after all, I considered, have been but the suggestion of a vivid imagination, rendered morbidly active by the terror of the lady, by the opium, and by the hour.

Yet I cannot conceal it from myself that, after this period, a rapid change for the worse took place in the disorder of my wife, so that, on the third subsequent night, the hands of her menials prepared her for the tomb, and on the fourth, I sat alone, with her shrouded body, in that fantastical chamber which had received her as my bride. Wild visions, opium-engendered, flitted, shadow-like, before me. I gazed with unquiet eye upon the sarcophagi in the angles of the room, upon the varying figures of the drapery, and upon the writhing of the parti-coloured fires in the censer overhead. My eyes then fell, as I called to mind the circumstances of a former night, to the spot beneath the glare of the censer where I had beheld the faint traces of the shadow. It was there, however, no longer, and, breathing with greater freedom, I turned my glances to the pallid and rigid figure upon the bed. Then rushed upon me a thousand memories of Ligeia – and then came back upon my heart, with the turbulent violence of a flood, the whole of that unutterable woe with which I had regarded *her* thus enshrouded. The night waned; and still, with a bosom full of bitter thoughts of the one only and supremely beloved, I remained with mine eyes rivetted upon the body of Rowena.

It might have been midnight, or perhaps earlier, or later, for I had taken no note of time, when a sob, low, gentle, but very distinct, startled me from my revery. I *felt* that it came from the bed of ebony – the bed of death. I listened in an agony of superstitious terror – but there was no repetition of the sound; I strained my vision to detect any motion in the corpse, but there was not the slightest perceptible. Yet I could not have been deceived. I had heard the noise, however faint, and my whole soul was awakened within me, as I resolutely and perseveringly kept my attention rivetted upon the body. Many minutes elapsed before any circumstance occurred tending to throw light upon the mystery. At length it became evident that a slight, a very faint, and barely noticeable tinge of colour had flushed up within the cheeks, and along the sunken small veins of the eyelids. Through a species of unutterable horror and awe, for which the language of mortality has no sufficiently energetic expression, I felt my brain reel, my heart cease to beat, my limbs grow rigid where I sat. Yet a sense of duty finally operated to restore my self-possession. I could no longer doubt that we had been precipitate in our preparations for interment – that Rowena still lived. It was necessary that some immediate exertion be made; yet the turret was altogether apart from the portion of the abbey tenanted by the servants – there were none within call, and I had no means of summoning them to my aid without leaving the room for many minutes – and this I could not venture to do. I therefore struggled alone in my endeavors to call back the spirit still hovering. In a short period it became evident, however, that a relapse had taken place; the colour utterly disappeared from both eyelid and cheek, leaving a wanness even more than that of marble; the lips became doubly shrivelled and pinched up in the ghastly expression of death; a coldness overspread rapidly the surface of the body, and all the usual rigorous stiffness immediately supervened. I fell back with a shudder upon the ottoman from which I had been so startlingly aroused, and again gave myself up to passionate waking visions of Ligeia.

An hour thus elapsed, when, (could it be possible?) I was a second time aware of some vague sound issuing from the region of the bed. I listened – in extremity of horror. The sound

came again – it was a sigh. Rushing to the corpse, I saw –
distinctly saw – a tremor upon the lips. In a minute after they
slightly relaxed, disclosing a bright line of the pearly teeth.
Amazement now struggled in my bosom with the profound
awe which had hitherto reigned therein alone. I felt that my
vision grew dim, that my brain wandered, and it only by a
violent effort that I at length succeeded in nerving myself to
the task which duty thus, once more, had pointed out. There
was now a partial glow upon the forehead, upon the cheek and
throat – a perceptible warmth pervaded the whole frame – there
was even a slight pulsation at the heart. The lady lived, and
with redoubled ardor I betook myself to the task of restoration.
I chafed and bathed the temples and the hands, and used
every exertion which experience, and no little medical reading,
could suggest. But in vain. Suddenly, the colour fled, the
pulsation ceased, the lips resumed the expression of the dead,
and, in an instant afterwards, the whole body took upon itself
the icy chillness, the livid hue, the intense rigidity, the sunken
outline, and each and all of the loathsome peculiarities of that
which has been, for many days, a tenant of the tomb.

And again I sunk into visions of Ligeia – and again (what
marvel I shudder while I write?) *again* there reached my ears a
low sob from the region of the ebony bed. But why shall I
minutely detail the unspeakable horrors of that night? Why
shall I pause to relate how, time after time, until near the
period of the gray dawn, this hideous drama of revivification
was repeated, and how each terrific relapse was only into a
sterner and apparently more irredeemable death? Let me hurry
to a conclusion.

The greater part of the fearful night had worn away, and
the corpse of Rowena once again stirred – and now more
vigorously than hitherto, although arousing from a dissolution
more appalling in its utter hopelessness than any. I had long
ceased to struggle or to move, and remained sitting rigidly

upon the ottoman, a helpless prey to a whirl of violent emotions, of which extreme awe was perhaps the least terrible, the least consuming. The corpse, I repeat, stirred, and now more vigorously than before. The hues of life flushed up with unwonted energy into the countenance – the limbs relaxed – and, save that the eyelids were yet pressed heavily together, and that the bandages and draperies of the grave still imparted their charnel character to the figure, I might have dreamed that Rowena had indeed shaken off, utterly, the fetters of Death. But if this idea was not, even then, altogether adopted, I could, at least, doubt no longer, when, arising from the bed, tottering, with feeble steps, with closed eyes, and with the air of one bewildered in a dream, the lady of Tremaine stood bodily and palpably before me.

I trembled not – I stirred not – for a crowd of unutterable fancies connected with the air, the demeanor of the figure, rushing hurriedly through my brain, had sent the purple blood ebbing in torrents from the temples to the heart. I stirred not – but gazed upon her who was before me. There was a mad disorder in my thoughts – a tumult unappeasable. Could it, indeed, be the *living* Rowena who confronted me? Why, *why* should I doubt it? The bandage lay heavily about the mouth – but then it was the mouth of the breathing lady of Tremaine. And the cheeks – there were the roses as in her noon of health – yes, these were indeed the fair cheeks of the living lady of Tremaine. And the chin, with its dimples, as in health, was it not hers? – but – but *had she grown taller since her malady?* What inexpressible madness seized me with that thought? One bound, and I had reached her feet! Shrinking from my touch, she let fall from her head, unloosened, the ghastly cerements which had confined it, and there streamed forth, into the rushing atmosphere of the chamber, huge masses of long and dishevelled hair. *It was blacker than the raven wings of the midnight!* And now the eyes opened of the figure which stood before me. "Here then at least," I shrieked aloud, "can I never – can I never be mistaken – these are the full, and the black, and the wild eyes of the lady – of the lady Ligeia!"

[September, 1838]

The Fall of the House of Usher

Son cœur est un luth suspendu;
Sitôt qu'on le touche il résonne.
[His heart is a hanging lute;
As soon as touched, it reverberates.]

—De Béranger.

DURING THE WHOLE of a dull, dark, and soundless day in the
autumn of the year, when the clouds hung oppressively low in
the heavens, I had been passing alone, on horseback, through
a singularly dreary tract of country; and at length found
myself, as the shades of the evening drew on, within view of
the melancholy House of Usher. I know not how it was–but,
with the first glimpse of the building, a sense of insufferable
gloom pervaded my spirit. I say insufferable; for the feeling
was unrelieved by any of that half-pleasurable, because poetic,
sentiment, with which the mind usually receives even the
sternest natural images of the desolate or terrible. I looked
upon the scene before me–upon the mere house, and the
simple landscape features of the domain–upon the bleak
walls–upon the vacant eye-like windows–upon a few rank
sedges–and upon a few white trunks of decayed trees–with an
utter depression of soul which I can compare to no earthly
sensation more properly than to the after-dream of the reveller
upon opium–the bitter lapse into common life–the hideous
dropping off of the veil. There was an iciness, a sinking, a
sickening of the heart–an unredeemed dreariness of thought
which no goading of the imagination could torture into aught
of the sublime. What was it–I paused to think–what was it
that so unnerved me in the contemplation of the House of
Usher? It was a mystery all insoluble; nor could I grapple with

the shadowy fancies that crowded upon me as I pondered. I was forced to fall back upon the unsatisfactory conclusion, that while, beyond a doubt, there *are* combinations of very simple natural objects which have the power of thus affecting us, still the reason, and the analysis of this power lies among considerations beyond our depth. It was possible, I reflected, that a mere different arrangement of the particulars of the scene, of the details of the picture, would be sufficient to modify, or perhaps to annihilate its capacity for sorrowful impression; and, acting upon this idea, I reined my horse to the precipitous brink of a black and lurid tarn that lay in unruffled lustre by the dwelling, and gazed down – but with a shudder even more thrilling than before – upon the remodelled and inverted images of the gray sedge, and the ghastly tree-stems, and the vacant and eye-like windows.

Nevertheless, in this mansion of gloom I now proposed to myself a sojourn of some weeks. Its proprietor, Roderick Usher, had been one of my boon companions in boyhood; but many years had elapsed since our last meeting. A letter, however, had lately reached me in a distant part of the country – a letter from him – which, in its wildly importunate nature, had admitted of no other than a personal reply. The MS. gave evidence of nervous agitation. The writer spoke of acute bodily illness – of a pitiable mental idiosyncrasy which oppressed him – and of an earnest desire to see me, as his best, and indeed his only personal friend, with a view of attempting, by the cheerfulness of my society, some alleviation of his malady. It was the manner in which all this, and much more, was said – it was the apparent *heart* that went with his request – which allowed me no room for hesitation; and I accordingly obeyed what I still considered a very singular summons, forthwith.

Although, as boys, we had been even intimate associates, yet I really knew little of my friend. His reserve had been always excessive and habitual. I was aware, however, that his very ancient family had been noted, time out of mind, for a peculiar sensibility of temperament, displaying itself, through long ages, in many works of exalted art, and manifested, of late, in repeated deeds of munificent yet unobtrusive charity, as well as in a passionate devotion to the intricacies, perhaps even more than to the orthodox and easily recognisable beauties, of musical science. I had learned, too, the very remarkable fact, that the stem of the Usher race, all time-honored as it was, had put forth, at no period, any enduring branch; in other words, that the entire family lay in the direct line of descent, and had always, with very trifling and very temporary variation, so lain. It was this deficiency, I considered, while running over in thought the perfect keeping of the character of the premises with the accredited character of the people, and while speculating upon the possible influence which the one, in the long lapse of centuries, might have exercised upon the other – it was this deficiency, perhaps, of collateral issue, and the consequent undeviating transmission, from sire to son, of the patrimony with the name, which had, at length, so identified the two as to merge the original title of the estate in the quaint and equivocal appellation of the "House of Usher" – an appellation which seemed to include, in the minds of the peasantry who used it, both the family and the family mansion.

I have said that the sole effect of my somewhat childish experiment – of looking down within the tarn – had been to deepen the first singular impression. There can be no doubt that the consciousness of the rapid increase of my superstition – for why should I not so term it? – served mainly to accelerate the increase itself. Such, I have long known, is the paradoxical law of all sentiments having terror as a basis. And it might have been for this reason only, that when I again uplifted my eyes to the house itself, from its image in the pool, there grew in my mind a strange fancy – a fancy so ridiculous, indeed, that

I but mention it to show the vivid force of the sensations which oppressed me. I had so worked upon my imagination as really to believe that around about the whole mansion and domain there hung an atmosphere peculiar to themselves and their immediate vicinity – an atmosphere which had no affinity with the air of heaven, but which had reeked up from the decayed trees, and the gray walls and in the silent tarn, in the form of an inelastic vapor or gas – dull, sluggish, faintly discernible, and leaden-hued.

Shaking off from my spirit what *must* have been a dream, I scanned more narrowly the real aspect of the building. Its principal feature seemed to be that of an excessive antiquity. The discoloration of ages had been great. Minute fungi over-spread the whole exterior, hanging in a fine tangled web-work from the eaves. Yet all this was apart from any extraordinary dilapidation. No portion of the masonry had fallen; and there appeared to be a wild inconsistency between its still perfect adaptation of parts, and the utterly porous, and evidently decayed condition of the individual stones. In this there was much that reminded me of the specious totality of old wood-work which has rotted for long years in some neglected vault, with no disturbance from the breath of the external air. Beyond this indication of extensive decay, however, the fabric gave little token of instability. Perhaps the eye of a scrutinizing observer might have discovered a barely perceptible fissure, which, extending from the roof of the building in front, made its way down the wall in a zigzag direction, until it became lost in the sullen waters of the tarn.

Noticing these things, I rode over a short causeway to the house. A servant in waiting took my horse, and I entered the Gothic archway of the hall. A valet, of stealthy step, thence conducted me, in silence, through many dark and intricate passages in my progress to the studio of his master. Much that I encountered on the way contributed, I know not how, to heighten the vague sentiments of which I have already spoken. While the objects around me–while the carvings of the ceilings, the sombre tapestries of the walls, the ebon blackness of the floors, and the phantasmagoric armorial trophies which rattled as I strode, were but matters to which, or to such as which, I had been accustomed from my infancy–while I hesitated not to acknowledge how familiar was all this–I still wondered to find how unfamiliar were the fancies which ordinary images were stirring up. On one of the staircases, I met the physician of the family. His countenance, I thought, wore a mingled expression of low cunning and perplexity. He accosted me with trepidation and passed on. The valet now threw open a door and ushered me into the presence of his master.

The room in which I found myself was very large and excessively lofty. The windows were long, narrow, and pointed, and at so vast a distance from the black oaken floor as to be altogether inaccessible from within. Feeble gleams of encrimsoned light made their way through the trellised panes, and served to render sufficiently distinct the more prominent objects around; the eye, however, struggled in vain to reach the remoter angles of the chamber, or the recesses of the vaulted and fretted ceiling. Dark draperies hung upon the walls. The general furniture was profuse, comfortless, antique, and tattered. Many books and musical instruments lay scattered about, but failed to give any vitality to the scene. I felt that I breathed an atmosphere of sorrow. An air of stern, deep, and irredeemable gloom hung over and pervaded all.

Upon my entrance, Usher arose from a sofa upon which he had been lying at full length, and greeted me with a vivacious warmth which had much in it, I at first thought, of an overdone cordiality–of the constrained effort of the *ennuyé* man of the world. A glance, however, at his countenance, convinced me of his perfect sincerity. We sat down; and for some moments, while he spoke not, I gazed upon him with a feeling half of pity, half of awe. Surely, man had never before so terribly altered, in so brief a period, as had Roderick Usher! It was with difficulty that I could bring myself to admit the identity of the wan being before me with the companion of my early boyhood. Yet the character of his face had been at all times remarkable. A cadaverousness of complexion; an eye large, liquid, and luminous beyond comparison; lips somewhat thin and very pallid, but of a surpassingly beautiful curve; a nose of a delicate Hebrew model, but with a breadth of nostril unusual in similar formations; a finely moulded chin, speaking, in its want of prominence, of a want of moral energy; hair of a more than web-like softness and tenuity; these features, with an inordinate expansion above the regions of the temple, made up altogether a countenance not easily to be forgotten. And now in the mere exaggeration of the prevailing character of these features, and of the expression they were wont to convey, lay so much of change that I doubted to whom I spoke. The now ghastly pallor of the skin, and the now miraculous lustre of the eye, above all things startled and even awed me. The silken hair, too, had been suffered to grow all unheeded, and as, in its wild gossamer texture, it floated rather than fell about the face, I could not, even with effort, connect its Arabesque expression with any idea of simple humanity.

In the manner of my friend I was at once struck with an incoherence – an inconsistency; and I soon found this to arise from a series of feeble and futile struggles to overcome an habitual trepidancy – an excessive nervous agitation. For something of this nature I had indeed been prepared, no less by his letter, than by reminiscences of certain boyish traits, and by conclusions deduced from his peculiar physical conformation and temperament. His action was alternately vivacious and sullen. His voice varied rapidly from a tremulous indecision (when the animal spirits seemed utterly in abeyance) to that species of energetic concision – that abrupt, weighty, unhurried, and hollow-sounding enunciation – that leaden, self-balanced and perfectly modulated guttural utterance, which may be observed in the moments of the intensest excitement of the lost drunkard, or the irreclaimable eater of opium.

It was thus that he spoke of the object of my visit, of his earnest desire to see me, and of the solace he expected me to afford him. He entered, at some length, into what he conceived to be the nature of his malady. It was, he said, a constitutional and a family evil, and one for which he despaired to find a remedy – a mere nervous affection, he added in a breath, which would undoubtedly soon pass. It displayed itself in a host of unnatural sensations. Some of these, as he detailed them, interested and bewildered me; although, perhaps, the terms, and the general manner of the narration had their weight. He suffered much from a morbid acuteness of the senses; the most insipid food was alone endurable; he could wear only garments of certain texture; the odors of all flowers were oppressive; his eyes were tortured by even a faint light; and there were but peculiar sounds, and these from stringed instruments, which did not inspire him with horror.

To an anomalous species of terror I found him a bounden slave. "I shall perish," said he, "I *must* perish in this deplorable folly. Thus, thus, and not otherwise, shall I be lost. I dread the events of the future, not in themselves, but in their results. I shudder at the thought of any, even the most trivial, incident, which may operate upon this intolerable agitation of soul. I have, indeed, no abhorrence of danger, except in its absolute effect – in terror. In this unnerved – in this pitiable condition – I feel that I must inevitably abandon life and reason together, in my struggles with some fatal demon of fear."

I learned, moreover, at intervals, and through broken and equivocal hints, another singular feature of his mental condition. He was enchained by certain superstitious impressions in regard to the dwelling which he tenanted, and from which, for many years, he had never ventured forth–in regard to an influence whose supposititious force was conveyed in terms too shadowy here to be restated–an influence which some peculiarities in the mere form and substance of his family mansion, had, by dint of long sufferance, he said, obtained over his spirit–an effect which the *physique* of the gray walls and turrets, and of the dim tarn into which they all looked down, had, at length, brought about upon the *morale* of his existence.

He admitted, however, although with hesitation, that much of the peculiar gloom which thus afflicted him could be traced to a more natural and far more palpable origin–to the severe and long-continued illness–indeed to the evidently approaching dissolution–of a tenderly beloved sister–his sole companion for long years–his last and only relative on earth. "Her decease," he said, with a bitterness which I can never forget, "would leave him (him the hopeless and the frail) the last of the ancient race of the Ushers." As he spoke, the lady Madeline (for so was she called) passed slowly through a remote portion of the apartment, and without having noticed my presence, disappeared. I regarded her with an utter astonishment not unmingled with dread. Her figure, her air, her features–all, in their very minutest development were those–were identically (I can use no other sufficient term) were identically those of the Roderick Usher who sat beside me. A feeling of stupor oppressed me, as my eyes followed her retreating steps. As a door, at length, closed upon her exit, my glance sought instinctively and eagerly the countenance of the brother–but he had buried his face in his hands, and I could only perceive that a far more than ordinary wanness had overspread the emaciated fingers through which trickled many passionate tears.

The disease of the lady Madeline had long baffled the skill of her physicians. A settled apathy, a gradual wasting away of the person, and frequent although transient affections of a partially cataleptical character, were the unusual diagnosis. Hitherto she had steadily borne up against the pressure of her malady, and had not betaken herself finally to bed; but, on the closing in of the evening of my arrival at the house, she succumbed (as her brother told me at night with inexpressible agitation) to the prostrating power of the destroyer; and I learned that the glimpse I had obtained of her person would thus probably be the last I should obtain – that the lady, at least while living, would be seen by me no more.

For several days ensuing, her name was unmentioned by either Usher or myself: and during this period I was busied in earnest endeavors to alleviate the melancholy of my friend. We painted and read together; or I listened, as if in a dream, to the wild improvisations of his speaking guitar. And thus, as a closer and still closer intimacy admitted me more unreservedly into the recesses of his spirit, the more bitterly did I perceive the futility of all attempt at cheering a mind from which darkness, as if an inherent positive quality, poured forth upon all objects of the moral and physical universe, in one unceasing radiation of gloom.

I shall ever bear about me, as Moslemin their shrouds at Mecca, a memory of the many solemn hours I thus spent alone with the master of the House of Usher. Yet I should fail in any attempt to convey an idea of the exact character of the studies, or of the occupations, in which he involved me, or led me the way. An excited and highly distempered ideality threw a sulphurous lustre over all. His long improvised dirges will ring forever in my ears. Among other things, I bear painfully in mind a certain singular perversion and amplification of the wild air of the last waltz of Von Weber. From the paintings over which his elaborate fancy brooded, and which grew, touch by touch, into vaguenesses at which I shuddered the more thrillingly, because I shuddered knowing not why;–from these paintings (vivid as their images now are before me) I would in vain endeavor to educe more than a small portion which would lie within the compass of merely written words. By the utter simplicity, by the nakedness of his designs, he arrested and overawed attention. If ever mortal painted an idea, that mortal was Roderick Usher. For me at least–in the circumstances then surrounding me–there arose out of the pure abstractions which the hypochondriac contrived to throw upon his canvas an intensity of intolerable awe, no shadow of which felt I ever yet in the contemplation of the certainly glowing yet too concrete reveries of Fuseli.

One of the phantasmagoric conceptions of my friend, partaking not so rigidly of the spirit of abstraction, may be shadowed forth, although feebly, in words. A small picture presented the interior of an immensely long and rectangular vault or tunnel, with low walls, smooth, white, and without interruption or device. Certain accessory points of the design served well to convey the idea that this excavation lay at an exceeding depth below the surface of the earth. No outlet was observed in any portion of its vast extent, and no torch, or other artificial source of light was discernible; yet a flood of intense rays rolled throughout, and bathed the whole in a ghastly and inappropriate splendor.

I have just spoken of that morbid condition of the auditory nerve which rendered all music intolerable to the sufferer with the exception of certain effects of stringed instruments. It was, perhaps, the narrow limits to which he thus confined himself upon the guitar, which gave birth, in great measure, to the fantastic character of his performances. But the fervid *facility* of his impromptus could not be so accounted for. They must have been, and were, in the notes, as well as in the words of his wild fantasias (for he not unfrequently accompanied

himself with rhymed verbal improvisations), the result of that
intense mental collectedness and concentration to which I
have previously alluded as observable only in particular
moments of the highest artificial excitement. The words of one
of these rhapsodies I have easily borne away in memory. I was,
perhaps, the more forcibly impressed with it, as he gave it,
because, in the under or mystic current of its meaning, I
fancied that I perceived, and for the first time, a full consciousness on the part of Usher, of the tottering of his lofty
reason upon her throne. The verses, which were entitled "The
Haunted Palace," ran very nearly, if not accurately, thus:

[THE HAUNTED PALACE]

I

In the greenest of our valleys
    By good angels tenanted,
Once a fair and stately palace –
    Snow-White palace – reared its head.
In the monarch Thought's dominion –
    It stood there!
Never seraph spread his pinion
    Over fabric half so fair!

II

Banners yellow, glorious, golden,
    On its roof did float and flow –
(This – all this – was in the olden
    Time long ago)
And every gentle air that dallied,
    In that sweet day,
Along the rampart plumed and pallid,
    A winged odor went away.

III

All wanderers in that happy valley,
     Through two luminous windows, saw
Spirits moving musically,
     To a lute's well-tuned law,
Round about a throne where, sitting,
     Porphyrogene,
In state his glory well befitting
     The sovereign of the realm was seen.

IV

And with all pearl and ruby flowing
     Was the fair palace door,
Through which came flowing, flowing, flowing,
     And sparkling evermore,
A troop of Echoes whose sweet duty
     Was but to sing,
In voices of surpassing beauty,
     The wit and wisdom of their king.

V

But evil things, in robes of sorrow,
     Assailed the monarch's high estate.
(Ah, let us mourn! – for never morrow
     Shall dawn upon him, desolate!)
And round about his home the glory
     That blushed and bloomed,
Is but a dim-remembered story
     Of the old-time entombed.

VI

And travellers, now, within that valley,
     Through the encrimsoned windows see

Vast forms that move fantastically
To a discordant melody,
While, like a rapid ghastly river,
Through the pale door
A hideous throng rush out forever
And laugh – but smile no more.

I well remember that suggestions arising from this ballad led us into a train of thought wherein there became manifest an opinion of Usher's which I mention not so much on account of its novelty, (for other men have thought thus,) as on account of the pertinacity with which he maintained it. This opinion, in its general form, was that of the sentience of all vegetable things. But, in his disordered fancy, the idea had assumed a more daring character, and trespassed under certain conditions, upon the kingdom of inorganization. I lack words to express the full extent, or the earnest *abandon* of his persuasion. The belief, however, was connected (as I have previously hinted) with the gray stones of the home of his forefathers. The condition of the sentience had been here, he imagined, fulfilled in the method of collocation of these stones – in the order of their arrangement, as well as in that of the many fungi which overspread them, and of the decayed trees which stood around – above all, in the long undisturbed endurance of this arrangement, and in its reduplication in the still waters of the tarn. Its evidence – the evidence of the sentience – was to be seen, he said, (and I here started as he spoke,) in *the gradual yet certain condensation of an atmosphere of their own about the waters and the walls.* The result was discoverable, he added, in that silent, yet importunate and terrible influence which for centuries had moulded the destinies of his family, and which made *him* what I now saw him – what he was. Such opinions need no comment and I will make none.

Our books—the books which, for years, had formed no
small portion of the mental existence of the invalid—were, as
might be supposed, in strict keeping with this character of
phantasm. We pored together over such works as the *Ververt et
Chartreuse* of Gresset; the *Belphegor of Machiavelli; the
Selenography* of Brewster; the *Heaven and Hell* of Swedenborg;
the *Subterranean Voyage* of Nicholas Klimm de Holberg; the
Chiromancy of Robert Flud, of Jean D'Indaginé, and of De la
Chambre; the *Journey into the Blue Distance* of Tieck; and the
City of the Sun of Campanella. One favorite volume was a small
octavo edition of the *Directorium Inquisitorum* [Office of the
Chief Inquisitor] by the Dominican Eymeric de Gironne, and
there were passages in Pomponius Mela, about the old African
Satyrs and Œgipans, over which Usher would sit dreaming for
hours. His chief delight, however, was found in the earnest and
repeated perusal of an exceedingly rare and curious book in
quarto Gothic—the manual of a forgotten church—the *Vigilae
Mortuorum secundum Chorum Ecclesiae Maguntinae* [Vigils of
the Dead According to the Chorus of the Church of Minz].

I could not help thinking of the wild ritual of this work,
and of its probable influence upon the hypochondriac, when,
one evening, having informed me abruptly that the lady
Madeline was no more, he stated his intention of preserving
her corpse for a fortnight, (previously to its final interment,) in
one of the numerous vaults within the main walls of the building. The worldly reason, however, assigned for this singular
proceeding, was one which I did not feel at liberty to dispute.
The brother had been led to his resolution (so he told me) by
considerations of the unusual character of the malady of the
deceased, of certain obtrusive and eager inquiries on the part
of her medical men, and of the remote and exposed situation
of the burial-ground of the family. I will not deny that when I
called to mind the sinister countenance of the person whom
I met upon the staircase, on the day of my arrival at the house,

I had no desire to oppose what I regarded as at best but a harmless, and not by any means an unnatural, precaution.

At the request of Usher, I personally aided him in the arrangements for the temporary entombment. The body having been encoffined, we two alone bore it to its rest. The vault in which we placed it (and which had been so long unopened that our torches, half smothered in its oppressive atmosphere, gave us little opportunity for investigation) was small, damp, and utterly without means of admission for light; lying, at great depth, immediately beneath that portion of the building in which was my own sleeping apartment. It had been used, apparently, in remote feudal times, for the worst purposes of a donjon-keep, and, in later days, as a place of deposit for powder, or other highly combustible substance, as a portion of its floor, and the whole interior of a long archway through which we reached it, were carefully sheathed with copper. The door, of massive iron, had been, also, similarly protected. Its immense weight caused an unusually sharp grating sound, as it moved upon its hinges.

Having deposited our mournful burden upon tressels within this region of horror, we partially turned aside the yet unscrewed lid of the coffin, and looked upon the face of the tenant. The exact similitude between the brother and sister even here again startled and confounded me. Usher, divining, perhaps, my thought, murmured out some few words from which I learned that the deceased and himself had been twins, and that sympathies of a scarcely intelligible nature had always existed between them. Our glances, however, rested not long upon the dead – for we could not regard her unawed. The disease which had thus entombed the lady in the maturity of youth, had left, as usual in all maladies of a strictly cataleptical character, the mockery of a faint blush upon the bosom and the face, and that suspiciously lingering smile upon the lip which is so terrible in death. We replaced and screwed down the lid, and having secured the door of iron, made our way, with toil, into the scarcely less gloomy apartments of the upper portion of the house.

And now, some days of bitter grief having elapsed, an observable change came over the features of the mental disorder of my friend. His ordinary manner had vanished. His ordinary occupations were neglected or forgotten. He roamed from chamber to chamber with hurried, unequal, and objectless step. The pallor of his countenance had assumed, if possible, a more ghastly hue–but the luminousness of his eye had utterly gone out. The once occasional huskiness of his tone was heard no more; and a tremulous quaver, as if of extreme terror, habitually characterized his utterance. There were times, indeed, when I thought his mind was laboring with an oppressive secret, to divulge which he struggled for the necessary courage. At times, again, I was obliged to resolve all into the mere inexplicable vagaries of madness, as I beheld him gazing upon vacancy for long hours, in an attitude of the profoundest attention, as if listening to some imaginary sound. It was no wonder that his condition terrified–that it infected me. I felt creeping upon me, by slow yet certain degrees, the wild influences of his own fantastic yet impressive superstitions.

It was, most especially, upon retiring to bed late in the night of the seventh or eighth day after the entombment of the lady Madeline, that I experienced the full power of such feelings. Sleep came not near my couch–while the hours waned and waned away. I struggled to reason off the nervousness which had dominion over me. I endeavored to believe that much, if not all of what I felt, was due to the phantasmagoric influence of the gloomy furniture of the room–of the dark and tattered draperies, which, tortured into motion by the breath of a rising tempest, swayed fitfully to and fro upon the walls, and rustled uneasily about the decorations of the bed. But my efforts were fruitless. An irrepressible tremor gradually pervaded my frame; and, at length, there sat upon my very heart an incubus of utterly causeless alarm. Shaking this off with a gasp and a struggle, I uplifted myself upon the pillows, and peering earnestly within the intense darkness of the chamber, harkened – I know not why, except that an instinctive spirit prompted me – to certain low and indefinite sounds which came, through the pauses of the storm, at long intervals, I knew not whence. Overpowered by an intense sentiment of horror, unaccountable yet unendurable, I threw on my clothes with haste (for I felt that I should sleep no more during the night), and endeavored to arouse myself from the pitiable condition into which I had fallen, by pacing rapidly to and fro through the apartment.

I had taken but few turns in this manner, when a light step on an adjoining staircase arrested my attention. I presently recognised it as that of Usher. In an instant afterwards he rapped, with a gentle touch, at my door, and entered, bearing a lamp. His countenance was, as usual, cadaverously wan – but there was a species of mad hilarity in his eyes – an evidently restrained hysteria in his whole demeanor. His air appalled me – but anything was preferable to the solitude which I had so long endured, and I even welcomed his presence as a relief.

"And you have not seen it?" he said abruptly, after having stared about him for some moments in silence –"you have not then seen it? – but, stay! you shall." Thus speaking, and having carefully shaded his lamp, he hurried to one of the gigantic casements, and threw it freely open to the storm.

The impetuous fury of the entering gust nearly lifted us from our feet. It was, indeed, a tempestuous yet sternly beautiful night, and one wildly singular in its terror and its beauty. A whirlwind had apparently collected its force in our vicinity; for there were frequent and violent alterations in the direction of the wind; and the exceeding density of the clouds (which hung so low as to press upon the turrets of the house) did not prevent our perceiving the life-like velocity with which they flew careering from all points against each other, without passing away into the distance. I say that even their exceeding density did not prevent our perceiving this–yet we had no glimpse of the moon or stars–nor was there any flashing forth of the lightning. But the under surfaces of the huge masses of agitated vapor, as well as all terrestrial objects immediately around us, were glowing in the unnatural light of a faintly luminous and distinctly visible gaseous exhalation which hung about and enshrouded the mansion.

"You must not–you shall not behold this!" said I, shudderingly, to Usher, as I led him, with a gentle violence, from the window to a seat. "These appearances, which be- wilder you, are merely electrical phenomena not uncommon – or it may be that they have their ghastly origin in the rank miasma of the tarn. Let us close this casement;–the air is chilling and dangerous to your frame. Here is one of your favorite romances. I will read, and you shall listen;–and so we will pass away this terrible night together."

The antique volume which I had taken up was the *Mad Trist* of Sir Launcelot Canning; but I had called it a favorite of Usher's more in sad jest than in earnest; for, in truth, there is little in its uncouth and unimaginative prolixity which could have had interest for the lofty and spiritual ideality of my friend. It was, however, the only book immediately at hand; and I indulged a vague hope that the excitement which now agitated the hypochondriac, might find relief (for the history of mental disorder is full of similar anomalies) even in the utterness of the folly which I should read. Could I have judged, indeed, by the wild overstrained air of vivacity with which he harkened, or apparently harkened, to the words of the tale, I might have well congratulated myself upon the success of my design.

I had arrived at the well-known portion of the story where
Ethelred, the hero of the *Trist,* having sought in vain for peace-
able admission into the dwelling of the hermit, proceeds to
make good an entrance by force. Here, it will be remembered,
the words of the narrative run thus:

"And Ethelred, who was by nature of a doughty heart, and
who was now mighty withal, on account of the powerfulness
of the wine which he had drunken, waited no longer to hold
parley with the hermit, who, in sooth, was of an obstinate and
maliceful turn, but, feeling the rain upon his shoulders, and
fearing the rising of the tempest, uplifted his mace outright,
and, with blows, made quickly room in the plankings of the
door for his gauntleted hand; and now pulling therewith
sturdily, he so cracked, and ripped, and tore all asunder, that
the noise of the dry and hollow-sounding wood alarummed
and reverberated throughout the forest."

At the termination of this sentence I started, and for a
moment, paused; for it appeared to me (although I at once
concluded that my excited fancy had deceived me) – it
appeared to me that, from some very remote portion of the
mansion or of its vicinity, there came, indistinctly, to my ears,
what might have been, in its exact similarity of character, the
echo (but a stifled and dull one certainly) of the very cracking
and ripping sound which Sir Launcelot had so particularly
described. It was, beyond doubt, the coincidence alone which
had arrested my attention; for, amid the rattling of the sashes
of the casements, and the ordinary commingled noises of the
still increasing storm, the sound, in itself, had nothing, surely,
which should have interested or disturbed me. I continued
the story:

"But the good champion Ethelred, now entering within the
door, was sore enraged and amazed to perceive no signal of
the maliceful hermit; but, in the stead thereof, a dragon of a
scaly and prodigious demeanor, and of a fiery tongue, which

sate in guard before a palace of gold, with a floor of silver; and
upon the wall there hung a shield of shining brass with this
legend enwritten –

Who entereth herein, a conqueror hath bin;
Who slayeth the dragon, the shield he shall win;

And Ethelred uplifted his mace, and struck upon the head of
the dragon, which fell before him, and gave up his pesty
breath, with a shriek so horrid and harsh, and withal so
piercing, that Ethelred had fain to close his ears with his
hands against the dreadful noise of it, the like whereof was
never before heard."

Here again I paused abruptly, and now with a feeling of
utter amazement – for there could be no doubt whatever that,
in this instance, I did actually hear (although from what
direction it proceeded I found it impossible to say) a low and
apparently distant, but harsh, protracted, and most unusual
screaming or grating sound – the exact counterpart of what my
fancy had already conjured up as the sound of the dragon's
unnatural shriek as described by the romancer.

Oppressed, as I certainly was, upon the occurrence of this
second and most extraordinary coincidence, by a thousand
conflicting sensations, in which wonder and extreme terror
were predominant, I still retained sufficient presence of mind
to avoid exciting, by any observation, the sensitive nervousness
of my companion. I was by no means certain that he had
noticed the sounds in question; although, assuredly, a strange
alteration had, during the last few minutes, taken place in his
demeanor. From a position fronting my own, he had gradually
brought round his chair, so as to sit with his face to the door
of the chamber; and thus I could but partially perceive his
features, although I saw that his lips trembled as if he were
murmuring inaudibly. His head had dropped upon his
breast – yet I knew that he was not asleep, from the wide and

rigid opening of the eye as I caught a glance of it in profile. The motion of his body, too, was at variance with this idea – for he rocked from side to side with a gentle yet constant and uniform sway. Having rapidly taken notice of all this, I resumed the narrative of Sir Launcelot, which thus proceeded:

"And now, the champion, having escaped from the terrible fury of the dragon, bethinking himself of the brazen shield, and of the breaking up of the enchantment which was upon it, removed the carcass from out of the way before him, and approached valorously over the silver pavement of the castle to where the shield was upon the wall; which in sooth tarried not for his full coming, but fell down at his feet upon the silver floor, with a mighty great and terrible ringing sound."

No sooner had these syllables passed my lips, than – as if a shield of brass had indeed, at the moment, fallen heavily upon a floor of silver – I became aware of a distinct, hollow, metallic, and clangorous, yet apparently muffled reverberation. Utterly unnerved, I started convulsively to my feet; but the measured rocking movement of Usher was undisturbed. I rushed to the chair in which he sat. His eyes were bent fixedly before him, and throughout his whole countenance there reigned a more than stony rigidity. But, as I laid my hand upon his shoulder, there came a strong shudder over his frame; a sickly smile quivered about his lips; and I saw that he spoke in a low, hurried, and gibbering murmur, as if unconscious of my presence. Bending closely over his person, I at length drank in the hideous import of his words.

"Not hear it? – yes, I hear it, and *have* heard it. Long – long – long – many minutes, many hours, many days, have I heard it – yet I dared not – oh, pity me, miserable wretch that I am! – I dared not – I *dared* not speak! We *have put her living in the tomb!* Said I not that my senses were acute? I *now* tell you that I heard her first feeble movements in the hollow coffin. I heard them – many, many days ago – yet I dared not – I *dared*

not speak! And now–tonight–Ethelred–ha! ha!–the breaking
of the hermit's door, and the death-cry of the dragon, and the
clangor of the shield!–say, rather, the rending of the coffin,
and the grating of the iron hinges and her struggles within the
coppered arch-way of the vault! Oh whither shall I fly? Will
she not be here anon? Is she not hurrying to upbraid me for
my haste? Have I not heard her footsteps on the stair? Do I not
distinguish that heavy and horrible beating of her heart?
Madman!"–here he sprung violently to his feet, and shrieked
out his syllables, as if in the effort he were giving up his
soul–"Madman! *I tell you that she now stands without the door!*"

As if in the superhuman energy of his utterance there had
been found the potency of a spell–the huge antique pannels
to which the speaker pointed, threw slowly back, upon the
instant, their ponderous and ebony jaws. It was the work of the
rushing gust–but then without those doors there *did* stand the
lofty and enshrouded figure of the lady Madeline of Usher.
There was blood upon her white robes, and the evidence of
some bitter struggle upon every portion of her emaciated
frame. For a moment she remained, trembling and reeling to
and fro upon the threshold–then, with a low moaning cry, fell
heavily inward upon the person of her brother, and in her
horrible and now final death-agonies bore him to the floor a
corpse, and a victim to the terrors he had dreaded.

From that chamber, and from that mansion, I fled aghast.
The storm was still abroad in all its wrath as I found myself
crossing the old causeway. Suddenly there shot along the path
a wild light, and I turned to see whence a gleam so unusual
could have issued; for the vast house and its shadows were
alone behind me. The radiance was that of the full, setting,
and blood-red moon, which now shone vividly through that
once barely-discernible fissure, of which I have before spoken
as extending from the roof of the building, in a zigzag
direction, to the base. While I gazed, this fissure rapidly

widened – there came a fierce breath of the whirlwind – the entire orb of the satellite burst at once upon my sight – my brain reeled as I saw the mighty walls rushing asunder – there was a long tumultuous shouting sound like the voice of a thousand waters – and the deep and dank tarn at my feet closed sullenly and silently over the fragments of the *"House of Usher."*

[September, 1839]

WILLIAM WILSON – A TALE

What say of it? what say of CONSCIENCE *grim,*
That spectre in my path?

— CHAMBERLAYNE'S *Pharonnida.*

LET ME CALL myself, for the present, William Wilson. The fair page now lying before me need not be sullied with my real appellation. This has been already too much an object for the scorn – for the horror – for the detestation of my race. To the uttermost regions of the globe have not the indignant winds bruited its unparalleled infamy? Oh, outcast of all outcasts most abandoned! – to the earth art thou not for ever dead? to its honors, to its flowers, to its golden aspirations? – and a cloud, dense, dismal, and limitless, does it not hang eternally between thy hopes and heaven?

I would not, if I could, here or to-day, embody a record of my later years of unspeakable misery, and unpardonable crime. This epoch – these later years – took unto themselves a sudden elevation in turpitude, whose origin alone it is my present purpose to assign. Men usually grow base by degrees. From me, in an instant, all virtue dropped bodily as a mantle. I shrouded my nakedness in triple guilt. From comparatively trivial wickedness I passed, with the stride of a giant, into more than the enormities of an Elah-Gabalus. What chance – what one event brought this evil thing to pass, bear with me while I relate. Death approaches; and the shadow which foreruns him has thrown a softening influence over my spirit. I long, in passing through the dim valley, for the sympathy – I had nearly said for the pity – of my fellow men. I would fain have them believe that I have been, in some measure, the slave of circumstances beyond human control. I would wish them to seek out for me, in the details I am about to give, some little oasis of *fatality* amid a wilderness of error. I would have them allow – what they cannot refrain from allowing – that, although temptation may have erewhile existed as great, man was never *thus*, at least, tempted before – certainly, never *thus* fell. And therefore has he never thus suffered. Have I not indeed been living in a dream? And am I not now dying a victim to the horror and the mystery of the wildest of all sublunary visions?

I am come of a race whose imaginative and easily excitable temperament has at all times rendered them remarkable; and, in my earliest infancy, I gave evidence of having fully inherited the family character. As I advanced in years it was more strongly developed; becoming, for many reasons, a cause of serious disquietude to my friends, and of positive injury to myself. I grew self-willed, addicted to the wildest caprices, and a prey to the most ungovernable passions. Weak-minded, and beset with constitutional infirmities akin to my own, my parents could do but little to check the evil propensities which distinguished me. Some feeble and ill-directed efforts resulted in complete failure on their part, and, of course, in total triumph on mine. Thenceforward my voice was a household law; and at an age when few children have abandoned their leading-strings, I was left to the guidance of my own will, and became, in all but name, the master of my own actions.

My earliest recollections of a school-life are connected with a large, rambling, cottage-built, and somewhat decayed building in a misty-looking village of England, where were a vast number of gigantic and gnarled trees, and where all the houses were excessively ancient and inordinately tall. In truth, it was a dream-like and spirit-soothing place, that venerable old town. At this moment, in fancy, I feel the refreshing chilliness of its deeply-shadowed avenues, inhale the fragrance of its thousand shrubberies, and thrill anew with undefinable delight, at the deep hollow note of the church-bell, breaking, each hour, with sullen and sudden roar, upon the stillness of the dusky atmosphere in which the old, fretted Gothic steeple lay imbedded and asleep.

It gives me, perhaps, as much of pleasure as I can now in any manner experience, to dwell upon minute recollections of the school and its concerns. Steeped in misery as I am – misery, alas! only too real – I shall be pardoned for seeking relief, however slight and temporary, in the weakness of a few rambling details. These, moreover, utterly trivial, and even ridiculous in themselves, assume, to my fancy, adventitious importance, as connected with a period and a locality when and where I recognise the first ambiguous monitions of the destiny which afterwards so full overshadowed me. Let me then remember.

The house, I have said, was old, irregular, and cottage-built. The grounds were extensive, and an enormously high and solid brick wall, topped with a bed of mortar and broken glass, encompassed the whole. This prison-like rampart formed the limit of our domain; beyond it we saw but thrice a week – once every Saturday afternoon, when, attended by two ushers, we were permitted to take brief walks in a body through some of the neighboring fields – and twice during Sunday, when we were paraded in the same formal manner to the morning and evening service in the one church of the village. Of this church the principal of our school was pastor. With how deep a spirit of wonder and perplexity was I wont to regard him from our remote pew in the gallery, as, with step solemn and slow, he ascended the pulpit! This reverend man, with countenance so demurely benign, with robes so glossy and so clerically flowing, with wig so minutely powdered, so rigid and so vast, – could this be he who, of late, with sour visage, and in snuffy habiliments, administered, ferule in hand, the Draconian Laws of the academy? Oh, gigantic paradox, too utterly monstrous for solution!

At an angle of the ponderous wall frowned a more ponderous gate. It was riveted and studded with iron bolts, and surmounted with jagged iron spikes. What impressions of

deep awe it inspired! It was never opened save for the three
periodical egressions and ingressions already mentioned; then,
in every creak of its mighty hinges, we found a plenitude of
mystery−a world of matter for solemn remark, or for far more
solemn meditation.

The extensive enclosure was irregular in form, having
many capacious recesses. Of these, three or four of the largest
constituted the play-ground. It was level, and covered with fine
hard gravel. I well remember it had no trees, nor benches, nor
anything similar within it. Of course it was in the rear of the
house. In front lay a small parterre, planted with box and
other shrubs; but through this sacred division we passed only
upon rare occasions indeed−such as a first advent or final
departure from school or perhaps, when a parent or friend
having called for us, we joyfully took our way home for the
Christmas or Midsummer holydays.

But the house!−how quaint an old building was this!−to
me how veritably a palace of enchantment! There was really
no end to its windings−to its incomprehensible subdivisions.
It was impossible, at any given time, to say with certainty upon
which of its two stories one happened to be. From each room
to every other there were sure to be found three or four steps
either in ascent or descent. Then the lateral branches were
innumerable−inconceivable−and so returning in upon themselves, that our most exact ideas in regard to the whole
mansion were not very far different from those with which we
pondered upon infinity. During the five years of my residence
here, I was never able to ascertain with precision, in what
remote locality lay the little sleeping apartment assigned to
myself and some eighteen or twenty other scholars.

The school-room was the largest in the house−I could not
help thinking, in the world. It was very long, narrow, and
dismally low, with pointed Gothic windows and a ceiling of
oak. In a remote and terror-inspiring angle was a square

enclosure of eight or ten feet, comprising the *sanctum,* "during hours," of our principal, the Reverend Dr. Bransby. It was a solid structure, with massy door, sooner than open which in the absence of the "Dominie," we would all have willingly perished by the *peine forte et dure* [torture]. In other angles were two other similar boxes, far less reverenced, indeed, but still greatly matters of awe. One of these was the pulpit of the "classical" usher, one of the "English and mathematical." Interspersed about the room, crossing and recrossing in endless irregularity, were innumerable benches and desks, black, ancient, and time-worn, piled desperately with much-bethumbed books, and so beseamed with initial letters, names at full length, meaningless gashes, grotesque figures, and other multiplied efforts of the knife, as to have utterly lost what little of original form might have been their portion in days long departed. A huge bucket with water stood at one extremity of the room, and a clock of stupendous dimensions at the other.

Encompassed by the massy walls of this venerable academy, I passed, yet not in tedium or disgust, the years of the third lustrum of my life. The teeming brain of childhood requires no external world of incident to occupy or amuse it; and the apparently dismal monotony of a school was replete with more intense excitement than my riper youth has derived from luxury, or my full manhood from crime. Yet I must believe that my first mental development had in it much of the uncommon—even much of the *outré.* Upon mankind at large the events of very early existence rarely leave in mature age any definite impression. All is gray shadow—a weak and irregular remembrance—an indistinct regathering of feeble pleasures and phantasmagoric pains. With me this is not so. In childhood I must have felt with the energy of a man what I now find stamped upon memory in lines as vivid, as deep, and as durable as the exergues of the Catharginian medals.

Yet in fact—in the fact of the world's view—how little was

there to remember! The morning's awakening, the nightly
summons to bed; the connings, the recitations; the periodical
half-holidays, and perambulations; the play-ground, with its
broils, its pastimes, its intrigues; – these, by a mental sorcery
long forgotten, were made to involve a wilderness of sensation,
a world of rich incident, an universe of varied emotion, of
excitement the most passionate and spirit-stirring. *"Oh, le bon
temps, que ce siecle de fer* [Oh, the age of iron was such a
good time]!"

In truth, the ardency, the enthusiasm, and the imperious-
ness of my disposition, soon rendered me a marked character
among my schoolmates, and by slow, but natural gradations,
gave me an ascendancy over all not greatly older than myself; –
over all with one single exception. This exception was found in
the person of a scholar, who, although no relation, bore the
same Christian and surname as myself; – a circumstance, in
truth, little remarkable; for, notwithstanding a noble descent,
mine was one of those everyday appellations which seem, by
prescriptive right, to have been, time out of mind, the common
property of the mob. In this narrative I have therefore
designated myself as William Wilson, – a fictitious title not
very dissimilar to the real. My namesake alone, of those who
in school phraseology constituted "our set," presumed to
compete with me in the studies of the class – in the sports and
broils of the play-ground – to refuse implicit belief in my
assertions, and submission to my will – indeed, to interfere
with my arbitrary dictation in any respect whatsoever. If there
be on earth a supreme and unqualified despotism, it is the
despotism of a master mind in boyhood over the less energetic
spirits of his companions.

Wilson's rebellion was to me a source of the greatest
embarrassment; the more so as, in spite of the bravado with
which in public I made a point of treating him and his
pretensions, I secretly felt that I feared him, and could not

help thinking the equality which he maintained so easily with myself, a proof of his true superiority; since not to be overcome cost me a perpetual struggle. Yet this superiority – even this equality – was in truth acknowledged by no one but myself; our companions, by some unaccountable blindness, seemed not even to suspect it. Indeed, his competition, his resistance, and especially his impertinent and dogged interference with my purposes, were not more pointed than private. He appeared to be utterly destitute alike of the ambition which urged, and of the passionate energy of mind which enabled me to excel. In his rivalry he might have been supposed actuated solely by a whimsical desire to thwart, astonish, or mortify myself; although there were times when I could not help observing, with a feeling made up of wonder, abasement, and pique, that he mingled with his injuries, his insults, or his contradictions, a certain most inappropriate, and assuredly most unwelcome *affectionateness* of manner. I could only conceive this singular behavior to arise from a consummate self-conceit assuming the vulgar airs of patronage and protection.

Perhaps it was this latter trait in Wilson's conduct, conjoined with our identity of name, and the mere accident of our having entered the school upon the same day, which set afloat the notion that we were brothers, among the senior classes in the academy. These do not usually inquire with much strictness into the affairs of their juniors. I have before said, or should have said, that Wilson was not, in the most remote degree, connected with my family. But assuredly if we *had* been brothers we must have been twins; for, since leaving Dr. Bransby's, I casually learned that my namesake – a somewhat remarkable coincidence – was born on the nineteenth of January, 1811 – and this is precisely the day of my own nativity.

It may seem strange that in spite of the continual anxiety occasioned me by the rivalry of Wilson, and his intolerable spirit of contradiction, I could not bring myself to hate him altogether. We had, to be sure, nearly every day, a quarrel in which, yielding me publicly the palm of victory, he, in some manner, contrived to make me feel that it was he who had deserved it; yet a sense of pride upon my part, and a veritable dignity upon his own, kept us always upon what are called "speaking terms," while there were many points of strong congeniality in our tempers, operating to awake in me a sentiment which our position alone, perhaps, prevented from ripening into friendship. It is difficult, indeed, to define, or even to describe, my real feelings towards him. They were formed of a heterogeneous mixture—some petulant animosity, which was not yet hatred, some esteem, more respect, much fear, with a world of uneasy curiosity. To the moralist fully acquainted with the minute springs of human action, it will be unnecessary to say, in addition, that Wilson and myself were the most inseparable of companions.

It was no doubt the anomalous state of affairs existing between us, which turned all my attacks upon him, (and they were many, either open or covert) into the channel of banter or practical joke (giving pain while assuming the aspect of mere fun) rather than into that of a more serious and determined hostility. But my endeavors on this head were by no means uniformly successful, even when my plans were the most wittily concocted; for my namesake had much about him, in character, of that unassuming and quiet austerity which, while enjoying the poignancy of its own jokes, has no heel of Achilles in itself, and absolutely refuses to be laughed at. I could find, indeed, but one vulnerable point, and that, lying in a personal peculiarity, arising, perhaps, from constitutional disease, would have been spared by an antagonist less at his wit's end than myself;—my rival had a weakness in the faucial or guttural organs, which precluded him from raising his voice at any time *above a very low whisper.*

Of this defect I did not fail to take what poor advantage lay
in my power.

Wilson's retaliations in kind were many; and there was one
form of his practical wit that disturbed me beyond measure.
How his sagacity first discovered at all that so petty a thing
would vex me, is a question I never could solve; but, having
discovered, he habitually practised the annoyance. I had
always felt aversion to my uncourtly patronymic, and its very
common, if not plebeian praenomen. The words were venom
in my ears; and when, upon the day of my arrival, a second
William Wilson came also to the academy, I felt angry with
him for bearing the name, and doubly disgusted with the
name because a stranger bore it, who would be the cause of its
twofold repetition, who would be constantly in my presence,
and whose concerns, in the ordinary routine of the school
business, must inevitably, on account of the detestable
coincidence, be often confounded with my own.

The feeling of vexation thus engendered grew stronger with
every circumstance tending to show resemblance, moral or
physical, between my rival and myself. I had not then discovered the remarkable fact that we were of the same age; but I
saw that we were of the same height, and I perceived that we
were not altogether unlike in general contour of person and
outline of feature. I was galled, too, by the rumor touching a
relationship, which had grown current in the upper forms. In a
word, nothing could more seriously disturb me, (although I
scrupulously concealed such disturbance,) than any allusion to
a similarity of mind, person, or condition existing between us.
But, in truth, I had no reason to believe that (with the
exception of the matter of relationship, and in the case of
Wilson himself,) this similarity had ever been made a subject
of comment, or even observed at all by our schoolfellows.
That *he* observed it in all its bearings, and as fixedly as I, was
apparent; but that he could discover in such circumstances so

fruitful a field of annoyance for myself can only be attributed, as I said before, to his more than ordinary penetration.

His cue, which was to perfect an imitation of myself, lay both in words and in actions; and most admirably did he play his part. My dress it was an easy matter to copy; my gait and general manner were, without difficulty, appropriated; in spite of his constitutional defect, even my voice did not escape him. My louder tones were, of course, unattempted, but then the key, it was identical; *and his singular whisper, it grew the very echo of my own.*

How greatly this most exquisite portraiture harrassed me, (for it could not justly be termed a caricature,) I will not now venture to describe. I had but one consolation – in the fact that the imitation, apparently, was noticed by myself alone, and that I had to endure only the knowing and strangely sarcastic smiles of my namesake himself. Satisfied with having produced in my bosom the intended effect, he seemed to chuckle in secret over the sting he had inflicted, and was characteristically disregardful of the public applause which the success of his witty endeavors might have so easily elicited. That the school, indeed, did not feel his design, perceive its accomplishment, and participate in his sneer, was, for many anxious months, a riddle I could not resolve. Perhaps the *gradation* of his copy rendered it not so readily perceptible; or, more possibly, I owed my security to the masterly air of the copyist, who, disdaining the letter, (which in a painting is all the obtuse can see,) gave but the full spirit of his original for my individual contemplation and chagrin.

I have already more than once spoken of the disgusting air of patronage which he assumed towards me, and of his frequent officious interference with my will. This interference often took the ungracious character of advice; advice not openly given, but hinted or insinuated. I received it with a repugnance which gained strength as I grew in years. Yet, at

this distant day, let me do him the simple justice to acknowledge that I can recall no occasion when the suggestions of my
rival were on the side of those errors or follies so usual to his
immature age and seeming inexperience; that his moral sense,
at least, if not his general talents and worldly wisdom, was far
keener than my own; and that I might, to-day, have been a
better, and thus a happier man, had I more seldom rejected
the counsels embodied in those meaning whispers which I
then but too cordially hated and too bitterly derided.

As it was, I at length grew restive in the extreme under his
distasteful supervision, and daily resented more and more
openly what I considered his intolerable arrogance. I have said
that, in the first years of our connexion as schoolmates, my
feelings in regard to him might have been easily ripened into
friendship: but, in the latter months of my residence at the
academy, although the intrusion of his ordinary manner had,
beyond doubt, in some measure, abated, my sentiments, in
nearly similar proportion, partook very much of positive
hatred. Upon one occasion he saw this, I think, and afterwards
avoided, or made a show of avoiding me.

It was about the same period, if I remember aright, that, in
an altercation of violence with him, in which he was more
than usually thrown off his guard, and spoke and acted with
an openness of demeanor rather foreign to his nature, I
discovered, or fancied I discovered, in his accent, his air, and
general appearance, a something which first startled, and then
deeply interested me, by bringing to mind dim visions of my
earliest infancy—wild, confused and thronging memories of a
time when memory herself was yet unborn. I cannot better
describe the sensation which oppressed me, than by saying
that I could with difficulty shake off the belief that myself and
the being who stood before me had been acquainted at some
epoch very long ago—some point of the past even infinitely
remote. The delusion, however, faded rapidly as it came; and I

mention it at all but to define the day of the last conversation I there held with my singular namesake.

The huge old house, with its countless subdivisions, had several enormously large chambers communicating with each other, where slept the greater number of the students. There were, however, (as must necessarily happen in a building so awkwardly planned,) many little nooks or recesses, the odds and ends of the structure; and these the economic ingenuity of Dr. Bransby had also fitted up as dormitories; although, being the merest closets, they were capable of accommodating only a single individual. One of these small apartments was occupied by Wilson.

It was upon a gloomy and tempestuous night of an early autumn, about the close of my fifth year at the school, and immediately after the altercation just mentioned, that, finding every one wrapped in sleep, I arose from bed, and lamp in hand, stole through a wilderness of narrow passages from my own bedroom to that of my rival, I had been long plotting one of those ill-natured pieces of practical wit at his expense in which I had hitherto been so uniformly unsuccessful. It was my intention, now, to put my scheme in operation, and I resolved to make him feel the whole extent of the malice with which I was imbued. Having reached his closet, I noiselessly entered, leaving the lamp, with a shade over it, on the outside. I advanced a step, and listened to the sound of his tranquil breathing. Assured of his being asleep, I returned, took the light, and with it again approached the bed. Close curtains were around it, which, in the prosecution of my plan, I slowly and quietly withdrew, when the bright rays fell vividly upon the sleeper, and my eyes, at the same moment, upon his countenance. I looked;–and a numbness, an iciness of feeling instantly pervaded my frame. My breast heaved, my knees tottered, my whole spirit became possessed with on objectless yet intolerable horror. Gasping for breath, I lowered the lamp

in still nearer proximity to the face. Were these,—*these the*
lineaments of William Wilson? I saw, indeed, that they were
his, but I shook as with a fit of the ague, in fancying they were
not. What *was* there about them to confound me in this
manner? I gazed;—while my brain reeled with a multitude of
incoherent thoughts. Not thus he appeared—assuredly not
thus—in the vivacity of his waking hours. The same name! the
same contour of person! the same day of arrival at the
academy! And then his dogged and meaningless imitation of
my gait, my voice, my habits, and my manner! Was it, in truth,
within the bounds of human possibility, that *what I now
witnessed* was the result of the habitual practice of this sarcastic
imitation? Awe-stricken, and with a creeping shudder, I extinguished the lamp, passed silently from the chamber, and left, at
once, the halls of that old academy, never to enter them again.

After a lapse of some months, spent at home in mere
idleness, I found myself a student at Eton. The brief interval
had been sufficient to enfeeble my remembrance of the events
at Dr. Bransby's, or at least to effect a material change in the
nature of the feelings with which I remembered them. The
truth—the tragedy—of the drama was no more. I could now
find room to doubt the evidence of my senses; and seldom
called up the subject at all but with wonder at the extent of
human credulity, and a smile at the vivid force of the
imagination which I hereditarily possessed. Neither was this
species of skepticism likely to be diminished by the character
of the life I led at Eton. The vortex of thoughtless folly into
which I there so immediately and so recklessly plunged,
washed away all but the froth of my past hours, engulfed at
once every solid or serious impression, and left to memory
only the veriest levities of a former existence.

I do not wish, however, to trace the course of my miserable
profligacy here—a profligacy which set at defiance the laws,
while it eluded the vigilance of the institution. Three years of

folly, passed without profit, had but given me rooted habits of vice, and added, in a somewhat unusual degree, to my bodily stature, when, after a week of soulless dissipation, I invited a small party of the most dissolute students to a secret carousal in my chamber. We met at a late hour for the night; for our debaucheries were to be faithfully protracted until morning. The wine flowed freely, and there were not wanting other, perhaps more dangerous seductions; so that the gray dawn had already faintly appeared in the east, while our delirious extravagance was at its height. Madly flushed with cards and intoxication, I was in the act of insisting upon a toast of more than intolerable profanity, when my attention was suddenly diverted by the violent, although partial unclosing of the door of the apartment, and by the eager voice from without of a servant. He said that some person, apparently in great haste, demanded to speak with me in the hall.

Wildly excited with the potent *Vin de Barac,* the unexpected interruption rather delighted than surprised me. I staggered forward at once, and a few steps brought me to the vestibule of the building. In this low and small room there hung no lamp; and now no light at all was admitted, save that of the exceedingly feeble dawn which made its way through a semi-circular window. As I put my foot over the threshold, I became aware of the figure of a youth about my own height, and (what then peculiarly struck my mad fancy) habited in a white cassimere morning frock, cut in the novel fashion of the one I myself wore at the moment. This the faint light enabled me to perceive; but the features of his face I could not distinguish. Immediately upon my entering, he strode hurriedly up to me, and seizing me by the arm with a gesture of petulant impatience, whispered the words "William Wilson!" in my ear.

I grew perfectly sober in an instant.

There was that in the manner of the stranger, and in the tremulous shake of his uplifted finger, as he held it between

my eyes and the light, which filled me with unqualified
amazement; but it was not this which had so violently moved
me. It was the pregnancy of solemn admonition in the
singular, low, hissing utterance; and, above all, it was the
character, the tone, *the key,* of those few, simple, and familiar,
yet whispered syllables, which came with a thousand thronging memories of by-gone days, and struck upon my soul with
the shock of a galvanic battery. Ere I could recover the use of
my senses he was gone.

Although this event failed not of a vivid effect upon my
disordered imagination, yet was it evanescent as vivid. For
some weeks, indeed, I busied myself in earnest inquiry, or was
wrapped in a cloud of morbid speculation. I did not pretend
to disguise from my perception the identity of the singular
individual who thus perseveringly interfered with my affairs,
and harrassed me with his insinuated counsel. But who and
what was this Wilson? – and whence came he? – and what
were his purposes? Upon neither of these points could I be
satisfied – merely ascertaining, in regard to him, that a sudden
accident in his family had caused his removal from Dr.
Bransby's academy on the afternoon of the day in which I
myself had eloped. But in a brief period I ceased to think upon
the subject, my attention being all absorbed in a contemplated
departure for Oxford. Thither I soon went, the uncalculating
vanity of my parents furnished me with an outfit and annual
establishment, which would enable me to indulge at will in
the luxury already so dear to my heart – to vie in profuseness
of expenditure with the haughtiest heirs of the wealthiest
earldoms in Great Britain.

Excited by such appliances to vice, my constitutional
temperament broke forth with redoubled ardor, and I spurned
even the common restraints of decency in the mad infatuation
of my revels. But it were absurd to pause in the detail of my
extravagance. Let it suffice, that among spendthrifts I out-

heroded Herod, and that, giving name to a multitude of novel follies, I added no brief appendix to the long catalogue of vices then usual in the most dissolute university of Europe.

It could hardly be credited, however, that I had, even here, so utterly fallen from the gentlemanly estate, as to seek acquaintance with the vilest arts of the gambler by profession, and, having become an adept in his despicable science, to practise it habitually as a means of increasing my already enormous income at the expense of the weak-minded among my fellow-collegians. Such, nevertheless, was the fact. And the very enormity of this offense against all manly and honorable sentiment proved, beyond doubt, the main if not the sole reason of the impunity with which it was committed. Who, indeed, among my most abandoned associates, would not rather have disputed the clearest evidence of his senses, than have suspected of such courses, the gay, the frank, the generous William Wilson—the noblest and most liberal commoner at Oxford—him whose follies (said his parasites) were but the follies of youth and unbridled fancy—whose errors but inimitable whim—whose darkest vice but a careless and dashing extravagance?

I had been now two years successfully busied in this way, when there came to the university a young *parvenu* nobleman, Glendinning—rich, said report, as Herodes Atticus—his riches, too, as easily acquired. I soon found him of weak intellect, and, of course, marked him as a fitting subject for my skill. I frequently engaged him in play, and contrived, with a gambler's usual art, to let him win considerable sums, the more effectually to entangle him in my snares. At length, my schemes being ripe, I met him (with the full intention that this meeting should be final and decisive) at the chambers of a fellow-commoner, (Mr. Preston,) equally intimate with both, but who, to do him justice, entertained not even a remote suspicion of my design. To give to this a better coloring, I had contrived to have assembled a party of some eight or ten, and was solicitously careful that the introduction of cards should appear accidental, and originate in the proposal of my contemplated dupe himself. To be brief upon a vile topic, none of the low finesse was omitted, so customary upon similar occasions that it is a just matter for wonder how any are still found so besotted as to fall its victim.

We had protracted our sitting far into the night, and I had at length effected the manœuvre of getting Glendinning as my sole antagonist. The game, too, was my favorite *écarté*. The rest of the company, interested in the extent of our play, had abandoned their own cards, and were standing around us as spectators. The *parvenu,* who had been induced by my artifices in the early part of the evening, to drink deeply, now shuffled, dealt, or played, with a wild nervousness of manner for which his intoxication, I thought, might partially, but could not altogether account. In a very short period he had became my debtor to a large amount of money; when, having taken a long draught of port, he did precisely what I had been coolly anticipating—proposed to double our already extravagant stakes. With a well-feigned show of reluctance, and not until after my repeated refusal had seduced him into some angry words which gave a color of *pique* to my compliance, did I finally comply. The result, of course, did but prove how entirely the prey was in my toils: in less than a single hour he had quadrupled his debt. For some time his countenance had been losing the florid tinge lent it by the wine; but now, to my astonishment, I perceived that it had grown to a pallor truly fearful. I say, to my astonishment. Glendinning had been represented to my eager inquiries as immeasurably wealthy; and the sums which he had as yet lost, although in themselves vast, could not, I supposed, very seriously annoy, much less so violently affect him. That he was overcome by the wine just swallowed, was the idea which most readily presented itself;

and, rather with a view to the preservation of my own character in the eyes of my associates, than from any less interested motive, I was about to insist, peremptorily, upon a discontinuance of the play, when some expressions at my elbow from among the company, and an ejaculation evincing utter despair on the part of Glendinning, gave me to understand that I had effected his total ruin under circumstances which, rendering him an object for the pity of all, should have protected him from the ill offices even of a fiend.

What now might have been my conduct it is difficult to say. The pitiable condition of my dupe had thrown an air of embarrassed gloom over all; and, for some moments, a profound and unbroken silence was maintained, during which I could not help feeling my cheeks tingle with the many burning glances of scorn or reproach cast upon me by the less abandoned of the party. I will even own that an intolerable weight of anxiety was for a brief instant lifted from my bosom by the sudden and extraordinary interruption which ensued. The wide, heavy folding doors of the apartment were all at once thrown open, to their full extent, with a vigorous and rushing impetuosity that extinguished, as if by magic, every candle in the room. Their light, in dying, enabled us just to perceive that a stranger had entered, of about my own height, and closely muffled in a cloak. The darkness, however, was now total; and we could only feel that he was standing in our midst. Before any one of us could recover from the extreme astonishment into which this rudeness had thrown all, we heard the voice of the intruder.

"Gentlemen," he said, in a low, distinct, and never-to-be-forgotten *whisper* which thrilled to the very marrow of my bones, "Gentlemen, I make no apology for this behavior, because in thus behaving, I am but fulfilling a duty. You are, beyond doubt, uninformed of the true character of the person who has to-night won at *écarté* a large sum of money from

Lord Glendinning. I will therefore put you upon an expeditious and decisive plan of obtaining this very necessary information. Please to examine, at your leisure, the inner linings of the cuff of his left sleeve, and the several little packages which may be found in the somewhat capacious pockets of his embroidered morning wrapper."

While he spoke, so profound was the stillness that one might have heard a pin dropping upon the floor. In ceasing, he at once departed and as abruptly as he had entered. Can I – shall I describe my sensations? – must I say that I felt all the horrors of the damned? Most assuredly I had but little time given for reflection. Many hands roughly seized me upon the spot, and lights were immediately reprocured. A search ensued. In the lining of my sleeve were found all of the court cards essential in *écarté*, and, in the pockets of my wrapper, a number of packs, fac-similes of those used at our sittings, with the single exception that mine were of the species called, technically, *arrondées*, the honors being slightly convex at the ends, the lower cards slightly convex at the sides. In this disposition, the dupe who cuts, as customary, at the breadth, of the pack, will invariably find that he cuts his antagonist an honor; while the gambler, cutting at the length will, as certainly, cut nothing for his victim which may count in the records of the game.

Any outrageous burst of indignation upon this shameful discovery would have affected me less than the silent contempt, or the sarcastic composure, with which it was received.

"Mr. Wilson," said our host, stooping to remove from beneath his feet an exceedingly luxurious cloak of rare furs, "Mr. Wilson, this is your property." (The weather was cold; and, upon quitting my own room, I had thrown a cloak over my dressing wrapper, putting it off upon reaching the scene of play.) "I presume it is supererogatory to seek here (eyeing the folds of the garment with a bitter smile) for any farther evidence of your skill. Indeed, we have had enough. You will see the necessity, I hope, of quitting Oxford—at all events, of quitting instantly my chambers."

Abased, humbled to the dust as I then was, it is probable that I should have resented this galling language by immediate personal violence, had not my whole attention been immediately arrested by a fact of the most startling character. The cloak which I had worn was of a rare description of fur; how rare, how extravagantly cost, I shall not venture to say. Its fashion, too, was of my own fantastic invention; for I was fastidious to a degree of absurd coxcombry, in matters of this frivolous nature. When, therefore, Mr. Preston reached me that which he had picked up upon the floor, and near the folding-doors of the apartment, it was with an astonishment nearly bordering upon terror, that I perceived my own already hanging on my arm, (where I had no doubt unwittingly placed it,) and that the one presented me was but its exact counter-part in every, in even the minutest possible particular. The singular being who had so disastrously exposed me, had been muffled, I remember, in a cloak; and none had been worn at all by any of the members of our party, with the exception of myself. Retaining some presence of mind, I took the one offered me by Preston; placed it, unnoticed, over my own; left the apart-ment with a resolute scowl of defiance; and, next morning ere dawn of day, commenced a hurried journey from Oxford to the continent, in a perfect agony of horror and shame.

I fled in vain. My evil destiny pursued me as if in exul-tation, and proved, indeed, that the exercise of its mysterious dominion had as yet only begun. Scarcely had I set foot in Paris, ere I had fresh evidence of the detestable interest taken by this Wilson in my concerns. Years flew, while I experienced no relief. Villain!—at Rome, with how untimely, yet with how spectral an officiousness stepped he in between me and my ambition! At Vienna, too—at Berlin—and at Moscow!

Where, in truth, had I *not* bitter cause to curse him within my heart? From his inscrutable tyranny did I at length flee, panic-stricken, as from a pestilence; and to the very ends of the earth I *fled in vain.*

And again, and again, in secret communion with my own spirit, would I demand the questions "Who is he?–whence came he?–and what are his objects?" But no answer was there found. And now I scrutinized, with a minute scrutiny, the forms, and the methods, and the leading traits of his impertinent supervision. But even here there was very little upon which to base a conjecture. It was noticeable, indeed, that, in no one of the multiplied instances in which he had of late crossed my path, had he so crossed it except to frustrate those schemes, or to disturb those actions, which, fully carried out, might have resulted in bitter mischief. Poor justification this, in truth, for an authority so imperiously assumed! Poor indemnity for natural rights of self-agency so pertinaciously, so insultingly denied!

I had also been forced to notice that of my tormentor, for a very long period of time, (while scrupulously and with miraculous dexterity maintaining his whim of an identity of apparel with myself,) had so contrived it, in the execution of his varied interference with my will, that I saw not, at any moment, the features of his face. Be Wilson what he might, *this* at least, was but the veriest of affectation, or of folly. Could he, for an instant, have supposed that, in my admonisher at Eton–in the destroyer of my honor at Oxford–in him who thwarted my ambition at Rome, my revenge in Paris, my passionate love at Naples, or what he falsely termed my avarice in Egypt,–that in this, my arch-enemy and evil genius, I could fail to recognise the William Wilson of my schoolboy days,–the namesake, the companion, the rival,–the hated and dreaded rival at Dr. Bransby's? Impossible!–But let me hasten to the last eventful scene of the drama.

Thus far I had succumbed supinely to this imperious domination. The sentiments of deep awe with which I habitually regarded the elevated character, the majestic wisdom, the apparent omnipresence and omnipotence of Wilson, added to a feeling of even terror, with which certain other traits in his nature and assumptions inspired me, had operated, hitherto, to impress me with an idea of my own utter weakness and helplessness, and to suggest an implicit, although bitterly reluctant submission to his arbitrary will. But, of late days, I had given myself up entirely to wine; and its maddening influence upon my hereditary temper rendered me more and more impatient of control. I began to murmur,– to hesitate,– to resist. And was it only fancy which induced me to believe that, with the increase of my own firmness, that of my tormentor underwent a proportional diminution? Be this as it may, I now began to feel the inspirations of a burning hope, and at length nurtured in my secret thoughts a stern and desperate resolution that I would submit no longer to be enslaved.

It was at Rome, during the Carnival of 18 –, that I attended a masquerade in the palazzo of the Neapolitan Duke Di Broglio. I had indulged more freely than usual in the excesses of the winetable; and now the suffocating atmosphere of the crowded rooms irritated me beyond endurance. The difficulty, too, of forcing my way through the mazes of the company contributed not a little to the ruffling of my temper; for I was anxiously seeking (let me not say with what unworthy motive) the gay, the beautiful wife of the aged and doting Di Broglio. With a too unscrupulous confidence she had previously communicated to me the secret of the costume in which she would be habited, and now, having caught a glimpse of her person, I was hurrying up to make my way into her presence. At this moment I felt a light hand laid upon my shoulder, and that ever-remembered, low, damnable whisper within my ear.

In a perfect whirlwind of wrath, I turned at once upon him who had thus interrupted me, and seized him violently by the collar. He was attired, as I expected, like myself; wearing a large Spanish cloak, and a mask of black silk which entirely covered his features.

"Scoundrel!" I said, in a voice husky with rage, while every syllable I uttered seemed as new fuel to my fury; "scoundrel! imposter! accursed villain! you shall not–you shall *not* dog me unto death! Follow me, or I stab you where you stand!"–and I broke my way from the room into a small ante-chamber adjoining, dragging him unresistingly with me as I went.

Upon entering, I thrust him furiously from me. He staggered against the wall, while I closed the door with an oath, and commanded him to draw. He hesitated but an instant; then, with a slight sigh, drew in silence, and put himself upon his defence.

The contest was brief indeed. I was frantic with every species of wild excitement, and felt within my single arm the energy and the power of a multitude. In a few seconds I forced him by sheer strength against the wainscoting, and thus, getting him at mercy, plunged my sword, with brute ferocity, repeatedly through and through his bosom.

At this instant some person tried the latch of the door. I hastened to prevent an intrusion, and then immediately returned to my dying antagonist. But what human language can adequately portray *that* astonishment, *that* horror which possessed me at the spectacle then presented to view? The brief moment in which I averted my eyes had been sufficient to produce, apparently, a material change in the arrangements at the upper or farther end of the room. A large mirror, it appeared to me, now stood where none had been perceptible before; and, as I stepped up to it in extremity of terror, mine own image, but with features all pale and dabbled in blood, advanced, with a feeble and tottering gait, to meet me.

Thus it appeared, I say, but was not. It was my antagonist—it was Wilson, who then stood before me in the agonies of his dissolution. Not a line in all the marked and singular lineaments of that face which was not, even identically, mine own! His mask and cloak lay, where he had thrown them, upon the floor.

It was Wilson; but he spoke no longer in a whisper, and I could have fancied that I myself was speaking while he said:

"You have conquered, and I yield. Yet, henceforward art thou also dead—dead to the world and its hopes. In me didst thou exist—and, in my death, see by this image, which is thine, how utterly thou hast murdered thyself."

[October, 1839]

THE MURDERS IN THE RUE MORGUE

What song the Syrens sang, or what name Achilles assumed when he hid himself among women, although puzzling questions, are not beyond all conjecture.

—SIR THOMAS BROWNE.

IT IS NOT improbable that a few farther steps in phrenological science will lead to a belief in the existence, if not to the actual discovery and location of an organ of *analysis*. If this power (which may be described, although not defined, as the capacity for resolving thought into its elements) be not, in fact, an essential portion of what late philosophers term ideality, then there are indeed many good reasons for supposing it a primitive faculty. That it may be a constituent of ideality is here suggested in opposition to the vulgar dictum (founded upon the assumptions of grave authority), that the calculating and discriminating powers (causality and comparison) are at variance with the imaginative—that the three, in short, can hardly coexist. But, although thus opposed to received opinion, the idea will not appear ill-founded when we observe that the processes of invention or creation are strictly akin with the processes of resolution—the former being nearly, if not absolutely, the latter conversed.

It cannot be doubted that the mental features discoursed of as the analytical are, in themselves, but little susceptible of analysis. We appreciate them only in their effects. We know of them, among other things, that they are always to their possessor, when inordinately possessed, a source of the liveliest enjoyment. As the strong man exults in his physical ability, delighting in such exercises as call his muscles into action, so glories the analyst in that moral activity which *disentangles.* He derives pleasure from even the most trivial occupations bringing his talent into play. He is fond of enigmas, of conundrums, of hieroglyphics; exhibiting in his solutions of each and all a degree of acumen which appears to the ordinary apprehension præternatural. His results, brought about by the very soul and essence of method, have, in truth, the whole air of intuition.

The faculty in question is possibly much invigorated by mathematical study, and especially by that highest branch of it which, unjustly, and merely on account of its retrograde operations, has been called, as if *par excellence,* analysis. Yet to calculate is not in itself to analyse. A chess-player, for example, does the one without effort at the other. If follows that the game of chess, in its effects upon mental character, is greatly misunderstood. I am not now writing a treatise, but simply prefacing a somewhat peculiar narrative by observations very much at random; I will, therefore, take occasion to assert that the higher powers of the reflective intellect are more decidedly and more usefully taxed by the unostentatious game of draughts than by all the elaborate frivolity of chess. In this latter, where the pieces have different and bizarre motions, with various and variable values, that which is only complex is mistaken (a not unusual error) for that which is profound. The *attention* is here called powerfully into play. If it flag for an instant, an oversight is committed, resulting in injury or defeat. The possible moves being not only manifold but involute, the chances of such oversights are multiplied; and in nine cases out of ten it is the more concentrative rather than the more acute player who conquers. In draughts, on the contrary, where the moves are unique and have but little variation, the prob-abilities of inadvertence are diminished, and the mere attention being left comparatively unemployed, what advantages are obtained by either party are obtained by superior acumen. To be less abstract—Let us suppose a game of draughts where the pieces are reduced to four kings, and where, of course, no oversight is to be expected. It is obvious that here the victory can be decided (the players being at all equal) only by some *recherché* movement, the result of some strong exertion of the intellect. Deprived of ordinary resources, the analyst throws himself into the spirit of his opponent, identifies himself therewith, and not unfrequently sees thus, at a glance, the sole methods (sometimes indeed absurdly simple ones) by which he may seduce into miscalculation or hurry into error.

Whist has long been noted for its influence upon what are termed the calculating powers; and men of the highest order of intellect have been known to take an apparently unaccountable delight in it, while eschewing chess as frivolous. Beyond doubt there is nothing of a similar nature so greatly tasking the faculty of analysis. The best chess-player in Christendom *may* be little more than the best player of chess; but proficiency in whist implies capacity for success in all those more important undertakings where mind struggles with mind. When I say proficiency, I mean that perfection in the game which includes a comprehension of all the sources (whatever be their character) from which legitimate advantage may be derived. These are not only manifold but multiform, and lie frequently among recesses of thought altogether inaccessible to the ordinary understanding. To observe attentively is to remember distinctly; and, so far, the concentrative chess-player will do very well at whist; while the rules of Hoyle (themselves based upon the mere mechanism of the game) are sufficiently and generally comprehensible. Thus to have a retentive memory, and to proceed by "the book," are points commonly regarded as the sum total of good playing. But it is in matters beyond the limits of mere rule where the skill of the analyst is evinced. He makes, in silence, a host of observations and inferences. So, perhaps, do his companions; and the difference in the extent of the information obtained lies not so much in the falsity of the inference as in the quality of the observation. The necessary knowledge is that of *what* to observe. Our player confines himself not at all; nor, because the game is the object, does he reject deductions from things external to the game. He examines the countenance of his partner, comparing it carefully with that of each of his opponents. He considers the mode of assorting the cards in each hand; often counting trump by trump, and honor by honor, through the glances bestowed by their holders upon each. He notes every variation of face as the play progresses, gathering a fund of thought from the differences in the expression of certainty, of surprise, of triumph, or of chagrin. From the manner of gathering up a trick he judges whether the person taking it can make another in the suit. He recognises what is played through feint, by the air with which it is thrown upon the table. A casual or inadvertent word; the accidental dropping or turning of a card, with the accompanying anxiety or carelessness in regard to its concealment; the counting of the tricks, with the order of their arrangement; embarrassment, hesitation, eagerness or trepidation – all afford, to his apparently intuitive perception, indications of the true state of affairs. The first two or three rounds having been played, he is in full possession of the contents of each hand, and thenceforward puts down his cards with as absolute a precision of purpose as if the rest of the party had turned outward the faces of their own.

The analytical power should not be confounded with simple ingenuity; for while the analyst is necessarily ingenious, the ingenious man is utterly incapable of analysis.

I have spoken of this latter faculty as that of resolving thought into its elements, and it is only necessary to glance upon this idea to perceive the necessity of the distinction just mentioned. The constructive or combining power, by which ingenuity is usually manifested, and to which the phrenologists (I believe erroneously) have assigned a separate organ, supposing it a primitive faculty, has been so frequently seen in those whose intellect bordered otherwise upon idiocy, as to have attracted general observation among writers on morals. Between ingenuity and the analytic ability there exists a difference far greater, indeed, than that between the fancy and the imagination, but of a character very strictly analogous. It will be found, in fact, that the ingenious are always fanciful, and the *truly* imaginative never otherwise than profoundly analytic.

The narrative which follows will appear to the reader somewhat in the light of a commentary upon the propositions just advanced.

Residing in Paris during the spring and part of the summer of 18–, I there contracted an intimacy with a Monsieur C. Auguste Dupin. This young gentleman was of an excellent– indeed of an illustrious family, but, by a variety of untoward events, had been reduced to such poverty that the quondam energy of his character succumbed beneath it, and he ceased to bestir himself in the world, or to care for the retrieval of his fortunes. By courtesy of his creditors, there still remained in his possession a small remnant of his patrimony; and, upon the income arising from this, he managed, by means of a rigorous economy, to procure the necessaries of life, without troubling himself about its superfluities. Books, indeed, were his sole luxuries, and in Paris these are easily obtained.

Our first meeting was at an obscure library in the Rue Montmartre, where the accident of our both being in search of the same very rare and very remarkable volume brought us into closer communion. We saw each other again and again. I was deeply interested in the little family history which he detailed to me with all the candor which a Frenchman indulges only when self is his theme. I was astonished, too, at the vast extent of his reading; and, above all, I felt my soul enkindled within me by the wild fervor, and what I could only term the vivid freshness of his imagination. Seeking in Paris the objects I then sought, I felt that the society of such a man would be to me a treasure beyond price; and this feeling I frankly confided to him. It was at length arranged that we should live together during my stay in the city; and as my worldly circumstances were somewhat less embarrassed than his own, I was permitted to be at the expense of renting, and furnishing in a style which suited the rather fantastic gloom of our common temper, a time-eaten and grotesque mansion, long deserted through superstitions into which we did not inquire, and tottering to its fall in a retired and desolate portion of the Faubourg St. Germain.

Had the routine of our life at this place been known to the world, we should have been regarded as madmen – although, perhaps, as madmen of a harmless nature. Our seclusion was perfect. We admitted no visitors whomsoever. Indeed the locality of our retirement had been carefully kept a secret from my own former associates; and it had been many years since Dupin had ceased to know or be known in Paris. We existed within ourselves alone.

It was a freak of fancy in my friend (for what else shall I call it?) to be enamored of the Night for her own sake; and into this *bizarrerie,* as into all his others, I quietly fell; giving myself up to his wild whims with an utter *abandon.* The sable divinity would not herself dwell with us always; but we could counterfeit her presence. At the first dawn of the morning we closed all the massy shutters of our old building, lighting a couple of tapers which, strongly perfumed, threw out only the ghastliest and feeblest of rays. By the aid of these we then busied our souls in dreams – reading, writing, or conversing, until warned by the clock of the advent of the true Darkness. Then we sallied forth into the streets, arm in arm, continuing the topics of the day, or roaming far and wide until a late hour, seeking, amid the wild lights and shadows of the populous city, that infinity of mental excitement which quiet observation could afford.

At such times I could not help remarking and admiring (although from his rich ideality I had been prepared to expect) a peculiar analytic ability in Dupin. He seemed, too, to take an eager delight in its exercise – if not exactly in its display – and did not hesitate to confess the pleasure thus derived. He boasted to me, with a low chuckling laugh, that most men, in respect to himself, wore windows in their bosoms, and was wont to follow up such assertions by direct and very startling proofs of his intimate knowledge of my own. His manner at these moments was frigid and abstract; his eyes were vacant in expression; while his voice, usually a rich tenor, rose into a treble which would have sounded petulantly but for the deliberateness and entire distinctness of the enunciation. Observing him in these moods, I often dwelt meditatively upon the old philosophy of the Bi-Part Soul, and amused myself with the fancy of a double Dupin – the creative and resolvent.

Let it not be supposed, from what I have just said, that I am detailing any mystery, or penning any romance. What I have described in the Frenchman was but the result of an excited, or perhaps of a diseased intelligence. But of the character of his remarks at the periods in question an example will best convey the idea.

We were strolling one night down a long dirty street, in the vicinity of the Palais Royal. Being both, apparently, occupied with thought, neither of us had spoken a syllable for fifteen minutes at least. All at once Dupin broke forth with these words:

"He is a very little fellow, that's true, and would do better for the *Théâtre des Variétés*."

"There can be no doubt of that," I replied unwittingly, and not at first observing (so much had I been absorbed in reflection) the extraordinary manner in which the speaker had chimed in with my meditations. In an instant afterward I recollected myself, and my astonishment was profound.

"Dupin," said I, gravely, "this is beyond my comprehension. I do not hesitate to say that I am amazed, and can scarcely credit my senses. How was it possible you should know I was thinking of – – –?" Here I paused, to ascertain beyond a doubt whether he really knew of whom I thought.

"– – –of Chantilly," said he, "why do you pause? You were remarking to yourself that his diminutive figure unfitted him for tragedy."

That was precisely what had formed the subject of my reflections. Chantilly was a quondam cobbler of the Rue St. Denis, who, becoming stage-mad, had attempted the rôle of Xerxes, in Crébillon's tragedy so called, and been notoriously Pasquinaded for his pains.

"Tell me, for God's sake," I exclaimed, "the method – if method there be – by which you have been enabled to fathom my soul in this matter." In fact, I was even more startled than I would have been willing to express.

"It was the fruiterer," replied my friend, "who brought you to the conclusion that the mender of soles was not of sufficient height for Xerxes *et id genus omne* [and all that sort]."

"The fruiterer! – you astonish me – I know no fruiterer whomsoever."

"The man who ran up against you as we entered the street – it may have been fifteen minutes ago."

I now remembered that, in fact, a fruiterer, carrying upon his head a large basket of apples, had nearly thrown me down, by accident, as we passed from the Rue C– – – into the thoroughfare where we now stood; but what this had to do with Chantilly I could not possibly understand.

There was not a particle of *charlatanerie* about Dupin. "I will explain," he said, "and that you may comprehend all clearly, we will first retrace the course of your meditations,

from the moment in which I spoke to you until that of the
recontre with the fruiterer in question. The larger links of the
chain run thus–Chantilly, Orion, Dr. Nichol, Epicurus,
Stereotomy, the street stones, the fruiterer."

There are few persons who have not, at some period of
their lives, amused themselves in retracing the steps by which
particular conclusions of their own minds have been attained.
The occupation is often full of interest; and he who attempts it
for the first time is astonished by the apparently illimitable
distance and incoherence between the starting-point and the
goal. What, then, must have been my amazement when I heard
the Frenchman speak what he had just spoken, and when I
could not help acknowledging that he had spoken the truth.
He continued:

"We had been talking of horses, if I remember aright, just
before leaving the Rue C– – –. This was the last subject we
discussed. As we crossed into this street, a fruiterer, with a
large basket upon his head, brushing quickly past us, thrust
you upon a pile of paving-stones collected at a spot where the
causeway is undergoing repair. You stepped upon one of the
loose fragments, slipped, slightly strained your ankle, appeared
vexed or sulky, muttered a few words, turned to look at the
pile, and then proceeded in silence. I was not particularly
attentive to what you did; but observation has become with
me, of late, a species of necessity.

"You kept your eyes upon the ground–glancing, with a
petulant expression, at the holes and ruts in the pavement, (so
that I saw you were still thinking of the stones,) until we
reached the little alley called Lamartine, which has been
paved, by way of experiment, with the overlapping and riveted
blocks. Here your countenance brightened up, and, perceiving
your lips move, I could not doubt that you murmured to
yourself the word stereotomic. You continued the same
inaudible murmur, with a knit brow, as is the habit of a man

tasking his memory, until I considered that you sought the Greek derivation of the word stereotomy. I knew that you could not find this without being brought to think of atomies, and thus of the theories of Epicurus; and as, when we discussed this subject not very long ago, I mentioned to you how singularly, yet with how little notice, the vague guesses of that noble Greek had met with confirmation in the late nebular cosmogony, I felt that you could not avoid casting your eyes upward to the great nebula in Orion, and I certainly expected that you would do so. You did look up; and I now was assured that I had correctly followed your steps. But in that bitter *tirade* upon Chantilly, which appeared in yesterday's *Musée,* the satirist, making some disgraceful allusions to the cobbler's change of name upon assuming the buskin, quoted a very peculiar Latin line upon whose meaning we have often conversed. I mean the line

> *Perdidit antiquum litera prima sonum* [The first letter has lost its old sound].

I had told you that this was in reference to Orion, formerly written Urion; and, from certain pungencies connected with this explanation, I was aware that you could not have forgotten it. It was clear, therefore, that you would not fail to combine the two ideas of Orion and Chantilly. That you did combine them I saw by the character of the smile which passed over your lips. You thought of the poor cobbler's immolation. So far, you had been stooping in your gait; but now I saw you draw yourself up to your full height. I was then sure that you reflected upon the diminutive figure of Chantilly. At this point I interrupted your meditations to remark that as, in fact, he *was* a very little fellow—that Chantilly—he would do better at the *Théâtre des Variétés."*

Not long after this, we were looking over an edition of *Le Tribunal* when the following paragraphs arrested our attention.

"Extraordinary Murders.—This morning, about three o'clock, the inhabitants of the Quartier St. Roch were aroused from sleep by a succession of terrific shrieks, issuing, apparently, from the fourth story of a house in the Rue Morgue, known to be in the sole occupancy of one Madame L'Espanaye, and her daughter, Mademoiselle Camille L'Espanaye. After some delay, occasioned by a fruitless attempt to procure admission in the usual manner, the gateway was broken in with a crow-bar, and eight or ten of the neighbors entered, accompanied by two *gendarmes*. By this time the cries had ceased; but, as the party rushed up the first flight of stairs, two or more rough voices, in angry contention, were distinguished, and seemed to proceed from the upper part of the house. As the second landing was reached, these sounds, also, had ceased, and everything remained perfectly quiet. The party spread themselves, and hurried from room to room. Upon arriving at a large back chamber in the fourth story, (the door of which, being found locked, with the key inside, was forced open,) a spectacle presented itself which struck every one present not less with horror than with astonishment.

"The apartment was in the wildest disorder—the furniture broken and thrown about in all directions. There was only one bedstead; and from this the bed had been removed, and thrown into the middle of the floor. On a chair lay a razor, besmeared with blood. On the hearth were two or three long and thick tresses of grey human hair, also dabbled in blood, and seeming to have been pulled out by the roots. Upon the floor were found four Napoleons, an ear-ring of topaz, three large silver spoons, three smaller of *métal d'Alger,* and two bags, containing nearly four thousand francs in gold. The drawers of a *bureau,* which stood in one corner, were open, and had been, apparently, rifled, although many articles still remained in them. A small iron safe was discovered under the *bed* (not under the bedstead). It was open, with the key still in the door.

It had no contents beyond a few old letters, and other papers of little consequence.

"Of Madame L'Espanaye no traces were here seen; but an unusual quantity of soot being observed in the fire-place, a search was made in the chimney, and (horrible to relate!) the corpse of the daughter, head downward, was dragged therefrom; it having been thus forced up the narrow aperture for a considerable distance. The body was quite warm. Upon examining it, many excoriations were perceived, no doubt occasioned by the violence with which it had been thrust up and disengaged. Upon the face were many severe scratches, and, upon the throat, dark bruises, and deep indentations of finger nails, as if the deceased had been throttled to death.

"After a thorough investigation of every portion of the house, without farther discovery, the party made its way into a small paved yard in the rear of the building, where lay the corpse of the old lady, with her throat so entirely cut that, upon an attempt to raise her, the head fell off and rolled to some distance. The body, as well as the head, was fearfully mutilated – the former so much so as scarcely to retain any semblance of humanity.

"To this horrible mystery there is not as yet, we believe, the slightest clew."

The next day's paper had these additional particulars.

"The Tragedy in the Rue Morgue. Many individuals have been examined in relation to this most extraordinary and frightful affair." [The word 'affaire' has not yet, in France, that levity of import which it conveys with us,] "but nothing whatever has transpired to throw light upon it. We give below all the material testimony elicited.

"Pauline Dubourg, laundress, deposes that she has known both the deceased for three years, having washed for them during that period. The old lady and her daughter seemed on good terms – very affectionate toward each other. They were

excellent pay. Could not speak in regard to their mode or means of living. Believed that Madame L. told fortunes for a living. Was reputed to have money put by. Never met any persons in the house when she called for the clothes or took them home. Was sure that they had no servant in employ. There appeared to be no furniture in any part of the building except in the fourth story.

"*Pierre Moreau,* tobacconist, deposes that he has been in the habit of selling small quantities of tobacco and snuff to Madame L'Espanaye for nearly four years. Was born in the neighborhood, and has always resided there. The deceased and her daughter had occupied the house in which the corpses were found, for more than six years. It was formerly occupied by a jeweller, who under-let the upper rooms to various persons. The house was the property of Madame L. She became dissatisfied with the abuse of the premises by her tenant and moved into them herself, refusing to let any portion. The old lady was childish. Witness had seen the daughter some five or six times during the six years. The two lived an exceedingly retired life—were reputed to have money. Had heard it said among the neighbors that Madame L. told fortunes—did not believe it. Had never seen any person enter the door except the old lady and her daughter, a porter once or twice, and a physician some eight or ten times.

"Many other persons, neighbors, gave evidence to the same effect. No one was spoken of as frequenting the house. It was not know whether there were any living connexions of Madame L. and her daughter. The shutters of the front windows were seldom opened. Those in the rear were always closed, with the exception of the large back room, fourth story. The house was a good house—not very old.

"*Isidore Musèt,* gendarme, deposes that he was called to the house about three o'clock in the morning, and found some twenty or thirty persons at the gateway, endeavoring to gain admittance. Forced it open, at length, with a bayonet – not with a crow-bar. Had but little difficulty in getting it open, on account of its being a double or folding gate, and bolted neither at bottom nor top. The shrieks were continued until the gate was forced – and then suddenly ceased. They seemed to be screams of some person (or persons) in great agony – were loud and drawn out, not short and quick. Witness led the way up stairs. Upon reaching the first landing, heard two voices in loud and angry contention – the one a gruff voice, the other much shriller – a very strange voice. Could distinguish some words of the former, which was that of a Frenchman. Was positive that it was not a woman's voice. Could distinguish the words 'sacré [holy]' and 'diable [devil].' The shrill voice was that of a foreigner. Could not be sure whether it was the voice of a man or of a woman. Could not make out what was said, but believed the language to be Spanish. Might have distinguished some words if he had been acquainted with the Spanish. The state of the room and of the bodies was described by this witness as we described them yesterday.

"Henri Duval, a neighbor, and by trade a silver-smith, deposes that he was one of the party who first entered the house. Corroborates the testimony of Musèt in general. As soon as they forced an entrance, they reclosed the door, to keep out the crowd, which collected very fast, notwithstanding the lateness of the hour. The shrill voice, this witness thinks, was that of an Italian. Was certain it was not French. Could not be sure that it was a man's voice. It might have been a woman's. Was not acquainted with the Italian language. Could not distinguish the words, but was convinced by the intonation that the speaker was an Italian. Knew Madame L. and her daughter. Had conversed with both frequently. Was sure that shrill voice was not that of either of the deceased.

" – –Odenheimer, restaurateur. This witness volunteered his testimony. Not speaking French, was examined through an interpreter. Is a native of Amsterdam. Was passing the house at the time of the shrieks. They lasted for several minutes – probably ten. They were long and loud – very awful and distressing. Was one of those who entered the building. Corroborated the previous evidence in every respect but one. Was sure that the shrill voice was that of a man – of a Frenchman. Could not distinguish the words uttered. They were loud and quick – unequal – sometimes quick, sometimes deliberate – spoken apparently in fear as well as in anger. The voice was harsh – not so much shrill as harsh. Could not call it a shrill voice. The gruff voice said repeatedly '*sacré*,' '*diable*,' and once '*mon Dieu*.'

"*Jules Mignaud*, banker, of the firm of Mignaud et Fils, Rue Deloraine. Is the elder Mignaud. Madame L'Espanaye had some property. Had opened an account with his banking house in the spring of the year – – –(eight years previously). Made frequent deposits in small sums. Had checked for nothing until the third day before her death, when she took out in person the sum of 4000 francs. This sum was paid in gold, and a clerk sent home with the money.

"*Adolphe Le Bon*, clerk to Mssrs. Mignaud et Fils, deposes that on the day in question, about noon, he accompanied Madame L'Espanaye to her residence with the 4000 francs, put up in two bags. Upon the door being opened, Mademoiselle L. appeared and took from his hands one of the bags, while the old lady relieved him of the other. He then bowed and departed. Did not see any person in the street at the time. It is a bye street – very lonely.

"*William Bird*, tailor, deposes that he was one of the party who entered the house. Is an Englishman. Has lived in Paris two years. Was one of the first to ascend the stairs. Heard the voices in contention. The gruff voice was that of a Frenchman. Could make out several words, but cannot now remember all. Heard distinctly '*sacré*' and '*mon Dieu*.' There was a sound at the moment as if of several persons struggling – a scraping and scuffling sound. The shrill voice was very loud – louder than the gruff one. Is sure that it was not the voice of an Englishman. Appeared to be that of a German. Might have been a woman's voice. Does not understand German.

"Four of the above-named witnesses, being recalled, deposed that the door of the chamber in which was found the body of Mademoiselle L. was locked on the inside when the party reached it. Every thing was perfectly silent – no groans or noises of any kind. Upon forcing the door no person was seen. The windows, both of the back and front room, were down and firmly fastened from within. A door between the two rooms was closed, but not locked. The door leading from the front room into the passage was locked, with the key on the inside. A small room in the front of the house, on the fourth story, at the head of the passage, was open, the door being ajar. This room was crowded with old beds, boxes, and so forth. These were carefully removed and searched. There was not an inch of any portion of the house which was not carefully searched. Sweeps were sent up and down the chimneys. The house was a four story one, with garrets (*mansardes*). A trap door on the roof was nailed down very securely – did not appear to have been opened for years. The time elapsing between the hearing of the voices in contention and the breaking open of the room door, was variously stated by the witnesses. Some made it as short as three minutes – some as long as five. The door was opened with difficulty.

"*Alfonzo Garcio,* undertaker, deposes that he resides in the Rue Morgue. Is a native of Spain. Was one of the party who entered the house. Did not proceed up stairs. Is nervous, and was apprehensive of the consequences of agitation. Heard the voices in contention. The gruff voice was that of a Frenchman. Could not distinguish what was said. The shrill voice was that of an Englishman – is sure of this. Does not understand the English language, but judges by the intonation.

"*Alberto Montani,* confectioner, deposes that he was among the first to ascend the stairs. Heard the voices in question. The gruff voice was that of a Frenchman. Distinguished several words. The speaker appeared to be expostulating. Could not make out the words of the shrill voice. Spoke quick and unevenly. Thinks it the voice of a Russian. Corroborates the general testimony. Is an Italian. Never conversed with a native of Russia.

"Several witnesses, recalled, here testified that the chimneys of all the rooms on the fourth story were too narrow to admit the passage of a human being. By 'sweeps' were meant cylindrical sweeping-brushes, such as are employed by those who clean chimneys. These brushes were passed up and down every flue in the house. There is no back passage by which any one could have descended while the party proceeded up stairs. The body of Mademoiselle L'Espanaye was so firmly wedged in the chimney that it could not be got down until four or five of the party united their strength.

"*Paul Dumas,* physician, deposes that he was called to view the bodies about day-break. They were both then lying on the sacking of the bedstead in the chamber where Mademoiselle L. was found. The corpse of the young lady was much bruised and excoriated. The fact that it had been thrust up the chimney would sufficiently account for these appearances. The throat was greatly chafed. There were several deep scratches just below the chin, together with a series of livid spots which were evidently the impression of fingers. The face was fearfully discolored, and the eye-balls protruded. The tongue had been partially bitten through. A large bruise was discovered upon the pit of the stomach, produced, apparently, by the pressure of a knee. In the opinion of M. Dumas, Mademoiselle L'Espanaye had been throttled to death by some person or persons unknown. The corpse of the mother was horribly mutilated. All the bones of the right leg

and arm were more or less shattered. The left tibia much
splintered, as well as all the ribs of the left side. Whole
body dreadfully bruised and discolored. It was not possible to
say how the injuries had been inflicted. A heavy club of wood,
or a broad bar of iron–a chair–any large, heavy, and obtuse
weapon would have produced such results, if wielded by the
hands of a very powerful man. No woman could have inflicted
the blows with any weapon. The head of the deceased, when
seen by witness, was entirely separated from the body,
and was also greatly shattered. The throat had evidently
been cut with some very sharp instrument–probably
with a razor.

"*Alexandre Etienne,* surgeon, was called with M. Dumas to
view the bodies. Corroborated the testimony, and the opinions
of M. Dumas.

"Nothing farther of importance was elicited, although
several other persons were examined. A murder so mysterious,
and so perplexing in all its particulars, was never before
committed in Paris–if indeed a murder has been committed at
all. The police are entirely at fault–an unusual occurrence in
affairs of this nature. There is not, however, the shadow of a
clew apparent."

The evening edition of the paper stated that the greatest
excitement still continued in the Quartier St. Roch–that the
premises in question had been carefully re-searched, and fresh
examinations of witnesses instituted, but all to no purpose. A
postscript, however, mentioned that Adolphe Le Bon had been
arrested and imprisoned–although nothing appeared to
criminate him, beyond the facts already detailed.

Dupin seemed singularly interested in the progress of this
affair–at least so I judged from his manner, for he made no
comments whatever. It was only after the announcement that
Le Bon had been imprisoned, that he asked me my opinion
respecting it.

I could merely agree with all Paris in considering it an insoluble mystery. I saw no means by which it would be possible to trace the murderer.

"We must not judge of the means," said Dupin, "by this shell of an examination. The Parisian police, so much extolled for acumen, are cunning, but no more. There is no method in their proceedings, beyond the method of the moment. They make a vast parade of measures; but, not unfrequently, these are so illy adapted to the objects proposed, as to put us in mind of Monsieur Jourdain's calling for his *robe-de-chambre – pour mieux entendre la musique* [dressing-gown – the better to hear the music]. The results attained by them are not unfrequently surprising, but, for the most part, are brought out by simple diligence and activity. When these qualities are unavailing, their schemes fail. Vidocq, for example, was a good guesser, and a persevering man. But, without educated thought, he erred continually by the very intensity of his investigations. He impaired his vision by holding the object too close. He might see, perhaps, one or two points with unusual clearness, but in so doing he, necessarily, lost sight of the matter as a whole. Thus there is such a thing as being too profound. Truth is not always in a well. In fact, as regards the more important knowledge, I do believe that she in invariably superficial. The depth lies in the valleys where we seek her, and not upon the mountain tops where she is found. The modes and sources of this kind of error are well typified in the contemplation of the heavenly bodies. To look at a star by glances – to view it in a side-long way, by turning toward it the exterior portions of the retina (more susceptible of feeble impressions of light than the interior), is to behold the star distinctly – is to have the best appreciation of its lustre – a lustre which grows dim just in proportion as we turn our vision *fully* upon it. A greater number of rays actually fall upon the eye in the latter case, but, in the former, there is the more refined capacity for comprehension. By undue profundity we perplex and enfeeble thought; and it is possible to make even Venus herself vanish from the firmament by a scrutiny too sustained, too concentrated, and too direct.

"As for these murders, let us enter into some examinations for ourselves, before we make up an opinion respecting them. An inquiry will afford us amusement," [I thought this an odd term, so applied, but said nothing] "and, besides, Le Bon once rendered me a service for which I am not ungrateful. We will go and see the premises with our own eyes. I know G– – –, the *Prefêt de Police,* and shall have no difficulty in obtaining the necessary permission."

This permission was obtained, and we proceeded at once to the Rue Morgue. This is one of those miserable thoroughfares which intervene between the Rue Richelieu and the Rue St. Roch. It was late in the afternoon when we reached it; for this Quartier is at a great distance from that in which we resided. The house we readily found; for there were still many persons gazing up at the closed shutters, with an objectless curiosity, from the opposite side of the way. It was an ordinary Parisian house, with a gateway, on one side of which was a glazed watch-box, with a sliding panel in the window, indicating a *loge de concierge* [concierge's booth]. Before going in we walked up the street, turned down an alley, and then, again turning, passed in the rear of the building – Dupin, meanwhile, examining the whole neighborhood, as well as the house, with a minuteness of attention for which I could see no possible object.

Retracing our steps, we came again to the front of the dwelling, rang, and, having shown our credentials, were admitted by the agents in charge. We went up stairs – into the chamber where the body of Mademoiselle L'Espanaye had been found, and where both the deceased still lay. The disorders of the room had, as usual, been suffered to exist. I saw nothing

beyond what had been stated in the *Tribunal*. Dupin
scrutinized every thing–not excepting the bodies of the
victims. We then went into the other rooms, and into the yard;
a gendarme accompanying us throughout. Our examination
occupied us until dark, when we took our departure. On our
way home my companion stepped in for a moment at the
office of one of the daily papers.

I have said that the whims of my friend were manifold,
and that *Je les ménageais* [I put up with them]:–for this phrase
there is no English equivalent. It was his humor, now, to
decline all conversation on the subject of the murder, until
after we had taken a bottle of wine together about noon the
next day. He then asked me, suddenly, if I had observed any
thing *peculiar* at the scene of the atrocity.

There was something in his manner of emphasizing the
word "peculiar," which caused me to shudder, without
knowing why.

"No, nothing *peculiar*," I said; "nothing more, at least, than
we both saw stated in the paper."

"*Le Tribunal*," he replied, "has not entered, I fear, into the
unusual horror of the thing. But we will not revert to the idle
opinions of this print. It appears to me that this mystery is
considered insoluble, for the very reasons which should cause
it to be regarded as easy of solution–I mean for the *outré*
character of its features. The police are confounded by the
seeming absence of motive–not for the murder itself–but for
the atrocity of the murder. They are puzzled by the seeming
impossibility of reconciling the voices heard in contention,
with the facts that no one was discovered upstairs but the
assassinated Mademoiselle L'Espanaye, and that there were no
means of egress without the notice of the party ascending. The
wild disorder of the room; the corpse thrust, with the head
downward, up the chimney; the frightful mutilation of the
body of the old lady; these considerations, with those just

mentioned, and others which I need not mention, have sufficed to paralyze the powers, by putting completely at fault the boasted acumen, of the government agents. They have fallen into the gross but common error of confounding the unusual with the abstruse. But it is by these deviations from the plane of the ordinary, that reason feels its way, if at all, in its search after the true. In investigations such as we are now pursuing, it should not be so much asked 'what has occurred,' as 'what has occurred which has never occurred before.' In fact, the facility with which I shall arrive, or have arrived, at the solution of this mystery, is in exact ratio with its apparent insolubility in the eyes of the police."

I stared at the speaker in mute astonishment.

He continued.

"I am now awaiting," continued he, looking toward the door of our apartment–"I am now awaiting a person who, although perhaps not the perpetrator of these butcheries, must have been in some measure implicated in their perpetration. Of the worst portion of the crimes committed, it is probable that he is innocent. I hope that I am right in this supposition; for upon it I build my expectation of reading the entire riddle. I look for the man here–in this room–every moment. It is true that he may not arrive; but the probability is that he will. Should he come, it will be necessary to detain him. Here are pistols; and we both know how to use them when occasion demands their use."

I took the pistols, scarcely knowing what I did, or believing what I heard, while Dupin went on, very much as if in a soliloquy. I have already spoken of his abstract manner at such times. His discourse was addressed to myself; but his voice, although by no means loud, had that intonation which is commonly employed in speaking to some one at a great distance. His eyes, vacant in expression, regarded only the wall.

"That the voices heard in contention," he said, "by the party upon the stairs, were not the voices of the women themselves, was fully proved by the evidence. This relieves us of all doubt upon the question whether the old lady could have first destroyed the daughter, and afterward have committed suicide. I speak of this point chiefly for the sake of method; for the strength of Madame L'Espanaye would have been utterly unequal to the task of thrusting her daughter's corpse up the chimney as it was found; and the nature of the wounds upon her own person entirely preclude the idea of self-destruction. Murder, then, has been committed by some third party; and the voices of this third party were those heard in contention. Let me now advert–not to the whole testimony respecting these voices–but to what was peculiar in that testimony. Did you observe any thing peculiar about it?"

I remarked that, while all the witnesses agreed in supposing the gruff voice to be that of a Frenchman, there was much disagreement in regard to the shrill, or, as one individual termed it, the harsh voice.

"That was the evidence itself," said Dupin, "but it was not the peculiarity of the evidence. You have observed nothing distinctive. Re-employing my own words I may say that you have pointed out no prominence above the plane of the ordinary, by which reason may feel her way. Yet there *was* something to be pointed out. The witnesses, as you remark, agreed about the gruff voice; they were here unanimous. But in regard to the shrill voice, the peculiarity is–not that they disagreed–but that, while an Italian, an Englishman, a Spaniard, a Hollander, and a Frenchman attempted to describe it, each one spoke of it as that *of a foreigner.* Each is sure that it was not the voice of one of his own countrymen. Each likens it–not to the voice of an individual of any nation with whose language he is conversant–but the converse. The Frenchman supposes it the voice of a Spaniard, and 'might have distinguished some words *had he been acquainted with Spanish.'* The Dutchman maintains it to have been that of a Frenchman; but we find it stated that *'not understanding French this witness was examined through an interpreter.'* The Englishman thinks it the voice of a German, and *'does not understand German.'* The Spaniard 'is sure' that it is that of an Englishman, but 'judges by the intonation' altogether, *'as he has no knowledge of the English.'* The Italian believes it the voice of a Russian, but *'has never conversed with a native of Russia.'* A second Frenchman differs, moreover, with the first, and is positive that the voice is that of an Italian; but, *'not being cognizant of that tongue,'* is, like the Spaniard, 'convinced by the intonation.' Now, how strangely unusual must that voice have really been, about which such testimony as this *could* have been elicited – in whose *tones,* even, denizens of the five great divisions of Europe could recognise nothing familiar! You will say that it might have been the voice of an Asiatic – of an African. Neither Asiatics nor Africans abound in Paris; but, without denying the inference, I will just now merely call your attention to three points which have relation to this topic. The voice is termed by one witness 'harsh rather than shrill.' It is represented by two others to have been 'quick and *unequal.'* No words – no sounds resembling words – were by any witness mentioned as distinguishable.

"I know not," continued Dupin, "what impression I may have made, so far, upon your own understanding; but I do not hesitate to say that legitimate deductions even from this portion of the testimony – the portion respecting the gruff and shrill voices – are in themselves sufficient to engender a suspicion which should bias, or give direction to all farther progress in the investigation of the mystery. I said 'legitimate deductions;' but my meaning is not thus fully expressed. I designed to imply that the deductions were the *sole* proper ones, and that the suspicion arose *inevitably* from them as the single result. What the suspicion is, however, I will not say just yet. I merely wish you to bear in mind that, with myself, it was sufficiently forcible to give a definite form—a certain tendency—to my inquiries in the chamber.

"Let us now transport ourselves, in fancy, to that chamber. What shall we first seek here? The means of egress employed by the murderers. It is not too much to say that we neither of us believe in præternatural events. Madame and Mademoiselle L'Espanaye were not destroyed by spirits. The doers of the dark deed were material, and escaped materially. Then how? Fortunately, there is but one mode of reasoning upon this point, and that mode *must* lead us to a definite decision.—Let us examine, each by each, the possible means of egress. It is clear that the assassins were in the room where Mademoiselle L'Espanaye was found, or at least in the room adjoining, when the party ascended the stairs. It is then only from these two apartments that we have to seek for issues. The police have laid bare the floors, the ceilings, and the masonry of the walls, in every direction. No *secret* issues could have escaped their vigilance. But, not trusting to their eyes. I examined with my own. There were, then, *no* secret issues. Both doors leading from the rooms into the passage were securely locked, with the keys inside. Let us turn to the chimneys. These, although of ordinary width for some eight or ten feet above the hearths, will not admit, throughout their extent, the body of a large cat. The impossibility of egress, by means already stated, being thus absolute, we are reduced to the windows. Through those of the front room no one could have escaped without notice from the crowd in the street. The murderers *must* have passed, then, through those of the back room. Now, brought to this conclusion in so unequivocal a manner as we are, it is not our part, as reasoners, to reject it on account of apparent impossibilities. It is only left for us to prove that these 'impossibilities' are not such.

"There are two windows in the chamber. One of them is unobstructed by furniture, and is wholly visible. The lower portion of the other is hidden from view by the head of the unwieldy bedstead which is thrust close up against it. The former was found securely fastened from within. It resisted the utmost force of those who endeavored to raise it. A large gimlet-hole had been pierced in its frame to the left, and a very stout nail was found fitted therein, nearly to the head. Upon examining the other window, a similar nail was seen similarly fitted in it; and a vigorous attempt to raise this sash failed also. The police were now entirely satisfied that egress had not been in these directions. And, *therefore,* it was thought a matter of supererogation to withdraw the nails and open the windows.

"My own examination was somewhat more particular, and was so for the reason I have just given – because here it was, I knew, that all apparent impossibilities *must* be proved to be not such in reality.

"I proceeded to think thus – *a posteriori.* The murderers *did* escape from one of these windows. This being so, they could not have re-fastened the sashes from the inside, as they were found fastened; – the consideration which put a stop, through its obviousness, to the scrutiny of the police in this quarter. Yet the sashes *were* fastened. They *must,* then, have the power of fastening themselves. There was no escape from this conclusion. I stepped to the unobstructed casement, withdrew the nail with some difficulty, and attempted to raise the sash. It resisted all my efforts, as I had anticipated. A concealed spring must, I now knew, exist; and this corroboration of my idea convinced me that my premises, at least, were correct, however mysterious still appeared the circumstances attending the nails. A careful search soon brought to light the hidden spring. I pressed it, and, satisfied with the discovery, forbore to upraise the sash.

"I now replaced the nail and regarded it attentively. A person passing out this window might have reclosed it, and the spring would have caught–but the nail could not have been replaced. The conclusion was plain, and again narrowed in the field of my investigations. The assassins *must* have escaped through the other window. Supposing, then, the springs upon each sash to be the same, as was probable, there *must* be found a difference between the nails, or at least between the modes of their fixture. Getting upon the sacking of the bedstead, I looked over the head-board minutely at the second casement. Passing my hand down behind the board, I readily discovered and pressed the spring, which was, as I had supposed, identical in character with its neighbor. I now looked at the nail. It was as stout as the other, and apparently fitted in the same manner–driven in nearly up to the head.

"You will say that I was puzzled; but, if you think so, you must have misunderstood the nature of the inductions. To use a sporting phrase, I had not been once 'at fault.' The scent had never for an instant been lost. There was no flaw in any link of the chain. I had traced the secret to its ultimate result,–and that result was *the nail*. It had, I say, in every respect, the appearance of its fellow in the other window; but this fact was an absolute nullity (conclusive as it might seem to be) when compared with the consideration that here, at this point, terminated the clew. 'There *must* be something wrong,' I said, 'about the nail.' I touched it; and the head, with about the eighth of an inch of the shank, came off in my fingers. The rest of the shank was in the gimlet-hole, where it had been broken off. The fracture was an old one (for its edges were incrusted with rust), and had apparently been accomplished by the blow of a hammer, which had partially imbedded, in the top of the bottom sash, the head portion of the nail. I now carefully replaced this head portion in the indentation whence I had taken it, and the resemblance to a perfect nail was complete. Pressing the spring, I gently raised the sash for a few inches; the head went up with it, remaining firm in its bed. I closed the window, and the semblance of the whole nail was again perfect.

"The riddle, so far, was now unriddled. The assassins had escaped through the window which looked upon the bed. Dropping of its own accord upon their exit (or perhaps purposely closed by them) it had become fastened by the spring; and it was the retention of this spring which had been mistaken by the police for that of the nail,–farther inquiry being thus considered unnecessary.

"The next question is that of the mode of descent. Upon this point I had been satisfied in my walk with you around the building. About five feet and a half from the casement in question there ran a lightning-rod. From this rod it would have been impossible for any one to reach the window itself, to say nothing of entering it. I observed, however, that the shutters of the fourth story were of the peculiar kind called by Parisian carpenters *ferrades*–a kind rarely employed at the present day, but frequently seen upon very old mansions at Lyons and Bourdeaux. They are in the form of an ordinary door, (a single, not a folding door) except that the lower half is latticed or worked in open trellis–thus affording an excellent hold for the hands. In the present instance these shutters are fully three feet and a half broad. When we saw them from the rear of the house, they were both about half open–that is to say, they stood off at right angles from the wall. It is probable that the police, as well as myself, examined the back of the tenement; but, if so, in looking at these *ferrades* in the line of their breadth (as they must have done), they did not perceive this great breadth itself, or at all events, failed to take it into due consideration. In fact, having once satisfied themselves that no egress could have been made in this quarter, they would naturally bestow here a very cursory examination.

It was clear to me, however, that the shutter belonging to the window at the head of the bed, would, if swung fully back to the wall, reach to within two feet of the lightning-rod. It was also evident that, by exertion of a very unusual degree of activity and courage, an entrance into the window, from the rod, might have been thus effected.–By reaching to the distance of two feet and a half (we now suppose the shutter open to its whole extent) a robber might have taken a firm grasp upon the trellis-work. Letting go, then, his hold upon the rod, placing his feet firmly against the wall, and springing boldly from it, he might have swung the shutter so as to close it, and, if we imagine the window open at the time, might even have swung himself into the room.

"I wish you to bear especially in mind that I have spoken of a *very* unusual degree of activity as requisite to success in so hazardous and so difficult a feat. It is my design to show you, first, that the thing might possibly have been accomplished: but, secondly and *chiefly*, I wish to impress upon your understanding the *very extraordinary*–the almost præternatural character of that agility which could have accomplished it.

"You will say, no doubt, using the language of the law, that 'to make out my case,' I should rather undervalue, than insist upon a full estimation of the activity required in this matter. This may be the practice in law, but it is not the usage of reason. My ultimate object is only the truth. My immediate purpose is to lead you to place in juxta-position, that *very unusual* activity of which I have just spoken, with that *very peculiar* shrill (or harsh) and *unequal* voice, about whose nationality no two persons could be found to agree, and in whose utterance no syllabification could be detected."

At these words a vague and half-formed conception of the meaning of Dupin flitted over my mind. I seemed to be upon the verge of comprehension, without power to comprehend – as men, at times, find themselves upon the brink of

remembrance, without being able, in the end, to remember.
My friend went on with his discourse.

"You will see," he said, "that I have shifted the question
from the mode of egress to that of ingress. It was my design to
convey the idea that both were effected in the same manner, at
the same point. Let us now revert in fancy to the interior of
the room. Let us survey the appearances here. The drawers of
the bureau, it is said, had been rifled, although many articles
of apparel still remained within them. The conclusion here is
absurd. It is a mere guess – a very silly one – and no more. How
are we to know that the articles found in the drawers were not
all these drawers had originally contained? Madame L'Espanaye
and her daughter lived an exceedingly retired life – saw no
company – seldom went out – had little use for numerous
changes of habiliment. Those found were at least of as good
quality as any likely to be possessed by these ladies. If a thief
had taken any, why did he not take the best – why did he not
take all? In a word, why did he abandon four thousand francs
in gold to encumber himself with a bundle of linen? The gold
was abandoned. Nearly the whole sum mentioned by Monsieur
Mignaud, the banker, was discovered, in bags, upon the floor. I
wish you, therefore, to discard from your thoughts the
blundering idea of *motive,* engendered in the brains of the
police by that portion of the evidence which speaks of money
delivered at the door of the house. Coincidences ten times as
remarkable as this (the delivery of the money, and murder
committed within three days upon the party receiving it),
happen to each and all of us every hour of our lives, without
attracting even a momentary notice. Coincidences, in general,
are great stumbling-blocks in the way of that class of thinkers
who have been educated to know nothing and care less of the
theory of probabilities – that theory to which the most glorious
objects of human research are indebted for the most glorious
of illustration. In the present instance, had the gold been gone,

the fact of its delivery three days before would have formed
something more than a coincidence. It would have been
corroborative of this idea of motive. But, under the real
circumstances of the case, if we are to suppose gold the motive
of this outrage, we must also imagine the perpetrator so
vacillating an idiot as to have abandoned his gold and his
motive together.

"Keeping now steadily in mind the points to which I have
drawn your attention–that peculiar voice, that unusual agility,
and that startling absence of motive in a murder so singularly
atrocious as this–let us glance at the butchery itself. Here is a
woman strangled to death by manual strength, and thrust up a
chimney, head downward. Ordinary assassins employ no such
modes of murder as this. Least of all, do they thus dispose of
the murdered. In the manner of thrusting the corpse up the
chimney, you will admit that there was something *excessively
outré*–something altogether irreconcilable with our common
notions of human action, even when we suppose the actors
the most depraved of men. Think, too, what must have been
the degree of that strength which could have thrust the body
up such an aperture so forcibly that the united vigor of several
persons was found barely sufficient to drag it *down!*

"Turn, now to other indications of the employment of a
vigor most marvellous. On the hearth were thick tresses–very
thick tresses–of grey human hair. These had been *torn out by
the roots*. You are aware of the great force necessary in tearing
thus from the head even twenty or thirty hairs together. You
saw the locks in question as well as myself. Their roots (a
hideous sight!) were clotted with fragments of the flesh of the
scalp–sure token of the prodigious power which had been
exerted in uprooting perhaps a million of hairs at a time. The
throat of the old lady was not merely cut, but the head absolutely severed from the body: the instrument was a mere razor.
Here again we have evidence of that vastness of strength upon

which I would fix your attention. I wish you also to look, and to look steadily, at the *brutal* ferocity of these deeds. Of the bruises upon the body of Madame L'Espanaye I do not speak. Monsieur Dumas, and his worthy coadjutor Monsieur Etienne, have pronounced that they were inflicted by some obtuse instrument; and so far these gentlemen are very correct. The obtuse instrument was clearly the stone pavement in the yard, upon which the victim had fallen from the window which looked in upon the bed. This idea, however simple it may now seem, escaped the police for the same reason that the breadth of the shutters escaped them – because, by the affair of the nails, their perceptions had been hermetically sealed against the possibility of the windows having ever been opened at all.

"If now, in addition to all these things, you have properly reflected upon the odd disorder of the chamber, we have gone so far as to combine the ideas of a strength superhuman, an agility astounding, a ferocity brutal, a butchery without motive, a *grotesquerie* in horror absolutely alien from humanity, and a voice foreign in tone to the ears of men of many nations, and devoid of all distinct or intelligible syllabification. What result, then, has ensued? What impression have I made upon your fancy?"

I shuddered as Dupin asked me the question. "A madman," I said, "has done this deed – some raving maniac, escaped from a neighboring *Maison de Santé.*"

"In some respects," he replied, "your idea is not irrelevant. But the voices of madmen, even in their wildest paroxysms, are never found to tally with that peculiar voice heard upon the stairs. Madmen are of some nation, and their language, however incoherent in its words, has always the coherence of syllabification. Besides, the hair of a madman is not such hair as I now hold in my hand. I disentangled this little tuft from among the tresses remaining upon the head of Madame L'Espanaye. Tell me what you can make of it."

"Good God," I said, completely unnerved; "this hair is most unusual – this is no *human* hair."

"I have not asserted that it was," said he; "but, before we decide upon this point, I wish you to glance at the little sketch I have here traced upon this paper. It is a *fac-simile* drawing of what has been described in one portion of the testimony as 'dark bruises, and deep indentations of finger-nails,' upon the throat of Mademoiselle L'Espanaye, and in another, (by Messrs. Dumas and Etienne,) as a 'series of livid spots, evidently the impression of fingers.'

"You will perceive," continued my friend, spreading out the paper upon the table before us, "you will perceive that this drawing gives the idea of a firm and fixed hold. There is no *slipping* apparent. Each finger has retained – possibly until the death of the victim – the fearful grasp by which it originally imbedded itself. Attempt, now, to place all your fingers, at one and the same time, in the impressions as you see them."

I made the attempt in vain.

"We are possibly not giving this matter a fair trial," he said. "The paper is spread out upon a plane surface; but the human throat is cylindrical. Here is a billet of wood, the circumference of which is about that of the throat. Wrap the drawing around it, and try the experiment again."

I did so; but the difficulty was even more obvious than before. "This," I said, "is the mark of no human hand."

"Assuredly it is not," replied Dupin –"read now this passage from Cuvier."

It was a minute anatomical and generally descriptive account of the large fulvous Ourang-Outang of the East Indian Islands. The gigantic stature, the prodigious strength and activity, the wild ferocity, and the imitative propensities of these mammalia are sufficiently well known to all. I understood the full horrors of the murder at once.

"The description of the digits," said I, as I made an end of reading, "is in exact accordance with this drawing. I see that no animal but an Ourang–Outang, of the species here mentioned, could have impressed the indentations as you have traced them. This tuft of yellow hair is identical in character with that of the beast of Cuvier. But I cannot possibly comprehend the particulars of this frightful mystery. Besides, there were *two* voices heard in contention, and one of them was unquestionably the voice of a Frenchman."

"True, and you will remember an expression attributed almost unanimously, by the evidence, to this voice,–the expression, 'mon Dieu!' This, under the circumstances, has been justly characterized by one of the witnesses (Montani, the confectioner,) as an expression of remonstrance or expostulation. Upon these two words, therefore, I have mainly built my hopes of a full solution of the riddle. A Frenchman was cognizant of the murder. It is possible–indeed it is far more than probable–that he was innocent of all participation in the bloody transactions which took place. The Ourang-Outang may have escaped from him. He may have traced it to this chamber; but, under the agitating circumstances which ensued, he could never have re-captured it. It is still at large. I will not pursue these guesses–for I have no right to call them more than guesses–since the shades of reflection upon which they are based are scarcely of sufficient depth to be appreciable by my own intellect, and since I could not pretend to make them intelligible to the understanding of another than myself. We will call them guesses then, and speak of them as such. If the Frenchman in question be indeed, as I suppose, innocent of this atrocity, this advertisement, which I left last night, upon our return home, at the office of Le Monde, (a paper devoted to the shipping interest, and much sought for by sailors,) will bring him to our residence."

He handed me a paper, and I read thus:

> CAUGHT—*In the Bois de Boulogne, early on the morning of the*
> *— — inst., (the morning of the murder,) a very large, tawny-colored*
> *Ourang-Outang of the Bornese species. The owner, (who is ascertained*
> *to be a sailor, belonging to a Maltese vessel,) may have the animal*
> *again, upon identifying it satisfactorily, and paying a few charges*
> *arising from its capture and keeping. Call at No. — —, Rue — —,*
> *Faubourg St. Germain—au troisième* [fourth floor].

"How was it possible," I asked, "that you should know the man to be a sailor, and belonging to a Maltese vessel?"

"I do *not* know it," said Dupin. "I am not *sure* of it. Here, however, is a small piece of ribbon, which has evidently, from its form, and from its greasy appearance, been used in tying the hair in one of those long *queues* of which sailors are so fond. Moreover, this knot is one which few besides sailors can tie, and is peculiar to the Maltese. I picked the ribbon up at the foot of the lightning-rod. It could not have belonged to either of the deceased. Now if, after all, I am wrong in my induction from this ribbon, that the Frenchman was a sailor belonging to a Maltese vessel, still I can have done no harm in stating what I did in the advertisement. If I am in error, he will merely suppose that I have been misled by some circumstance into which he will not take the trouble to inquire. But if I am right, a great point is gained. Cognizant of the murder, although not guilty, the Frenchman will naturally hesitate about replying to the advertisement—about demanding the Ourang-Outang. He will reason thus:—'I am innocent; I am poor; my Ourang-Outang is of great value—to one in my circumstances a fortune of itself—why should I lose it through idle apprehensions of danger? Here it is, within my grasp. It was found in the Bois de Boulogne—at a vast distance from the scene of that butchery. How can it ever be suspected that a brute beast should have done the deed? The police are at fault—they have failed to procur the slightest clew. Should they even trace the animal, it would be impossible to prove me cognizant of the murder, or to implicate me in guilt on account of that cognizance. Above all, *I am known.* The advertiser designates me as the possessor of the beast. I am not sure to what limit his knowledge may extend. Should I avoid claiming a property of so great a value, which it is known that I possess, I will render the animal at least, liable to suspicion. It is not my policy to attract attention either to myself or to the beast. I will answer the advertisement, get the Ourang-Outang, and keep it close until this matter has blown over.' "

At this moment we heard a step upon the stairs.

"Be ready," said Dupin, "with your pistols, but neither show them nor use them until at a signal from myself."

The front door of the house had been left open, and the visiter had entered, without ringing, or rapping, and advanced several steps upon the staircase. Now, however, he seemed to hesitate. Presently we heard him descending. Dupin was moving quickly to the door, when we again heard him coming up. He did not turn back a second time, but stepped up quickly and rapped at the door of our chamber.

"Come in," said Dupin, in a cheerful and hearty tone.

The visiter entered. He was a sailor, evidently,—a tall, stout, and muscular-looking man, with a certain dare-devil expression of countenance, not altogether unprepossessing. His face, greatly sunburnt, was more than half hidden by a world of whisker and *mustachio.* He had with him a huge oaken cudgel, but appeared to be otherwise unarmed. He bowed awkwardly, and bade us "good evening," in French accents, which, although somewhat Neufchatelish, were still sufficiently indicative of a Parisian origin.

"Sit down, my friend," said Dupin. "I suppose you have called about the Ourang-Outang. Upon my word, I almost envy you the possession of him; a remarkably fine, and no doubt a very valuable animal. How old do you suppose him to be?"

The sailor drew a long breath, with the air of a man relieved of some intolerable burden, and then replied, in an assured tone: "I have no way of telling–but he can't be more than four or five years old. Have you got him here?"

"Oh, no; we had no conveniences for keeping him here. He is at a livery stable in the Rue Dubourg, just by. You can get him in the morning. Of course you are prepared to identify the property?"

"To be sure I am, sir."

"I shall be sorry to part with him," said Dupin.

"I don't mean that you should be at all this trouble for nothing, sir," said the man. "Couldn't expect it. Am very willing to pay a reward for the finding of the animal–that is to say, any reward in reason."

"Well," replied my friend, "this is all very fair, to be sure. Let me think!–what reward ought I to have? Oh! I will tell you. My reward shall be this. You shall give me all the information in your power about that affair of the murder in the Rue Morgue."

Dupin said these last words in a very low tone, and very quietly. Just as quietly, too, he walked towards the door, locked it, and put the key in his pocket. He then drew a pistol from his bosom and placed it, without the least flurry, upon the table.

The sailor's face flushed up with an ungovernable tide of crimson. He started to his feet and grasped his cudgel; but the next moment he fell back into his seat, trembling convulsively, and with the countenance of death itself. He spoke not a single word. I pitied him from the bottom of my heart.

"My friend," said Dupin, in a kind tone, "you are alarming yourself unnecessarily–you are indeed. We mean you no harm whatever. I pledge you the honor of a gentleman, and of a Frenchman, that we intend you no injury. I perfectly well know that you are innocent of the atrocities in the Rue Morgue. It will not do, however, to deny that you are in some measure implicated in them. From what I have already said, you must know that I have had means of information about this matter – means of which you could never have dreamed. Now the thing stands thus. You have done nothing which you could have avoided – nothing, certainly, which renders you culpable. You were not even guilty of robbery, when you might have robbed with impunity. You have nothing to conceal. You have no reason for concealment. On the other hand, you are bound by every principle of honor to confess all that you know. An innocent man is now imprisoned, charged with that crime of which you can point out the perpetrator."

The sailor had recovered his presence of mind, in a great measure, while Dupin uttered these words; but his original boldness of bearing was all gone.

"So help me God," said he, after a brief pause, "I *will* tell you all that I know about this affair; – but I do not expect you to believe one half that I say – I would be a fool indeed if I did. Still, I *am* innocent, and I will make a clean breast if I die for it."

I do not propose to follow the man in the circumstantial narrative which he now detailed. What he stated was, in substance, this. He had lately made a voyage to the Indian Archipelago. A party, of which he formed one, landed at Borneo, and passed into the interior on an excursion of pleasure. Himself and a companion had captured the Ourang-Outang. This companion dying, the animal fell into his own exclusive possession. After great trouble, occasioned by the intractable ferocity of his captive during the home voyage, he at length succeeded in lodging it safely at his own residence in Paris, where, not to attract towards himself the unpleasant curiosity of his neighbors, he kept it carefully secluded, until such time as it should recover from a wound in the foot, received from a splinter on board ship. His ultimate design was to sell it.

Returning home from some sailors' frolic on the night, or rather in the morning of the murder, he found his prisoner occupying his own bed-room, into which he had broken from a closet adjoining, where he had been, as it was thought, securely confined. The beast, razor in hand, and fully lathered, was sitting before a looking-glass, attempting the operation of shaving, in which he had no doubt previously watched his master through the key-hole of the closet. Terrified at the sight of so dangerous a weapon in the possession of an animal so ferocious, and so well able to use it, the man, for some moments, was at a loss what to do. He had been accustomed, however, to quiet the creature, even in its fiercest moods, by the use of a strong wagoner's whip, and to this he now resorted. Upon sight of it, the Ourang-Outang sprang at once through the door of the chamber, down the stairs, and thence, through a window, unfortunately open, into the street.

The Frenchman followed in despair; the ape, razor still in hand, occasionally stopping to look back and gesticulate at his pursuer, until the latter had nearly come up with him. He then again made off. In this manner the chase continued for a long time. The streets were profoundly quiet, as it was nearly three o'clock in the morning. In passing down an alley in the rear of the Rue Morgue, the fugitive's attention was arrested by a light (the only one apparent except those of the town-lamps) gleaming from the open window of Madame L'Espanaye's chamber, in the fourth story of her house. Rushing to the building, he perceived the lightning-rod, clambered up with inconceivable agility, grasped the shutter, which was thrown fully back against the wall, and, by its means, swung himself directly upon the head-board of the bed. The whole feat did not occupy a minute. The shutter was kicked open again by the Ourang-Outang as he entered the room.

The sailor, in the meantime, was both rejoiced and perplexed. He had strong hopes of now recapturing the ape, as it could scarcely escape from the trap into which it had ventured, except by the rod, where it might be intercepted as it came down. On the other hand, there was much cause for anxiety as to what the brute might do in the house. This latter reflection urged the man still to follow the fugitive. A lightning-rod is ascended without difficulty, especially by a sailor; but, when he had arrived as high as the window, which lay far to his left, his career was stopped; the most that he could accomplish was to reach over so as to obtain a glimpse of the interior of the room. At this glimpse he nearly fell from his hold through excess of horror. Now it was that those hideous shrieks arose upon the night, which had startled from slumber the inmates of the Rue Morgue. Madame L'Espanaye and her daughter, habited in their night clothes, had apparently been occupied in arranging some papers in the iron chest already mentioned, which had been wheeled into the middle of the room. It was open, and its contents lay beside it on the floor. Their backs must have been towards the window; and by the time elapsing between the screams and the ingress of the ape, it seems probable that he was not immediately perceived. The flapping-to of the shutter they would naturally have attributed to the wind.

As the sailor looked in, the gigantic beast had seized Madame L'Espanaye by the hair, (which was loose, as she had been combing it,) and was flourishing the razor about her face, in imitation of the motions of a barber. The daughter lay prostrate and motionless; she had swooned. The screams and struggles of the old lady (during which the hair was torn from her head) had the effect of changing the probably pacific purposes of the Ourang-Outang into those of ungovernable wrath. With one determined sweep of his muscular arm he nearly severed her head from her body. The sight of blood inflames his anger into phrenzy. Gnashing his teeth, and flashing fire from his eyes, he flew upon the body of the girl, and imbedded his fearful talons in her throat, retaining his grasp until she expired. His wandering and wild glances fell at this moment upon the head of the bed, over which those of his master, glazed in horror, were just discernible. The fury of the beast, who no doubt bore still in mind the dreaded whip, was instantly converted into dread. Conscious of having deserved punishment, he seemed desirous to conceal his bloody deeds, and skipped about the chamber in an apparent agony of nervous agitation; throwing down and breaking the furniture as he moved, and dragging the bed from the bedstead. In conclusion, he seized first the corpse of the daughter, and thrust it up the chimney, as it was found; then that of the old lady, with which he rushed to the window precipitating it immediately therefrom.

As the ape approached him with his mutilated burden, the sailor shrunk aghast to the rod, and, rather gliding than clambering down it, hurried at once home – dreading the consequences of the butchery, and gladly abandoning, in his terror, all solicitude about the fate of the Ourang-Outang. The words heard by the party upon the staircase were the French-man's exclamations of horror and affright, commingled with the fiendish jabberings of the brute.

I have scarcely anything to add. The Ourang-Outang must have escaped from the chamber, by the rod, just before the breaking of the door. He must have closed the window as he passed through it. He was subsequently caught by the owner himself, who obtained for him a very large sum at the *Jardin des Plantes.* Le Bon was instantly released, upon our narration of the circumstances (with some comments from Dupin) at the *bureau* of the *Préfet de Police.* This functionary, however well disposed to my friend, could not altogether conceal his chagrin at the turn which affairs had taken, and was fain to indulge in a sarcasm or two, in regard to the propriety of every person minding his own business.

"Let him talk," said Dupin, who had not thought it
necessary to reply. "Let him discourse; it will ease his
conscience. I am satisfied with having defeated him in his
own castle. In truth, he is too cunning to be acute. There is no
stamen in his wisdom. It is all head and no body, like the
pictures of the Goddess Laverna,– or, at least, all head and
shoulders, like a codfish. But he is a good fellow after all. I like
him especially for one master stroke of cant, by which he has
attained that reputation for ingenuity which he possesses. I
mean the way he has '*de nier ce qui est, et d'expliquer ce qui n'est
pas* [of denying what is, and of explaining what is not].'"

[April, 1841]

THE MASK OF THE RED DEATH

A FANTASY

THE "RED DEATH" had long devastated the country. No pestilence had been ever so fatal, or so hideous. Blood was its Avatar and its seal – the redness and the horror of blood. There were sharp pains, and sudden dizziness, and then profuse bleedings at the pores, with dissolution. The scarlet stains upon the body and especially upon the face of the victim, were the pest ban which shut him out from the aid and from the sympathy of his fellow-men. And the whole seizure, progress and termination of the disease, were the incidents of half an hour.

But the Prince Prospero was happy and dauntless and sagacious. When his dominions were half depopulated, he summoned to his presence a thousand hale and light-hearted friends from among the knights and dames of his court, and with these retired to the deep seclusion of one of his castellated abbeys. This was an extensive and magnificent structure, the creation of the prince's own eccentric yet august taste. A strong and lofty wall girdled it in. This wall had gates of iron. The courtiers, having entered, brought furnaces and massy hammers and welded the bolts. They resolved to leave means neither of ingress or egress to the sudden impulses of despair from without or of frenzy from within. The abbey was amply provisioned. With such precautions the courtiers might bid defiance to contagion. The external world could take care of itself. In the meantime it was folly to grieve, or to think. The prince had provided all the appliances of pleasure. There were buffoons, there were improvisatori, there were ballet-dancers, there were musicians, there were cards, there was Beauty, there was wine. All these and security were within. Without was the "Red Death."

It was towards the close of the fifth or sixth month of his seclusion, and while the pestilence raged most furiously abroad, that the Prince Prospero entertained his thousand friends at a masked ball of the most unusual magnificence.

It was a voluptuous scene, that masquerade. But first let me tell of the rooms in which it was held. There were seven – an imperial suite. In many palaces, however, such suites form a long and straight vista, while the folding doors slide back nearly to the walls on either hand, so that the view of the whole extent is scarcely impeded. Here the case was very different; as might have been expected from the duke's love of the *bizarre*. The apartments were so irregularly disposed that the vision embraced but little more than one at a time. There was a sharp turn at every twenty or thirty yards, and at each turn a novel effect. To the right and left, in the middle of each wall, a tall and narrow Gothic window looked out upon a closed corridor which pursued the windings of the suite. These windows were of stained glass whose color varied in accordance with the prevailing hue of the decorations of the chamber into which it opened. That at the eastern extremity was hung, for example, in blue – and vividly blue were its windows. The second chamber was purple in its ornaments and tapestries, and here the panes were purple. The third was green throughout, and so were the casements. The fourth was furnished and litten with orange – the fifth with white – the sixth with violet. The seventh apartment was closely shrouded in black velvet tapestries that hung all over the ceiling and down the walls, falling in heavy folds upon a carpet of the same material and hue. But in this chamber only, the color of the windows failed to correspond with the decorations. The panes here were scarlet – a deep blood color. Now in no one of the seven apartments was there any lamp or candelabrum, amid the profusion of golden ornaments that lay scattered to and fro or depended from the roof. There was no light of any kind emanating from lamp or candle within the suite of chambers. But in the corridors that followed the suite, there stood, opposite to each window, a heavy tripod, bearing a brazier of fire that projected its rays through the tinted glass and so glaringly illumined the room. And thus were produced a multitude of gaudy and fantastic appearances. But in the western or black chamber the effect of the fire-light that streamed upon the dark hangings through the blood-tinted panes, was ghastly in the extreme, and produced so wild a look upon the countenances of those who entered, that there were few of the company bold enough to set foot within its precincts at all.

It was in this apartment, also, that there stood against the western wall, a gigantic clock of ebony. Its pendulum swung to and fro with a dull, heavy, monotonous clang; and when the minute-hand made the circuit of the face, and the hour was to be stricken, there came forth from the brazen lungs of the clock a sound which was clear and loud and deep and exceedingly musical, but of so peculiar a note and emphasis that, at each lapse of an hour, the musicians in the orchestra were constrained to pause, momently, in their performance, to harken to the sound; and thus the waltzers perforce ceased their evolutions; and there was a brief disconcert of the whole gay company; and, while the chimes of the clock yet rang, it was observed that the giddiest grew pale, and the more aged and sedate passed their hands over their brows as if in confused revery or meditation. But when the echoes had fully ceased, a light laughter at once pervaded the assembly; the musicians looked at each other and smiled as if at their own nervousness and folly, and made whispering vows, each to the other, that the next chiming of the clock should produce in them no similar emotion; and then, after the lapse of sixty minutes, (which embrace three thousand and six hundred seconds of the Time that flies,) there came yet another

chiming of the clock, and then there were the same disconcert
and tremulousness and meditation as before.

But, in spite of these things, it was a gay and magnificent
revel. The tastes of the duke were peculiar. He had a fine eye
for colors and effects. He disregarded the *decora* of mere
fashion. His plans were bold and fiery, and his conceptions
glowed with barbaric lustre. There are some who would have
thought him mad. His followers felt that he was not. It was
necessary to hear and see and touch him to be *sure* that
he was not.

He had directed, in great part, the moveable embellish-
ments of the seven chambers, upon occasion of this great *fête;*
and it was his own guiding taste which had given character to
the costumes of the masqueraders. Be sure they were
grotesque. There were much glare and glitter and piquancy
and phantasm – much of what has been seen in *Hernani.* There
were arabesque figures with unsuited limbs and appointments.
There were delirious fancies such as the madman fashions.
There was much of the beautiful, much of the wanton, much
of the *bizarre,* something of the terrible, and not a little of that
which might have excited disgust. To and fro in the seven
chambers there stalked, in fact, a multitude of dreams. And
these – the dreams – writhed in and about, taking hue from the
rooms, and causing the wild music of the orchestra to seem as
the echo of their steps. And, anon, there strikes the ebony
clock which stands in the hall of the velvet. And then,
momently, all is still, and all is silent save the voice of the
clock. The dreams are stiff-frozen as they stand. But the echoes
of the chime die away – they have endured but an instant – and
a light, half-subdued laughter floats after them as they depart.
And now again the music swells, and the dreams live, and
writhe to and fro more merrily than ever, taking hue from
the many tinted windows through which stream the rays from
the tripods. But to the chamber which lies most westwardly of

the seven, there are now none of the maskers who venture; for the night is waning away; and there flows a ruddier light through the blood-colored panes; and the blackness of the sable drapery appals; and to him whose foot falls upon the sable carpet, there comes from the near clock of ebony a muffled peal more solemnly emphatic than any which reaches *their* ears who indulge in the more remote gaieties of the other apartments.

But these other apartments were densely crowded, and in them beat feverishly the heart of life. And the revel went whirlingly on, until at length there was sounded the twelfth hour upon the clock. And then the music ceased, as I have told; and the evolutions of the waltzers were quieted; and there was an uneasy cessation of all things as before. But now there were twelve strokes to be sounded by the bell of the clock; and thus it happened, perhaps, that more of thought crept, with more of time, into the meditations of the thoughtful among those who revelled. And thus, again, it happened, perhaps, that before the last echoes of the last chime had utterly sunk into silence, there were many individuals in the crowd who had found leisure to become aware of the presence of a masked figure which had arrested the attention of no single individual before. And the rumor of this new presence having spread itself whisperingly around, there arose at length from the whole company a buzz, or murmur, expressive at first of disapprobation and surprise — then, finally, of terror, of horror, and of disgust.

In an assembly of phantasms such as I have painted, it may well be supposed that no ordinary appearance could have excited such sensation. In truth the masquerade license of the night was nearly unlimited; but the figure in question had out-Heroded Herod, and gone beyond the bounds of even the prince's indefinite decorum. There are chords in the hearts of the most reckless which cannot be touched without emotion.

Even with the utterly lost, to whom life and death are equally jests, there *are* matters of which no jest can be properly made. The whole company, indeed, seemed now deeply to feel that in the costume and bearing of the stranger neither wit nor propriety existed. The figure was tall and gaunt, and shrouded from head to foot in the habiliments of the grave. The mask which concealed the visage was made so nearly to resemble the countenance of a stiffened corpse that the closest scrutiny must have had difficulty in detecting the cheat. And yet all this might have been endured, if not approved, by the mad revellers around. But the mummer had gone so far as to assume the type of the Red Death. His vesture was dabbled in *blood* – and his broad brow, with all the features of the face, was besprinkled with the scarlet horror.

When the eyes of the Prince Prospero fell upon this spectral image (which with a slow and solemn movement, as if more fully to sustain its rôle, stalked to and fro among the waltzers) he was seen to be convulsed, in the first moment with a strong shudder either of terror or distaste; but, in the next, his brow reddened with rage.

"Who dares?" he demanded hoarsely of the group that stood around him –"who dares thus to make mockery of our woes? Uncase the varlet – that we may know whom we have to hang at sunrise, from the battlements. Will no one stir at my bidding? – stop and strip him, I say, of those reddened vestures of sacrilege!"

It was in the eastern or blue chamber in which stood the Prince Prospero as he uttered these words. They rang throughout the seven rooms loudly and clearly – for the prince was a bold and robust man, and the music had became hushed at the waving of his hand.

It was in the blue room where stood the prince, with a group of pale courtiers by his side. At first, as he spoke, there was a slight rushing movement of this group in the direction

of the intruder, who at the moment was also near at hand, and
now, with deliberate and stately step, made closer approach to
the speaker. But from a certain nameless awe with which the
mad assumptions of the mummer had inspired the whole
party, there were found none who put forth hand to seize him;
so that, unimpeded, he passed within a yard of the prince's
person; and, while the vast assembly, as if with one impulse,
shrank from the centres of the rooms to the walls, he made his
way uninterruptedly, but with the same solemn and measured
step which had distinguished him from the first, through the
blue chamber to the purple – through the purple to the
green – through the green to the orange – through this again to
the white – and even thence to the violet, ere a decided
movement had been made to arrest him. It was then, however,
that the Prince Prospero, maddening with rage and the shame
of his own momentary cowardice, rushed hurriedly through
the six chambers, while none followed him on account of a
deadly terror that had seized upon all. He bore aloft a drawn
dagger, and had approached, in rapid impetuosity, to within
three or four feet of the retreating figure, when the latter,
having attained the extremity of the velvet apartment, turned
suddenly round and confronted his pursuer. There was sharp
cry – and the dagger dropped gleaming upon the sable carpet,
upon which, instantly afterwards, fell prostrate in death the
Prince Prospero. Then, summoning the wild courage of
despair, a throng of the revellers at once threw themselves into
the black apartment, and, seizing the mummer, whose tall
figure stood erect and motionless within the shadow of the
ebony clock, gasped in unutterable horror at finding the grave
cerements and corpse-like mask which they handled with so
violent a rudeness, untenanted by any tangible form.

And now was acknowledged the presence of the Red
Death. He had come like a thief in the night. And one by one
dropped the revellers in the blood-bedewed halls of their revel,

and died each in the despairing posture of his fall. And the life of the ebony clock went out with that of the last of the gay. And the flames of the tripods expired. And Darkness and Decay and the Red Death held illimitable dominion over all.

[April 30, 1842]

THE PIT AND THE PENDULUM

Impia tortorum longas hic turba furores
Sanguinis innocui, non satiata, aluit,
Sospite nunc patria, fracto nunc funeris antro,
Mors ubi dira fuit, vita salusque patent.

[Here the wicked mob, unappeased,
long cherished a hatred of innocent blood.
Now that the fatherland is saved, and the cave of death demolished;
where grim death has been, life and health appear.]

[Quatrain composed for the gates of a market to be erected upon
the site of the Jacobin Club House in Paris.]

I WAS SICK – sick unto death with that long agony; and when
they at length unbound me, and I was permitted to sit, I felt
that my senses were leaving me. The sentence – the dread
sentence of death – was the last of distinct accentuation which
reached my ears. After that, the sound of the inquisitorial
voices seemed merged in one dreamy indeterminate hum. It
conveyed to my soul the idea of *revolution* – perhaps from its
association in fancy with the burr of a mill-wheel. This only
for a brief period; for presently I heard no more. Yet, for a
while, I saw; but with how terrible an exaggeration! I saw the
lips of the black-robed judges. They appeared to me white –
whiter than the sheet upon which I trace these words – and
thin even to grotesqueness; thin with the intensity of their
expression of firmness – of immoveable resolution – of stern
contempt of human torture. I saw that the decrees of what to
me was Fate, were still issuing from those lips. I saw them
writhe with a deadly locution. I saw them fashion the syllables
of my name; and I shuddered because no sound succeeded. I
saw, too, for a few moments of delirious horror, the soft and
nearly imperceptible waving of the sable draperies which

enwrapped the walls of the apartment. And then my vision fell
upon the seven tall candles upon the table. At first they wore
the aspect of charity, and seemed white slender angels who
would save me; but then, all at once, there came a most deadly
nausea over my spirit, and I felt every fibre in my frame thrill
as if I had touched the wire of a galvanic battery, while the
angel forms became meaningless spectres, with heads of flame,
and I saw that from them there would be no help. And there
stole into my fancy, like a rich musical note, the thought of
what sweet rest there must be in the grave. The thought came
gently and stealthily, and it seemed long before it attained full
appreciation; but just as my spirit came at length properly to
feel and entertain it, the figures of the judges vanished, as if
magically, from before me; the tall candles sank into
nothingness; their flames went out utterly; the blackness of
darkness supervened; all sensation appeared swallowed up in
that mad rushing descent as of the soul into Hades. Then
silence, and stillness, and night were the universe.

I had swooned; but will not say that all of consciousness
was lost. What of it there remained I will not attempt to
define, or even to describe; yet all was not lost. In the deepest
slumber—no! In delirium—no! In a swoon—no! In death—no!
even in the grave all *is not* lost. Else there is no immortality for
man. Arousing from the most profound of slumbers, we break
the gossamer web of *some* dream. Yet in a second afterwards,
(so frail may that web have been) we remember not that we
have dreamed. In the return to life from the swoon there are
two stages; first, that of the sense of mental or spiritual;
secondly, that of the sense of physical, existence. It seems
probable that if, upon reaching the second stage, we could
recall the impressions of the first, we should find these
impressions eloquent in memories of the gulf beyond. And
that gulf is—what? How at least shall we distinguish its
shadows from those of the tomb? But if the impressions of

what I have termed the first stage, are not, at will, recalled, yet, after long interval, do they not come unbidden, while we marvel whence they come? He who has never swooned is not he who finds strange palaces and wildly familiar faces in coals that glow; is not he who beholds floating in mid-air the sad visions that the many may not view; is not he who ponders over the perfume of some novel flower – is not he whose brain grows bewildered with the intense meaning of some musical cadence which has never before arrested his attention.

Amid frequent and thoughtful endeavors to remember; amid earnest struggles to regather some token of the state of seeming nothingness into which my soul had lapsed, there have been moments when I have dreamed of success; there have been brief, very brief periods when I have conjured up remembrances which the lucid reason of a later epoch assures me could have had reference only to that condition of what men term unconsciousness. These shadows of memory tell, indistinctly, of tall figures that lifted and bore me in silence down – down – still down – till a hideous dizziness oppressed me at the mere idea of the interminableness of the descent. They tell also of a vague horror at my heart on account of that heart's unnatural stillness. Then comes a sense of sudden motionlessness throughout all things; as if those who bore me (a ghastly train!) had outrun, in their descent, the limits of the limitless, and paused from the wearisomeness of their toil. After this I call to mind flatness and dampness; and then all is *madness* – the madness of a memory which busies itself among forbidden things.

Very suddenly there came back to my soul motion and sound – the tumultuous motion of the heart, and, in my ears, the sound of its beating. Then a pause in which all is blank. Then again sound, and motion, and touch – a tingling sensation pervading my frame. Then the mere consciousness of existence, without thought – a condition which lasted long.

Then, very suddenly, *thought,* and shuddering terror, and earnest endeavor to realize my true state. Then a strong desire to lapse into insensibility. Then a rushing revival of soul and a successful effort to move. And now a full memory of the trial, of the judges, of the tall candles, of the sable draperies, of the sentence, of the sickness, of the swoon. Then entire forgetfulness of all that followed; of all that a later day and much earnestness of endeavor have enabled me vaguely to recall.

So far, I had not opened my eyes. I felt that I lay upon my back, unbound. I reached out my hand, and it fell heavily upon something damp and hard. There I suffered it to remain for many minutes, while I strove to imagine where and *what* I could be. I longed, yet dared not to employ my vision. I dreaded the first glance at objects around. It was not that I feared to look upon things horrible, but that I grew aghast lest there should be *nothing* to see. At length, with a wild desperation at heart, I quickly unclosed my eyes. My worst thoughts, then, were confirmed. The blackness of the eternal night encompassed me. I gasped for breath. The intensity of the darkness seemed to oppress and stifle me. The atmosphere was intolerably close. I still lay quietly, and made effort to exercise my reason. I brought to mind the inquisitorial proceedings, and attempted from that point to deduce my real condition. The sentence had passed; and it appeared to me that a very long interval of time had since elapsed. Yet not for a moment did I suppose myself actually dead. Such a supposition, notwithstanding what we read in fiction, is altogether inconsistent with real existence;—but where and in what state was I? The condemned to death, I knew, perished usually at the *autos-da-fé,* and one of these had been held on the very night of the day of my trial. Had I been remanded to my dungeon, to await the next sacrifice, which would not take place for many months? This I at once saw could not be. Victims had been in immediate demand. Moreover, my

dungeon, as well as all the condemned cells at Toledo, had
stone floors, and light was not altogether excluded.

A fearful idea now suddenly drove the blood in torrents
upon my heart, and for a brief period, I once more relapsed
into insensibility. Upon recovering, I at once started to my feet,
trembling convulsively in every fibre. I thrust my arms wildly
above and around me in all directions. I felt nothing; yet
dreaded to move a step, lest I should be impeded by the walls
of *a tomb*. Perspiration burst from every pore, and stood in
cold big beads upon my forehead. The agony of suspense grew,
at length, intolerable, and I cautiously moved forward, with my
arms extended, and my eyes straining from their sockets, in
the hope of catching some faint ray of light. I proceeded for
many paces; but still all was blackness and vacancy. I breathed
more freely. It seemed evident that mine was not, at least, the
most hideous of fates.

And now, as I still continued to step cautiously onward,
there came thronging upon my recollection a thousand vague
rumors of the horrors at Toledo. Of the dungeons there had
been strange things narrated – fables I had always deemed
them – but yet strange, and too ghastly to repeat, save in a
whisper. Was I left to perish of starvation in this subterrene
world of darkness; or what fate, perhaps even more fearful
awaited me? That the result would be death, and a death of
more than customary bitterness, I knew too well the character
of my judges to doubt. The mode and the hour were all that
occupied or distracted me.

My outstretched hands at length encountered some solid
obstruction. It was a wall, seemingly of stone masonry – very
smooth, slimy, and cold. I followed it up; stepping with all the
careful distrust with which certain antique narratives had
inspired me. This process, however, afforded me no means of
ascertaining the dimensions of my dungeon; as I might make
its circuit, and return to the point whence I set out, without

being aware of the fact; so perfectly uniform seemed the wall. I therefore sought the knife which had been in my pocket, when led into the inquisitorial chamber; but it was gone; my clothes had been exchanged for a wrapper of coarse serge. I had thought of forcing the blade in some minute crevice of the masonry, so as to identify my point of departure. The difficulty, nevertheless, was but trivial; although, in the disorder of my fancy, it seemed at first insuperable. I tore a part of the hem from the robe and placed the fragment at full length, and at right angles to the wall. In groping my way around the prison, I could not fail to encounter this rag upon completing the circuit. So, at least, I thought: but I had not counted upon the extent of the dungeon, or upon my own weakness. The ground was moist and slippery. I staggered onwards for perhaps a half hour, when I stumbled and fell. My excessive fatigue induced me to remain prostrate; and sleep soon overtook me as I lay.

Upon awaking, and stretching forth an arm, I found beside me a loaf and a pitcher with water. I was too much exhausted to reflect upon this circumstance, but ate and drank with avidity. Shortly afterwards, I resumed my tour around the prison, and with much toil, came at last upon the fragment of serge. Up to the period when I fell, I had counted fifty-two paces, and, upon resuming my walk, I had counted forty-eight more—when I arrived at the rag. There were in all, then, a hundred paces; and, admitting two paces to the yard, I presumed the dungeon to be fifty yards in circuit. I had met, however, with many angles in the wall, and thus I could form no guess at the shape of the vault; for vault I could not help supposing it to be.

I had little object—certainly no hope—in these researches; but a vague curiosity prompted me to continue them. Quitting the wall, I resolved to cross the area of the enclosure. At first, I proceeded with extreme caution, for the floor, although seemingly of solid material, was treacherous with slime. At length, however, I took courage, and did not hesitate to step firmly – endeavoring to cross in as direct a line as possible. I had advanced some ten or twelve paces in this manner, when the remnant of the torn hem of my robe became entangled between my legs. I stepped on it, and fell violently on my face.

In the confusion attending my fall, I did not immediately apprehend a somewhat startling circumstance, which yet, in a few seconds afterwards, and while I still lay prostrate, arrested my attention. It was this: my chin rested upon the floor of the prison, but my lips, and the upper portion of my head, although seemingly at a less elevation than the chin, touched nothing. At the same time, my forehead seemed bathed in a clammy vapor, and the peculiar smell of decayed fungus arose to my nostrils. I put forward my arm, and shuddered to find that I had fallen at the very brink of a circular pit, whose extent, of course, I had no means of ascertaining at the moment. Groping about the masonry just below the margin, I succeeded in dislodging a small fragment, and let it fall into the abyss. For nearly a minute I hearkened to its reverberations as it dashed against the sides of the chasm in its descent: at length, there was a sullen plunge into water, succeeded by loud echoes. At the same moment, there came a sound resembling the quick opening, and as rapid closing of a door overhead, while a faint gleam of light flashed suddenly through the gloom, and as suddenly faded away.

I now saw clearly the doom which had been prepared for me, and congratulated myself upon the timely accident by which I had escaped. A step farther before my fall, and the world had seen me no more. And the death just avoided was of that very character which I had regarded as fabulous and frivolous in the tales respecting the Inquisition. To the victims of tyranny, there was the choice of death with its direst physical agonies, or death with its most hideous moral horrors.

I had been reserved for the latter. By long suffering my nerves had been unstrung, until I trembled at the sound of my own voice, and had become in every respect a fitting subject for the species of torture which awaited me.

Shaking in every limb, I groped my way back to the wall – resolving there to perish rather than risk the terrors of the wells, of which my imagination now pictured many in various positions about the dungeon. In other conditions of mind, I might have had courage to end my misery at once, by a plunge into one of these abysses; but now I was the veriest of cowards. Neither could I forget what I had read of these pits – that the *sudden* extinction of life formed no part of their most horrible plan.

Agitation of spirit kept me awake for many long hours; but at length I again slumbered. Upon arousing, I found by my side, as before, a loaf and a pitcher of water. A burning thirst consumed me, and I emptied the vessel at a draught. It must have been drugged – for scarcely had I drunk, before I became irresistibly drowsy. A deep sleep fell upon me – a sleep like that of death. How long it lasted I, of course, know not; but when, once again, I unclosed my eyes, the objects around me were visible. By a wild, sulphurous lustre, the origin of which I could not at first determine, I was enabled to see the extent and aspect of the prison.

In its size I had been greatly mistaken. The whole circuit of its walls did not exceed twenty-five yards. For some minutes this fact occasioned me a world of vain trouble; vain indeed – for what could be of less importance, under the terrible circumstances which environed me, than the mere dimension of my dungeon? But my soul took a wild interest in trifles, and I busied myself in endeavors to account for the error I had committed in my measurement. The truth at length flashed upon me. In my first attempt at exploration, I had counted fifty-two paces, up to the period when I fell: I must then have

been within a pace or two of the fragment of serge; in fact, I
had nearly performed the circuit of the vault. I then slept –
and, upon awaking, I must have returned upon my steps – thus
supposing the circuit nearly double what it actually was. My
confusion of mind prevented me from observing that I began
my tour with the wall to the left, and ended it with the wall
to the right.

I had been deceived, too, in respect to the shape of the
enclosure. In feeling my way, I had found many angles, and
thus deduced an idea of great irregularity; so potent is the
effect of total darkness upon our arousing from lethargy or
sleep! The angles were simply those of a few slight
depressions, or niches, at odd intervals. The general shape of
the prison was square. What I had taken for masonry seemed
now to be iron, or some other metal, in huge plates, whose
sutures or joints occasioned the depressions. The entire
surface of this metallic enclosure was rudely daubed in all the
hideous and repulsive devices to which the charnel
superstition of the monks has given rise. The figures of fiends
in aspects of menace, with skeleton forms, and other more
really fearful images, overspread and disfigured the walls. I
observed that the outlines of these monstrosities were
sufficiently distinct, but that the colors seemed faded and
blurred, as if from the effects of a damp atmosphere. I now
noticed the floor, too, which was of stone. In the centre
yawned the circular pit from whose jaws I had escaped; but it
was the only one in the dungeon.

All this I saw indistinctly and by much effort – for my
personal condition had been greatly changed during slumber. I
now lay upon my back, and at full length, on a species of low
framework of wood. To this I was securely bound by a long
strap resembling a surcingle. It passed in many convolutions
about my limbs and body, leaving at liberty only my head, and
my left arm to such extent, that I could, by dint of much

exertion, supply myself with food from an earthen dish which lay by my side on the floor. I saw, to my horror, that the pitcher was absent: to my horror – for I was consumed with intolerable thirst. This thirst it appeared to be the design of my persecutors to stimulate – for the food in the dish was meat pungently seasoned.

Looking upwards I surveyed the ceiling of my prison. It was some thirty or forty feet overhead, and constructed much as the side walls. In one of its panels a very singular figure riveted my whole attention. It was the painted figure of Time as he is commonly represented, save that, in lieu of a scythe, he held what, at a casual glance, I supposed to be the pictured image of a huge pendulum, such as we see on antique clocks. There was something, however, in the appearance of this machine which caused me to regard it more attentively. While I gazed directly upward at it, (for its position was immediately over my own,) I fancied that I saw it in motion. In an instant afterwards the fancy was confirmed. Its sweep was brief, and of course slow. I watched it for some minutes, somewhat in fear, but more in wonder. Wearied at length with observing its dull movement, I turned my eyes upon the other objects in the cell.

A slight noise attracted my notice, and, looking to the floor, I saw several enormous rats traversing it. They had issued from the well, which lay just within view to my right. Even then, while I gazed, they came up in troops, hurriedly, with ravenous eyes, allured by the scent of the meat. From this it required much effort and attention to scare them away.

It might have been half an hour, perhaps even an hour, (for I could take but imperfect note of time,) before I again cast my eyes upward. What I then saw confounded and amazed me. The sweep of the pendulum had increased in extent by nearly a yard. As a natural consequence, its velocity was also much greater. But what mainly disturbed me was the idea that it had perceptibly *descended*. I now observed – with what horror it is

needless to say – that its nether extremity was formed of a
crescent of glittering steel, about a foot in length from horn to
horn; the horns upward, and the under edge evidently as keen
as that of a razor. Like a razor also, it seemed massy and heavy,
tapering from the edge into a solid and broad structure above.
It was appended to a weighty rod of brass, and the whole
hissed as it swung through the air.

I could no longer doubt the doom prepared for me by
monkish ingenuity in torture. My cognizance of the pit had
become known to the inquisitorial agents – the *pit,* whose
horrors had been destined for so bold a recusant as myself –
the pit, typical of hell, and regarded by rumor as the Ultima
Thule of all their punishments. The plunge into this pit I had
avoided by the merest of accidents. I knew that surprise, or
entrapment into torment, formed an important portion of all
the grotesquerie of these dungeon deaths. Having failed to fall,
it was no part of the demon plan to hurl me into the abyss;
and thus (there being no alternative) a different and a milder
destruction awaited me. Milder! I half smiled in my agony as I
thought of such application of such a term.

What boots it to tell of the long, long hours of horror
more than mortal, during which I counted the rushing
vibrations of the steel! Inch by inch – line by line – with a
descent only appreciable at intervals that seemed ages – down
and still down it came! Days passed – it might have been that
many days passed – ere it swept so closely over me as to fan
me with its acrid breath. The odor of the sharp steel forced
itself into my nostrils. I prayed – I wearied heaven with prayer
for its more speedy descent. I grew frantically mad, and
struggled to force myself upwards against the sweep of the
fearful scimitar. And then I fell suddenly calm, and lay smiling
at the glittering death, as a child at some rare bauble.

There was an interval of utter insensibility; it was brief; for,
upon again lapsing into life, there had been no perceptible

descent in the pendulum. But it *might* have been long–for I knew there were demons who took note of my swoon, and who could have arrested the vibration at pleasure. Upon my recovery, too, I felt very–oh, inexpressibly–sick and weak, as if through long inanition. Even amid all the agonies of that period, the human nature *craved food*. With painful effort I outstretched my left arm as far as my bonds permitted, and took possession of the small remnant which had been spared me by the rats. As I put a portion of it within my lips, there rushed to my mind a half-formed thought of joy–of hope. Yet what business had *I* with hope? It was, as I say, a half-formed thought–man has many such, which are never completed. I felt that it was of joy–of hope; but I felt also that it had perished in its formation. In vain I struggled to realize–to regain it. Long suffering had nearly annihilated all my ordinary powers of mind. I was an imbecile–an idiot.

The vibration of the pendulum was at right angles to my length. I saw that the crescent was designed to cross the region of the heart. It would fray the serge of my robe–it would return and repeat its operation–again–and again. Notwith-standing its terrifically wide sweep, (some thirty feet or more,) and the hissing vigor of its descent, sufficient to sunder these very walls of iron, still the fraying of the serge of my robe would be all that, for several minutes, it would accomplish. And at this thought I paused. I dared not go farther than this reflection. I dwelt upon it with a pertinacity of attention–as if, in so dwelling, I could arrest *here* the descent of the steel. I forced myself to ponder upon the *sound* of the crescent as it should pass across the garment–upon the peculiar thrilling sensation which the friction of cloth produces in the nerves. I pondered upon all this frivolity until my teeth were on edge.

Down–steadily down it *crept*. I took a frenzied pleasure in contrasting its downward with its lateral velocity. To the right–to the left–far and wide–with the shriek and the plunge of a damned spirit! to my heart, with the stealthy pace of the tiger. I alternately laughed and howled, as the one or the other idea grew predominant.

Down – certainly, relentlessly down! It vibrated within three inches of my bosom! I struggled violently – furiously – to free my left arm. This was free only from the elbow to the hand. I could reach the latter, from the platter beside me, to my mouth, with great effort, but no farther. Could I have broken the fastenings above the elbow, I would have seized and attempted to arrest the pendulum. I might as well have attempted to arrest an avalanche!

Down – still unceasingly – still inevitably down! I gasped and struggled at each vibration. I shrunk convulsively at its every sweep. My eyes followed its outward or upward whirls with the eagerness of the most unmeaning despair; they closed themselves spasmodically at the descent, although death would have been a relief, oh, how unspeakable! I still quivered in every nerve to think how slight a sinking or slipping of the machinery would precipitate that keen, glistening axe upon my bosom. It was hope that prompted the nerve to quiver – the frame to shrink. It was hope – the hope that triumphs on the rack – that whispers to the death-condemned even in the dungeons of the Inquisition.

I saw that some ten or twelve vibrations would bring the steel in actual contact with my robe – and with this observation there suddenly came over my spirit all the keen, collected calmness of *despair*. For the first time during many hours – or perhaps days – I *thought*. It now at once occurred to me, that the bandage, or surcingle, which enveloped me, was *unique*. I was tied by no separate cords. The first stroke of the razor-like crescent athwart any portion of the band, would so detach it that it might be unwound from my person by means of my left hand. But how fearful, in that case, the proximity of the steel! The result of the slightest struggle, how deadly!

Was it likely, moreover, that the minions of the torturer had not foreseen and provided for this possibility? Was it probable that the bandage crossed my bosom *in the track* of the pendulum? Dreading to find my faint, and, as it seemed, my last hope frustrated, I so far elevated my head as to obtain a distinct view of my breast. The surcingle enveloped my limbs and body close in all directions—*save in the path of the destroying crescent.*

Scarcely had I dropped my head back in its original position, when there flashed upon my mind what I cannot better describe than as the *unformed half* of that idea of deliverance to which I have previously alluded, and of which a moiety only floated indeterminately through my brain when I raised *food* to my burning lips. The whole thought was now present—feeble, scarcely sane, scarcely definite—but still entire. I proceeded at once, with the nervous energy of despair, to attempt its execution.

For many hours the immediate vicinity of the low framework upon which I lay, had been literally swarming with rats. They were wild, bold, ravenous—their red eyes glaring upon me as if they waited but for motionlessness on my part to make me their prey. "To what food," I thought, "have they been accustomed in the well?"

They had devoured, in spite of all my efforts to prevent them, all but a small remnant of the contents of the dish. I had fallen into an habitual see-saw, or wave of the hand about the platter; and, at length, the unconscious uniformity of the movement deprived it of effect. In their voracity, the vermin frequently fastened their sharp fangs in my fingers. With the particles of the oily and spicy viand which now remained, I thoroughly rubbed the bandage wherever I could reach it; then, raising my hand from the floor, I lay breathlessly still.

At first, the ravenous animals were startled and terrified at the change—at the cessation of movement. They shrank alarmedly back; many sought the well. But this was only for a moment. I had not counted in vain upon their voracity. Observing that I remained without motion, one or two of the boldest leaped upon the framework, and smelt at the surcingle. This seemed the signal for a general rush. Forth from the well they hurried in fresh troops. They clung to the wood – they overran it, and leapt in hundreds upon my person. The measured movement of the pendulum disturbed them not at all. Avoiding its strokes, they busied themselves with the anointed bandage. They pressed – they swarmed upon me in ever accumulating heaps. They writhed upon my throat; their cold lips sought my own; I was half stifled by their thronging pressure; a disgust, for which the world has no name, swelled my bosom, and chilled, with a deadly clamminess, my heart. Yet one minute, and I felt that the struggle would be over. Plainly I perceived the loosening of the bandage. I knew that in more than one place it must already be severed. With a more than human resolution I lay *still*.

Nor had I erred in my calculations – nor had I endured in vain. I at length felt that I was *free*. The surcingle hung in ribands from my body. But the stroke of the pendulum already pressed upon my bosom. It had divided the serge of the robe. It had cut through the linen beneath. Twice again it swung, and a sharp sense of pain shot through every nerve. But the moment of escape had arrived. At a wave of my hand my deliverers hurried tumultuously away. With a steady movement – cautious, sidelong, shrinking, and slow – I slid from the embrace of the bandage and beyond the sweep of the scimitar. For the moment, at least, *I was free*.

Free! – and in the grasp of the Inquisition! I had scarcely stepped from my wooden bed of horror upon the stone floor of the prison, when the motion of the hellish machine ceased, and I beheld it drawn up, by some invisible force, through the ceiling. This was a lesson which I took desperately to heart.

My every motion was undoubtedly watched. Free!–I had but
escaped death in one form of agony, to be delivered unto
worse than death in some other. With that thought I rolled my
eyes nervously around on the barriers of iron that hemmed me
in. Something unusual–some change which, at first, I could
not appreciate distinctly–it was obvious, had taken place in
the apartment. For many minutes of a dreamy and trembling
abstraction, I busied myself in vain, unconnected conjecture.
During this period, I became aware, for the first time, of the
origin of the sulphureous light which illuminated the cell.
It proceeded from a fissure, about half an inch in width,
extending entirely around the prison at the base of the
walls, which thus appeared, and were completely separated
from the floor. I endeavored, but of course in vain, to look
through the aperture.

As I rose from the attempt, the mystery of the alteration in
the chamber broke at once upon my understanding. I have
observed that, although the outlines of the figures upon the
walls were sufficiently distinct, yet the colors seemed blurred
and indefinite. These colors had now assumed, and were
momentarily assuming, a startling and most intense brilliancy,
that gave to the spectral and fiendish portraitures an aspect
that might have thrilled ever firmer nerves than my own.
Demon eyes, of a wild and ghastly vivacity, glared upon me in
a thousand directions, where none had been visible before,
and gleamed with the lurid lustre of a fire that I could not
force my diseased imagination to regard as unreal.

Unreal!–Even while I gazed there came to my nostrils the
breath of the vapor of heated iron! A suffocating odor
pervaded the prison! A deeper glow settled each moment in
the eyes that glared at my agonies! A richer tint of crimson
diffused itself over the pictured horrors of blood. I panted! I
gasped for breath! There could be no doubt of the design of
my tormentors–oh! most unrelenting! oh! most demoniac of

men! I shrank from the glowing metal to the centre of the cell. Amid the thought of the fiery destruction that impended, the idea of the coolness of the well came over my soul like balm. I rushed to its deadly brink. I threw my straining vision below. The glare from the enkindled roof illumined its inmost recesses. Yet, for a wild moment, did my spirit refuse to comprehend the meaning of what I saw. At length it forced – it wrestled its way into my soul – it burned itself in upon my shuddering reason. Oh! for a voice to speak! – oh! horror! – oh! any horror but this! With a shriek, I rushed from the margin, and buried my face in my hands – weeping bitterly.

The heat rapidly increased, and once again I looked up, shuddering as with a fit of the ague. There had been a second change in the cell – and now the change was obviously in the *form*. As before, it was in vain that I at first endeavored to appreciate or understand what was taking place. But not long was I left in doubt. The Inquisitorial vengeance had been hurried by my two-fold escape, and there was to be no more dallying with the King of Terrors. The room had been square. I saw that two of its iron angles were now acute – two, consequently, obtuse. The fearful difference quickly increased with a low rumbling or moaning sound. In an instant the apartment had shifted its form into that of a lozenge. But the alteration stopped not here – I neither hoped nor desired it to stop. I could have clasped the red walls to my bosom as a garment of eternal peace. "Death," I said, "any death but that of the pit!" Fool! might I have not known that *into the pit* it was the object of the burning iron to urge me? Could I resist its glow? or if even that, could I withstand its pressure? And now, flatter and flatter grew the lozenge, with a rapidity that left me no time for contemplation. Its centre, and of course, its greatest width, came just over the yawning gulf. I shrank back – but the closing walls pressed me resistlessly onwards. At length for my seared and writhing body there was no longer an inch of foothold on the firm floor of the prison. I struggled no more, but the agony of my soul found vent in one loud, long, and final scream of despair. I felt that I tottered upon the brink – I averted my eyes –

There was a loud blast as of many trumpets! There was a discordant hum of human voices! There was a harsh grating as of a thousand thunders! The fiery walls rushed back! An outstretched arm caught my own as I fell, fainting, into the abyss. It was that of General Lasalle. The Inquisition was in the hands of its enemies. The French army had entered Toledo.

[Circa August, 1842]

THE TELL-TALE HEART

Motto: Art is long and Time is fleeting,
And our hearts, though stout and brave,
Still, like muffled drums, are beating
Funeral marches to the grave.
—LONGFELLOW.

TRUE!—NERVOUS—VERY, very dreadfully nervous I had been and am; but why *will* you say that I am mad? The disease had sharpened my senses—not destroyed—not dulled them. Above all was the sense of hearing acute. I heard all things in the heaven and in the earth. I heard many things in hell. How, then, am I mad? Hearken! and observe how healthily—how calmly I can tell you the whole story.

It is impossible to say how first the idea entered my brain; but, once conceived, it haunted me day and night. Object there was none. Passion there was none. I loved the old man. He had never wronged me. He had never given me insult. For his gold I had no desire. I think it was his eye! yes, it was this! He had the eye of a vulture—a pale blue eye, with a film over it. Whenever it fell upon me, my blood ran cold; and so by degrees—very gradually—I made up my mind to take the life of the old man, and thus rid myself of the eye forever.

Now this is the point. You fancy me mad. Madmen know nothing. But you should have seen *me*. You should have seen how wisely I proceeded—with what caution—with what foresight—with what dissimulation I went to work! I was never kinder to the old man than during the whole week before I killed him. And every night, about midnight, I turned the latch of his door and opened it—oh, so gently! And then, when I had made an opening sufficient for my head, I first put in a dark lantern, all closed, closed, so that no light shone out, and then I thrust in my head. Oh, you would have laughed to see how cunningly I thrust it in! I moved it slowly—very, very slowly, so that I might not disturb the old man's sleep. It took me an hour to place my whole head within the opening so far that I could see the old man as he lay upon his bed. Ha!— would a madman have been so wise as this? And then, when my head was well in the room, I undid the lantern cautiously—oh, so cautiously (for the hinges creaked)—I undid it just so much that a single thin ray fell upon the vulture eye. And this I did for seven long nights—every night just at midnight—but I found the eye always closed; and so it was impossible to do the work; for it was not the old man who vexed me, but his Evil Eye. And every morning, when the day broke, I went boldly into his chamber, and spoke courageously to him, calling him by name in a hearty tone, and inquiring how he had passed the night. So you see he would have been a very profound old man, indeed, to suspect that every night, just at twelve, I looked in upon him while he slept.

Upon the eighth night I was more than usually cautious in opening the door. A watch's minute hand moves more quickly than did mine. Never, before that night, had I *felt* the extent of my own powers—of my sagacity. I could scarcely contain my feelings of triumph. To think that there I was, opening the door, little by little, and the old man not even to dream of my secret deeds or thoughts. I fairly chuckled at the idea; and perhaps the old man heard me; for he moved in bed suddenly, as if startled. Now you may think that I drew back—but no. His room was as black as pitch with the thick darkness, (for the shutters were close fastened, through fear of robbers,) and so I knew that he could not see the opening of the door, and I kept on pushing it steadily, steadily.

I had got my head in, and was about to open the lantern, when my thumb slipped upon the tin fastening, and the old man sprang up in the bed, crying out—"Who's there?"

I kept quite still and said nothing. For another hour I did

not move a muscle, and in the meantime I did not hear the old man lie down. He was still sitting up in the bed, listening; – just as I have done, night after night, hearkening to the death-watches in the wall.

Presently I heard a slight groan, and I knew that it was the groan of mortal terror. It was not a groan of pain or of grief – oh, no! – it was the low stifled sound that arises from the bottom of the soul when overcharged with *awe*. I knew the sound well. Many a night, just at midnight, when all the world slept, it has welled up from my own bosom, deepening, with its dreadful echo, the terrors that distracted me. I say I knew it well. I knew what the old man felt, and pitied him, although I chuckled at heart. I knew that he had been lying awake ever since the first slight noise, when he had turned in the bed. His fears had been ever since growing upon him. He had been trying to fancy them causeless, but could not. He had been saying to himself – "It is nothing but the wind in the chimney – it is only a mouse crossing the floor," or "it is merely a cricket which has made a single chirp." Yes, he had been trying to comfort himself with these suppositions: but he had found all in vain. *All in vain;* because Death, in approaching the old man, had stalked with his black shadow before him, and the shadow had now reached and enveloped the victim. And it was the mournful influence of the unperceived shadow that caused him to feel – although he neither saw nor heard me – to *feel* the presence of my head within the room.

When I had waited a long time, very patiently, without hearing the old man lie down, I resolved to open a little – a very, very little crevice in the lantern. So I opened it – you cannot imagine how stealthily, stealthily – until, at length, a single dim ray, like the thread of the spider, shot from out the crevice and fell full upon the vulture eye.

It was open – wide, wide open – and I grew furious as I gazed upon it. I saw it with perfect distinctness – all a dull blue, with a hideous veil over it that chilled the very marrow in my bones; but I could see nothing else of the old man's face or person: for I had directed the ray as if by instinct, precisely upon the damned spot.

And now–have I not told you that what you mistake for madness is but over acuteness of the senses?–now, I say, there came to my ears *a low, dull, quick sound–much such a sound as a watch makes when enveloped in cotton.* I knew *that* sound well, too. It was the beating of the old man's heart. It increased my fury, as the beating of a drum stimulates the soldier into courage.

But even yet I refrained and kept still. I scarcely breathed. I held the lantern motionless. I tried how steadily I could maintain the ray upon the eye. Meantime the hellish tattoo of the heart increased. It grew quicker, and louder and louder every instant. The old man's terror *must* have been extreme! It grew louder, I say, louder every moment!–do you mark me well? I have told you that I am nervous: so I am. And now at the dead hour of the night, and amid the dreadful silence of that old house, so strange a noise as this excited me to uncontrollable wrath. Yet, for some minutes longer I refrained and kept still. But the beating grew louder, *louder!* I thought the heart must burst. And now a new anxiety seized me–the sound would be heard by a neighbor! The old man's hour had come! With a loud yell, I threw open the lantern and leaped into the room. He shrieked once–once only. In an instant I dragged him to the floor, and pulled the heavy bed over him. I then sat upon the bed and smiled gaily, to find the deed so far done. But, for many minutes, the heart beat on with a muffled sound. This, however, did not vex me; it would not be heard through the walls. At length it ceased. The old man was dead. I removed the bed and examined the corpse. Yes, he was stone, stone dead. I placed my hand upon the heart and held it there many minutes. There was no pulsation. The old man was stone dead. His eye would trouble *me* no more.

If still you think me mad, you will think so no longer when I describe the wise precautions I took for the concealment of the body. The night waned, and I worked hastily, but in silence. First of all I dismembered the corpse. I cut off the head and the arms and the legs.

I then took up three planks from the flooring of the chamber, and deposited all between the scantlings. I then replaced the boards so cleverly, so cunningly, that no human eye – not even *his* – could have detected anything wrong. There was nothing to wash out – no stain of any kind – no blood-spot whatever. I had been too wary for that. A tub had caught all – ha! ha!

When I had made an end of these labors, it was four o'clock – still dark as midnight. As the bell sounded the hour, there came a knocking at the street door. I went down to open it with a light heart, – for what had I *now* to fear? There entered three men, who introduced themselves, with perfect suavity, as officers of the police. A shriek had been heard by a neighbor during the night; suspicion of foul play had been aroused; information had been lodged at the police office, and they (the officers) had been deputed to search the premises.

I smiled, – for *what* had I to fear? I bade the gentlemen welcome. The shriek, I said, was my own in a dream. The old man, I mentioned, was absent in the country. I took my visiters all over the house. I bade them search – search *well*. I led them, at length, to *his* chamber. I showed them his treasures, secure, undisturbed. In the enthusiasm of my confidence, I brought chairs into the room, and desired them *here* to rest from their fatigues, while I myself, in the wild audacity of my perfect triumph, placed my own seat upon the very spot beneath which reposed the corpse of the victim.

The officers were satisfied. My *manner* had convinced them. I was singularly at ease. They sat, and while I answered cheerily, they chatted of familiar things. But, ere long, I felt myself getting pale and wished them gone. My head ached, and I fancied a ringing in my ears: but still they sat and still chatted. The ringing became more distinct: I talked more freely to get rid of the feeling: but it continued and gained definitiveness—until, at length, I found that the noise was *not* within my ears.

No doubt I now grew *very* pale;—but I talked more fluently, and with a heightened voice. Yet the sound increased—and what could I do? It was *a low, dull, quick sound—much such a sound as a watch makes when enveloped in cotton.* I gasped for breath—and yet the officers heard it not. I talked more quickly—more vehemently; but the noise steadily increased. I arose and argued about trifles, in a high key and with violent gesticulations; but the noise steadily increased. Why *would* they not be gone? I paced the floor to and fro with heavy strides, as if excited to fury by the observations of the men— but the noise steadily increased. Oh God! what *could* I do? I foamed—I raved—I swore! I swung the chair upon which I had sat, and grated it upon the boards, but the noise arose over all and continually increased. It grew louder—louder—*louder!* And still the men chatted pleasantly, and smiled. Was it possible they heard not? Almighty God!—no, no! They heard!—they suspected!—they *knew!*—they were making a mockery of my horror!—this I thought, and this I think. But anything better than this agony! Anything was more tolerable than this derision! I could bear those hypocritical smiles no longer! I felt that I must scream or die!—and now—again!—hark! louder! louder! louder! *louder!*—

"Villains!" I shrieked, "dissemble no more! I admit the deed!—tear up the planks!—here, here!—it is the beating of his hideous heart!"

[January, 1843]

L ENORE

AH, BROKEN IS the golden bowl!
  The spirit flown forever!
Let the bell toll—A saintly soul
  Glides down the Stygian river!
And let the burial rite be read—
  The funeral song be sung—
A dirge for the most lovely dead
  That ever died so young!
    And, Guy de Vere,
    Hast *thou* no tear?
      Weep now or nevermore!
    See, on yon drear
    And rigid bier,
      Low lies thy love Lenore!

"Yon heir, whose cheeks of pallid hue
  With tears are streaming wet,
Sees only, through
Their crocodile dew,
  A vacant coronet—
    False friends! ye loved her for her wealth
    And hated her for her pride,
And, when she fell in feeble health,
    Ye blessed her—that she died.
      How *shall* the ritual, then, be read?
      The requiem *how* be sung
      For her most wrong'd of all the dead
      That ever died so young?"

Peccavimus!
But rave not thus!
  And let the solemn song
Go up to God so mournfully that *she* may feel no wrong!
    The sweet Lenore
    Hath "gone before"
      With young hope at her side,
        And thou art wild
        For the dear child
      That should have been thy bride—
        For her, the fair
        And debonair,
          That now so lowly lies—
        The life still there
        Upon her hair,
          The death upon her eyes.

"Avaunt!—to-night
My heart is light—
  No dirge will I upraise,
But waft the angel on her flight
  With a Pæan of old days!
    Let *no* bell toll!
    Lest her sweet soul,
      Amid its hallow'd mirth,
        Should catch the note
        As it doth float
      Up from the damned earth—
        To friends above, from fiends below,
          Th' indignant ghost is riven—
        From grief and moan
        To a gold throne
      Beside the King of Heaven!"

[February, 1843]

THE GOLD-BUG

What ho! what ho! this fellow is dancing mad!
He hath been bitten by the Tarantula.
                                    —*All in the Wrong.*

MANY YEARS AGO, I contracted an intimacy with a Mr. William
Legrand. He was of an ancient Huguenot family, and had once
been wealthy; but a series of misfortunes had reduced him to
want. To avoid the mortification consequent upon his
disasters, he left New Orleans, the city of his forefathers, and
took up his residence at Sullivan's Island, near Charleston,
South Carolina.

This Island is a very singular one. It consists of little else
than the sea sand, and is about three miles long. Its breadth at
no point exceeds a quarter of a mile. It is separated from the
main land by a scarcely perceptible creek, oozing its way
through a wilderness of reeds and slime, a favorite resort of
the marsh-hen. The vegetation, as might be supposed, is scant,
or at least dwarfish. No trees of any magnitude are to be seen.
Near the western extremity, where Fort Moultrie stands, and
where are some miserable frame buildings, tenanted, during
summer, by the fugitives from Charleston dust and fever, may
be found, indeed, the bristly palmetto; but the whole island,
with the exception of this western point, and a line of hard,
white beach on the seacoast, is covered with a dense
undergrowth of the sweet myrtle, so much prized by the
horticulturists of England. The shrub here often attains the
height of fifteen or twenty feet, and forms an almost
impenetrable coppice, burthening the air with its fragrance.

In the inmost recesses of this coppice, not far from the
eastern or more remote end of the island, Legrand had built
himself a small hut, which he occupied when I first, by mere
accident, made his acquaintance. This soon ripened into

friendship–for there was much in the recluse to excite interest and esteem. I found him well educated, with unusual powers of mind, but infected with misanthropy, and subject to perverse moods of alternate enthusiasm and melancholy. He had with him many books, but rarely employed them. His chief amusements were gunning and fishing, or sauntering along the bank and through the myrtles, in quest of shells or entomological specimens;–his collection of the latter might have been envied by a Swammerdamm. In these excursions he was usually accompanied by an old negro, called Jupiter, who had been manumitted before the reverses of the family, but who could be induced, neither by threats nor by promises, to abandon what he considered his right of attendance upon the footsteps of his young "Massa Will." It is not improbable that the relatives of Legrand, conceiving him to be somewhat unsettled in intellect, had contrived to instil this obstinacy into Jupiter, with a view to the supervision and guardianship of the wanderer.

The winters in the latitude of Sullivan's Island are seldom very severe, and in the fall of the year it is a rare event indeed when a fire is considered necessary. About the middle of October, 18–, there occurred, however, a day of remarkable chilliness. Just before sunset I scrambled my way through the evergreens to the hut of my friend, whom I had not visited for several weeks–my residence being, at that time, in Charleston, a distance of nine miles from the island, while the facilities of passage and re-passage were very far behind those of the present day. Upon reaching the hut I rapped, as was my custom, and getting no reply, sought for the key where I knew it was secreted, unlocked the door and went in. A fine fire was blazing upon the hearth. It was a novelty, and by no means an unwelcome one. I threw off an overcoat, took an armchair by the crackling logs, and waited patiently the arrival of my hosts.

Soon after dark they arrived, and gave me a most cordial welcome. Jupiter, grinning from ear to ear, bustled about to prepare some marsh-hens for supper. Legrand was in one of his fits – how else shall I term them? – of enthusiasm. He had found an unknown bivalve, forming a new genus, and, more than this, he had hunted down and secured, with Jupiter's assistance, a *scarabœus* which he believed to be totally new, but in respect to which he wished to have my opinion on the morrow.

"And why not to-night?" I asked, rubbing my hands over the blaze, and wishing the whole tribe of *scarabœi* at the devil.

"Ah, if I had only known you were here!" said Legrand, "but it's so long since I saw you; and how could I foresee that you would pay me a visit this very night of all others? As I was coming home I met Lieutenant G––, from the fort, and, very foolishly, I lent him the bug; so it will be impossible for you to see it until the morning. Stay here to-night, and I will send Jup down for it at sunrise. It is the loveliest thing in creation!"

"What? – sunrise?"

"Nonsense! no! – the bug. It is of a brilliant color – about the size of a large hickory-nut – with two jet black spots near one extremity of the back, and another somewhat longer, at the other. The *antennœ* are – "

"Dey aint *no* tin in him, Massa Will, I keep a tellin on you," here interrupted Jupiter; "de bug is a goole bug, solid, ebery bit of him, inside and all, sep him wing – neber feel half so hebby a bug in my life."

"Well, suppose it is, Jup," replied Legrand, somewhat more earnestly, it seemed to me, than the occasion demanded, "is that any reason for your letting the birds burn? The color" – here he turned to me – "is really almost enough to warrant Jupiter's idea. You never saw a more brilliant metallic lustre than the scales emit – but of this you cannot judge till to-morrow. In the mean time I can give you some idea of the

shape." Saying this, he seated himself at a small table, on
which were a pen and ink, but no paper. He looked for some
in a drawer, but found none.

"Never mind," said he at length, "this will answer;" and he
drew from his waistcoat pocket a scrap of what I took to be
very dirty foolscap, and made upon it a rough drawing with
the pen. While he did this, I retained my seat by the fire, for I
was still chilly. When the design was complete, he handed it to
me without rising. As I received it, a loud growl was heard,
succeeded by a scratching at the door. Jupiter opened it, and a
large Newfoundland, belonging to Legrand, rushed in, leaped
upon my shoulders, and loaded me with caresses; for I had
shown him much attention during previous visits. When his
gambols were over, I looked at the paper, and, to speak the
truth, found myself not a little puzzled at what my friend
had depicted.

"Well!" I said, after contemplating it for some minutes,
"this is a strange *scarabæus*, I must confess: new to me: never
saw anything like it before–unless it was a skull, or a death's-
head–which it more nearly resembles than anything else that
has come under *my* observation."

"A death's-head!" echoed Legrand–"Oh–yes–well, it has
something of that appearance upon paper, no doubt. The two
upper black spots look like eyes, eh? and the longer one at the
bottom like a mouth–and then the shape of the whole is oval."

"Perhaps so," said I; "but, Legrand, I fear you are no artist. I
must wait until I see the beetle itself, if I am to form any idea
of its personal appearance."

"Well, I don't know," said he, a little nettled, "I draw
tolerably–*should* do it at least–have had good masters, and
flatter myself that I am not quite a blockhead."

"But, my dear fellow, you are joking then," said I, "this is a
very passable *skull*–indeed, I may say that it is a very *excellent*
skull, according to the vulgar notions about such specimens

of physiology—and your *scarabæus* must be the queerest
scarabæus in the world if it resembles it. Why, we may get up a
very thrilling bit of superstition upon this hint. I presume you
will call the bug *scarabæus caput hominis* [head-of-a-man
beetle], or something of that kind—there are many similar
titles in the Natural Histories. But where are the *antennæ*
you spoke of?"

"The *antennæ!*" said Legrand, who seemed to be getting
unaccountably warm upon the subject; "I am sure you must
see the *antennæ*. I made them as distinct as they are in the
original insect, and I presume that is sufficient."

"Well, well," I said, "perhaps you have—still I don't see
them;" and I handed him the paper without additional remark,
not wishing to ruffle his temper; but I was much surprised at
the turn affairs had taken; his ill humor puzzled me—and, as
for the drawing of the beetle, there were positively *no antennæ*
visible, and the whole *did* bear a very close resemblance to the
ordinary cut of a death's-head.

He received the paper very peevishly, and was about to
crumple it, apparently to throw it in the fire, when a casual
glance at the design seemed suddenly to rivet his attention. In
an instant his face grew violently red—in another as
excessively pale. For some minutes he continued to scrutinize
the drawing minutely where he sat. At length he arose, took a
candle from the table, and proceeded to seat himself upon a
sea-chest in the farthest corner of the room. Here again he
made an anxious examination of the paper; turning it in all
directions. He said nothing, however, and his conduct greatly
astonished me; yet I thought it prudent not to exacerbate the
growing moodiness of his temper by any comment. Presently
he took from his coat pocket a wallet, placed the paper
carefully in it, and deposited both in a writing-desk, which he
locked. He now grew more composed in his demeanor; but his
original air of enthusiasm had quite disappeared. Yet he

seemed not so much sulky as abstracted. As the evening wore away he became more and more absorbed in reverie, from which no sallies of mine could arouse him. It had been my intention to pass the night at the hut, as I had frequently done before, but, seeing my host in this mood, I deemed it proper to take leave. He did not press me to remain, but, as I departed, he shook my hand with even more than his usual cordiality.

It was about a month after this (and during the interval I had seen nothing of Legrand) when I received a visit, at Charleston, from his man, Jupiter. I had never seen the good old negro look so dispirited, and I feared that some serious disaster had befallen my friend.

"Well, Jup," said I, "what is the matter now? – how is your master?"

"Why, to speak de troof, massa, him not so berry well as mought be."

"Not well! I am truly sorry to hear it. What does he complain of?"

"Dar! dat's it! – him neber plain ob notin – but him berry sick for all dat."

"*Very* sick, Jupiter! – why didn't you say so at once? Is he confined to bed?"

"No, dat he aint! – he aint find nowhar – dat's just whar de shoe pinch – my mind is got to be berry hebby bout poor Massa Will."

"Jupiter, I should like to understand what it is you are talking about. You say your master is sick. Hasn't he told you what ails him?"

"Why, massa, taint worf while for to git mad about de matter – Massa Will say noffin at all aint de matter wid him – but den what make him go bout looking dis here way, wid he head down and he soldiers up, and as white as a gose? And den he keep a syphon all de time –"

"Keeps a what, Jupiter?"

"Keeps a syphon wid de figgurs on de slate–de queerest figgurs I ebber did see. Ise gitting to be skeered, I tell you. Hab for to keep mighty tight eye pon him noovers. Todder day he gib me slip fore de sun up and was gone de whole ob de blessed day. I had a big stick ready cut for to gib him d–n good beatin when he did come–but Ise sich a fool dat I hadn't de heart arter all–he look so berry poorly."

"Eh?–what?–ah yes!–upon the whole I think you had better not be too severe with the poor fellow–don't flog him, Jupiter–he can't very well stand it–but can you form no idea of what has occasioned this illness, or rather this change of conduct? Has anything unpleasant happened since I saw you?"

"No, massa, dey aint bin noffin onpleasant *since* den–'twas *fore* den I'm feared–'twas de berry day you was dare."

"How? what do you mean?"

"Why, massa, I mean de bug–dare now."

"The what?"

"De bug–I'm berry sartain dat Massa Will bin bit somewhere bout de head by dat d–n goole-bug."

"And what cause have you, Jupiter, for such a supposition?"

"Claws enuff, massa, and mouff too. I nebber did see sich a d–n bug–he kick and he bite ebery ting what cum near him. Massa Will cotch him fuss, but had for to let him go gin mighty quick, I tell you–den was de time he must ha got de bite. I didn't like de look ob de bug mouff, myself, no how, so I wouldn't take hold ob him wid my finger, but cotch him wid a piece ob paper dat I found. I rap up in de paper and stuff piece ob it in he mouff–dat was de way."

"And you think, then, that your master was really bitten by the beetle, and that the bite made him sick?"

"I don't tink noffin bout it–I nose it. What make him dream bout de goole so much, if taint cause he bit by de goole-bug? Ise heerd bout dem goole-bugs fore dis."

"But how do you know he dreams about gold?"

"How I know? why cause he talk about it in he sleep – dat's how I nose."

"Well, Jup, perhaps you are right; but to what fortunate circumstance am I to attribute the honor of a visit from you to-day?"

"What de matter, massa?"

"Did you bring any message from Mr. Legrand?"

"No, massa, I bring dis here pissel;" and here Jupiter handed me a note which ran thus:

My Dear ——

   Why have I not seen you for so long a time? I hope you have not been so foolish as to take offence at any little brusquerie of mine; but no, that is improbable.

   Since I saw you I have had great cause for anxiety. I have something to tell you, yet scarcely know how to tell it, or whether I should tell it at all.

   I have not been quite well for some days past, and poor old Jup annoys me, almost beyond endurance, by his well-meant attentions. Would you believe it? – he had prepared a huge stick, the other day, with which to chastise me for giving him the slip, and spending the day, solus, among the hills on the main land. I verily believe that my ill looks alone saved me a flogging.

   I have made no addition to my cabinet since we met.

   If you can, in any way, make it convenient, come over with Jupiter. Do come. I wish to see you to-night, upon business of importance. I assure you that it is of the highest importance.

   Ever yours,

                                        WILLIAM LEGRAND.

There was something in the tone of this note which gave me great uneasiness. Its whole style differed materially from that of Legrand. What could he be dreaming of? What new crotchet possessed his excitable brain? What "business of the highest importance" could *he* possibly have to transact? Jupiter's account of him boded no good. I dreaded lest the continued pressure of misfortune had, at length, fairly unsettled the reason of my friend. Without a moment's hesitation, therefore, I prepared to accompany the negro.

Upon reaching the wharf, I noticed a scythe and three spades, all apparently new, lying in the bottom of the boat in which we were to embark.

"What is the meaning of all this, Jup?" I inquired.

"Him syfe, massa, and spade."

"Very true; but what are they doing here?"

"Him de syfe and de spade which Massa Will sis pon my buying for him in de town, and de debbil's own lot of money I had to gib for em."

"But what, in the name of all that is mysterious, is your 'Massa Will' going to do with scythes and spades?"

"Dat's more dan I know, and debbil take me if I don't blieve 'tis more dan he know, too. But it's all cum ob de bug."

Finding that no satisfaction was to be obtained of Jupiter, whose whole intellect seemed to be absorbed by "de bug," I now stepped into the boat and made sail. With a fair and strong breeze we soon ran into the little cove to the northward of Fort Moultrie, and a walk of some two miles brought us to the hut. It was about three in the afternoon when we arrived. Legrand had been awaiting us in eager expectation. He grasped my hand with a nervous *empressement* which alarmed me and strengthened the suspicions already entertained. His countenance was pale even to ghastliness, and his deep-set eyes glared with unnatural lustre. After some inquiries respecting his health, I asked him, not knowing what better to say, if he had yet obtained the *scarabæus* from Lieutenant G――.

"Oh, yes," he replied, coloring violently, "I got it from him the next morning. Nothing should tempt me to part with that *scarabæus*. Do you know that Jupiter is quite right about it?"

"In what way?" I asked, with a sad foreboding at heart.

"In supposing it to be a bug of *real gold*." He said this with an air of profound seriousness, and I felt inexpressibly shocked.

"This bug is to make my fortune," he continued, with a triumphant smile, "to reinstate me in my family possessions. Is it any wonder, then, that I prize it? Since Fortune has thought fit to bestow it upon me, I have only to use it properly and I shall arrive at the gold of which it is the index. Jupiter, bring me that *scarabæus!*"

"What! de bug, massa? I'd rudder not go fer to trubble dat bug—you mus git him for your own self." Hereupon Legrand arose, with a grave and stately air, and brought me the beetle from a glass case in which it was enclosed. It was a beautiful *scarabæus*, and, at that time, unknown to naturalists—of course a great prize in a scientific point of view. There were two round, black spots near one extremity of the back, and a longer one near the other. The scales were exceedingly hard and glossy, with all the appearance of burnished gold. The weight of the insect was very remarkable, and, taking all things into consideration, I could hardly blame Jupiter for his opinion respecting it; but what to make of Legrand's concordance with that opinion, I could not, for the life of me, tell.

"I sent for you," said he, in a grandiloquent tone, when I had completed my examination of the beetle, "I sent for you, that I might have your counsel and assistance in furthering the views of Fate and of the bug"—

"My dear Legrand," I cried, interrupting him, "you are certainly unwell, and had better use some little precautions. You shall go to bed, and I will remain with you a few days, until you get over this. You are feverish and"—

"Feel my pulse," said he.

I felt it, and, to say the truth, found not the slightest indication of fever.

"But you may be ill and yet have no fever. Allow me this once to prescribe for you. In the first place, go to bed. In the next"—

"You are mistaken," he interposed, "I am as well as I can expect to be under the excitement which I suffer. If you really wish me well, you will relieve this excitement."

"And how is this to be done?"

"Very easily. Jupiter and myself are going upon an expedition into the hills, upon the main land, and, in this expedition, we shall need the aid of some person in whom we can confide. You are the only one we can trust. Whether we succeed or fail, the excitement which you now perceive in me will be equally allayed."

"I am anxious to oblige you in any way," I replied; "but do you mean to say that this infernal beetle has any connection with your expedition into the hills?"

"It has."

"Then, Legrand, I can become a party to no such absurd proceeding."

"I am sorry–very sorry–for we shall have to try it by ourselves."

"Try it by yourselves! The man is surely mad!–but stay!– how long do you propose to be absent?"

"Probably all night. We shall start immediately, and be back, at all events, by sunrise."

"And will you promise me, upon your honor, that when this freak of yours is over, and the bug business (good God!) settled to your satisfaction, you will then return home and follow my advice implicitly, as that of your physician?"

"Yes; I promise; and now let us be off, for we have no time to lose."

With a heavy heart I accompanied my friend. We started about four o'clock–Legrand, Jupiter, the dog, and myself. Jupiter had with him the scythe and spades–the whole of which he insisted upon carrying–more through fear, it seemed to me, of trusting either of the implements within reach of his master, than from any excess of industry or complaisance.

His demeanor was dogged in the extreme, and "dat d—n bug" were the sole words which escaped his lips during the journey. For my own part, I had charge of a couple of dark lanterns, while Legrand contented himself with the *scarabæus,* which he carried attached to the end of a bit of whip-cord; twirling it to and fro, with the air of a conjuror, as he went. When I observed this last, plain evidence of my friend's aberration of mind, I could scarcely refrain from tears. I thought it best, however, to humor his fancy, at least for the present, or until I could adopt some more energetic measures with a chance of success. In the mean time I endeavored, but all in vain, to sound him in regard to the object of the expedition. Having succeeded in inducing me to accompany him, he seemed unwilling to hold conversation upon any topic of minor importance, and to all my questions vouchsafed no other reply than "we shall see!"

We crossed the creek at the head of the island by means of a skiff, and, ascending the high grounds on the shore of the main land, proceeded in a northwesternly direction, through a tract of country excessively wild and desolate, where no trace of a human footstep was to be seen. Legrand led the way with decision; pausing only for an instant, here and there, to consult what appeared to be certain landmarks of his own contrivance upon a former occasion.

In this manner we journeyed for about two hours, and the sun was just setting when we entered a region infinitely more dreary than any yet seen. It was a species of table land, near the summit of an almost inaccessible hill, densely wooded from base to pinnacle, and interspersed with huge crags that appeared to lie loosely upon the soil, and in many cases were prevented from precipitating themselves into the valleys below, merely by the support of the trees against which they reclined. Deep ravines, in various directions, gave an air of still sterner solemnity to the scene.

The natural platform to which we had clambered was
thickly overgrown with brambles, through which we soon
discovered that it would have been impossible to force our way
but for the scythe; and Jupiter, by direction of his master,
proceeded to clear for us a path to the foot of an enormously
tall tulip-tree, which stood, with some eight or ten oaks, upon
the level, and far surpassed them all, and all other trees which
I had then ever seen, in the beauty of its foliage and form, in
the wide spread of its branches, and in the general majesty of
its appearance. When we reached this tree, Legrand turned to
Jupiter, and asked him if he thought he could climb it. The old
man seemed a little staggered by the question, and for some
moments made no reply. At length he approached the tree,
walked slowly round its huge trunk, and examined it with
minute attention. When he had completed his scrutiny, he
merely said,

"Yes, massa, Jup climb any tree he ebber see in he life."

"Then up with you as soon as possible, for it will soon be
too dark to see what we are about."

"How far mus go up, massa?" inquired Jupiter.

"Get up the main trunk first, and then I will tell you which
way to go – and here – stop! take this beetle up with you."

"De bug, Massa Will! – de goole bug!" cried the negro,
drawing back in dismay –"what for mus tote de bug way up de
tree? – d – n if I do!"

"If you are afraid, Jup, a great big negro like you, to take
hold of a harmless little dead beetle, why you can carry it up
by this string – but, if you do not take it up with you in some
way, I shall be under the necessity of breaking your head with
this shovel."

"What de matter now, massa?" said Jup, evidently shamed
into compliance; "always want for to raise fuss wid old nigger.
Was only funnin any how. *Me* feered de bug! what I keer for de
bug?" Here he took cautiously hold of the extreme end of the

string, and, maintaining the insect as far from his person as circumstances would permit, prepared to ascend the tree.

In youth, the tulip-tree, or *Liriodendron tulipiferum,* the most magnificent of American foresters, has a trunk peculiarly smooth, and often rises to a great height without lateral branches; but, in its riper age, the bark becomes gnarled and uneven, while many short limbs make their appearance on the stem. Thus the difficulty of ascension, in the present case, lay more in semblance than in reality. Embracing the huge cylinder, as closely as possible, with his arms and knees, seizing with his hands some projections, and resting his naked toes upon others, Jupiter, after one or two narrow escapes from falling, at length wriggled himself into the first great fork, and seemed to consider the whole business as virtually accomplished. The *risk* of the achievement was, in fact, now over, although the climber was some sixty or seventy feet from the ground.

"Which way mus go now, Massa Will?" he asked.

"Keep up the largest branch—the one on this side," said Legrand. The negro obeyed him promptly, and apparently with but little trouble; ascending higher and higher, until no glimpse of his squat figure could be obtained through the dense foliage which enveloped it. Presently his voice was heard in a sort of halloo.

"How much fudder is got for go?"

"How high up are you?" asked Legrand.

"Ebber so fur," replied the negro; "can see de sky fru de top of de tree."

"Never mind the sky, but attend to what I say. Look down the trunk and count the limbs below you on this side. How many limbs have you passed?"

"One, two, three, four, fibe—I done pass fibe big limb, massa, pon dis side."

"Then go one limb higher."

In a few minutes the voice was heard again, announcing that the seventh limb was attained.

"Now, Jup," cried Legrand, evidently much excited, "I want you to work your way out upon that limb as far as you can. If you see anything strange, let me know."

By this time what little doubt I might have entertained of my poor friend's insanity, was put finally at rest. I had no alternative but to conclude him stricken with lunacy, and I became seriously anxious about getting him home. While I was pondering upon what was best to be done, Jupiter's voice was again heard.

"Mos feerd for to ventur pon dis limb berry far—tis dead limb putty much all de way."

"Did you say it was a *dead* limb, Jupiter?" cried Legrand in a quavering voice.

"Yes, massa, him dead as de door-nail—done up for sartain—done departed dis here life."

"What in the name of heaven shall I do?" asked Legrand, seemingly in the greatest distress.

"Do!" said I, glad of an opportunity to interpose a word, "why come home and go to bed. Do—that's a fine fellow. It's getting late, and, besides, you remember your promise."

"Jupiter," cried he, without heeding me in the least, "do you hear me?"

"Yes, Massa Will, hear you ebber so plain."

"Try the wood well, then, with your knife, and see if you think it *very* rotten."

"Him rotten, massa, sure nuff," replied the negro in a few moments, "but not so berry rotten as mought be. Mought ventur out leetle way pon de limb by myself, dat's true."

"By yourself!—what do you mean?"

"Why I mean de bug. 'Tis *berry* hebby bug. Spose I drop him down fuss, and den de limb won't break wid just de weight ob one nigger."

"You infernal scoundrel!" cried Legrand, apparently much relieved, "what you mean by telling me such nonsense as that? As sure as you drop that beetle I'll break your neck. Look here, Jupiter, do you hear me?"

"Yes, massa, needn't hollo at poor nigger dat style."

"Well! now listen!—if you will venture out on the limb as far as you think safe, and not let go of the beetle, I'll make you a present of a silver dollar as soon as you get down."

"I'm gwine, Massa Will—deed I is," replied the negro very promptly—"mos out to de eend now."

"*Out to the end!*" here fairly screamed Legrand, "do you say you are out to the end of that limb?"

"Soon be to de eend, Massa—o-o-o-o-oh! Lor-gol-a-marcy! what *is* dis here pon de tree?"

"Well!" cried Legrand, highly delighted, "what is it?"

"Why taint noffin but a skull—somebody bin lef him head up de tree, and de crows done gobble ebery bit ob de meat off."

"A skull, you say!—very well!—how is it fastened to the limb?—what holds it on?"

"Sure nuff, massa; mus look. Why dis berry curous sarcumstance, pon my word—dare's a great big nail in de skull, what fastens ob it on to de tree."

"Well now, Jupiter, do exactly as I tell you—do you hear?"

"Yes, massa."

"Pay attention, then!—find the left eye of the skull."

"Hum! hoo! dat's good! why dare aint no eye lef at all."

"Curse your stupidity! do you know your right hand from your left?"

"Yes, I nose dat—nose all bout dat—tis my lef hand what I chops de wood wid."

"To be sure! you are left-handed; and your left eye is on the same side as your left hand. Now, I suppose, you can find the left eye of the skull, or the place where the left eye has been. Have you found it?"

Here was a long pause. At length the negro asked, "Is de lef
eye of de skull pon de same side as de lef hand of de skull,
too?–cause de skull aint got not a bit ob a hand at all–nebber
mind! I got de lef eye now–here de lef eye! what mus do
wid it?"

"Let the beetle drop through it, as far as the string will
reach–but be careful and not let go your hold of the string."

"All dat done, Massa Will; mighty easy ting for to put de
bug fru de hole–look out for him dare below!"

"Very well!–now just keep as you are for a few minutes."

During this colloquy no portion of Jupiter's person could
be seen; but the beetle, which he had suffered to descend, was
now visible at the end of the string, and glistened, like a globe
of burnished gold, in the last rays of the setting sun, some of
which still faintly illumined the eminence upon which we
stood. The *scarabæus* hung quite clear of any branches, and, if
allowed to fall, would have fallen at our feet. Legrand
immediately took the scythe, and cleared with it a circular
space, three or four yards in diameter, just beneath the insect,
and, having accomplished this, ordered Jupiter to let go the
string and come down from the tree.

Driving a peg, with great nicety, into the ground, at the
precise spot where the beetle lay, my friend now produced
from his pocket a tape-measure. Fastening one end of this at
that point of the trunk of the tree which was nearest the peg,
he unrolled it till it reached the peg, and thence farther
unrolled it, in the direction already established by the two
points of the tree and the peg, for the distance of fifty feet–
Jupiter clearing away the brambles with the scythe. At the spot
thus attained a second peg was driven, and about this, as a
centre, a rude circle, about four feet in diameter, described,
Taking now a spade himself, and giving one to Jupiter and one
to me, Legrand begged us to set about digging as quickly
as possible.

To speak the truth, I had no especial relish for such amusement at any time, and, at that particular moment, I would most willingly have declined it; for the night was coming on, and I felt much fatigued with the exercise already taken; but I saw no mode of escape, and was fearful of disturbing my poor friend's equanimity by a refusal. Could I have depended, indeed, upon Jupiter's aid, I would have had no hesitation in attempting to get the lunatic home by force; but I was too well assured of the old negro's disposition, to hope that he would assist me, under any circumstances, in a personal contest with his master. I made no doubt that the latter had been infected with some of the innumerable Southern superstitions about money buried, and that his phantasy had received confirmation by the finding of the *scarabæus,* or, perhaps, by Jupiter's obstinacy in maintaining it to be "a bug of real gold." A mind disposed to lunacy would readily be led away by such suggestions – especially if chiming in with favorite preconceived ideas – and then I called to mind the poor fellow's speech about the beetle's being "the index of his fortune." Upon the whole, I was sadly vexed and puzzled, but, at length, I concluded to make a virtue of necessity – to dig with a good will, and thus the sooner to convince him, by ocular demonstration, of the fallacy of the opinions he entertained.

The lanterns having been lit, we all fell to work with a zeal worthy a more rational cause; and, as the glare fell upon our persons and implements, I could not help thinking how picturesque a group we composed, and how strange and suspicious our labors must have appeared to any interloper who, by chance, might have stumbled upon our whereabouts.

We dug very steadily for two hours. Little was said; and our chief embarrassment lay in the yelpings of the dog, who took exceeding interest in our proceedings. He, at length, became so obstreperous that we grew fearful of his giving the alarm to some stragglers in the vicinity; – or, rather, this was the apprehension of Legrand; – for myself, I should have rejoiced at any interruption which might have enabled me to get the wanderer home. The noise was, at length, very effectually silenced by Jupiter, who, getting out of the hole with a dogged air of deliberation, tied the brute's mouth up with one of his suspenders, and then returned, with a grave chuckle, to his task.

When the time mentioned had expired, we had reached a depth of five feet, and yet no signs of any treasure became manifest. A general pause ensued, and I began to hope that the farce was at an end. Legrand, however, although evidently much disconcerted, wiped his brow thoughtfully and recommenced. We had excavated the entire circle of four feet diameter, and now we slightly enlarged the limit, and went to the farther depth of two feet. Still nothing appeared. The gold-seeker, whom I sincerely pitied, at length clambered from the pit, with the bitterest disappointment imprinted upon every feature, and proceeded, slowly and reluctantly, to put on his coat, which he had thrown off at the beginning of his labor. In the mean time I made no remark. Jupiter, at a signal from his master, began to gather up his tools. This done, and the dog having been unmuzzled, we turned in a profound silence towards home.

We had taken, perhaps, a dozen steps in this direction, when, with a loud oath, Legrand strode up to Jupiter, and seized him by the collar. The astonished negro opened his eyes and mouth to the fullest extent, let fall the spades, and fell upon his knees.

"You scoundrel," said Legrand, hissing out the syllables from between his clenched teeth –"you infernal black villain! – speak, I tell you! – answer me this instant, without prevarication! – which – which is your left eye?"

"Oh, my golly, Massa Will! aint dis here my lef eye for sartain?" roared the terrified Jupiter, placing his hand upon his *right* organ of vision, and holding it there with a desperate pertinacity, as if in immediate dread of his master's attempt at a gouge.

"I thought so!—I knew it!—hurrah!" vociferated Legrand, letting the negro go, and executing a series of curvets and caracols, much to the astonishment of his valet, who, arising from his knees, looked, mutely, from his master to myself, and then from myself to his master.

"Come! we must go back," said the latter, "the game's not up yet;" and he again led the way to the tulip-tree.

"Jupiter," said he, when we reached its foot, "come here! was the skull nailed to the limb with the face outwards or with the face to the limb?"

"De face was out, massa, so dat de crows could get at de eyes good, widout any trubble."

"Well, then, was it this eye or that through which you dropped the beetle?"– here Legrand touched each of Jupiter's eyes.

"Twas dis eye, massa—de lef eye—jis as you tell me," and here it was his right eye that the negro indicated.

"That will do—we must try it again."

Here my friend, about whose madness I now saw, or fancied that I saw, certain indications of method, removed the peg nearest the tree, to a spot about three inches to the westward of its former position. Taking, now, the tape-measure from the nearest point of the trunk, as before, and continuing the extension in a straight line to the distance of fifty feet, a spot was indicated, removed, by several yards, from the point at which we had been digging.

Around the new position a circle, somewhat larger than in the former instance, was now described, and we again set to work with the spades. I was dreadfully weary, but, scarcely understanding what had occasioned the change in my thoughts, I felt no longer any great aversion from the labor imposed. I had become most unaccountably interested—nay, even excited. Perhaps there was something, amid all the extravagant demeanor of Legrand – some air of forethought, or of deliberation, which impressed me. I dug eagerly, and now and then caught myself actually looking, with something that very much resembled expectation, for the fancied treasure, the vision of which had demented my unfortunate companion. At a period when such vagaries of thought most fully possessed me, and when we had been at work perhaps an hour and a half, we were again interrupted by the violent howlings of the dog. His uneasiness, in the first instance, had been, evidently, but the result of playfulness or caprice, but he now assumed a bitter and serious tone. Upon Jupiter's again attempting to muzzle him, he made furious resistance, and, leaping into the hole, tore up the mould frantically with his claws. In a few seconds he had uncovered a mass of human bones, forming two complete skeletons, and intermingled with several buttons of metal, and what appeared to be the dust of decayed woollen. One or two strokes of a spade upturned the blade of a large Spanish knife, and, as we dug farther, three or four loose pieces of gold and silver coin came to light.

At sight of these the joy of Jupiter could scarcely be restrained, but the countenance of his master wore an air of extreme disappointment. He urged us, however, to continue our exertions, and the words were hardly uttered when I stumbled and fell forward, having caught the toe of my boot in a large ring of iron that lay half buried in the loose earth.

We now worked in good earnest, and never did I pass ten minutes of more intense excitement. During this interval we had fairly unearthed an oblong chest of wood, which, from its perfect preservation and wonderful hardness, had plainly been subjected to some mineralizing process – perhaps that of the Bi-chloride of Mercury. This box was three feet and a half long, three feet broad, and two and a half feet deep. It was firmly secured by bands of wrought iron, riveted, and forming a kind of open trellis-work over the whole. On each side of the chest, near the top, were three rings of iron – six in all – by means of which a firm hold could be obtained by six persons. Our utmost united endeavors served only to disturb the coffer very slightly in its bed. We at once saw the impossibility of removing so great a weight. Luckily, the sole fastenings of the lid consisted of two sliding bolts. These we drew back – trembling and panting with anxiety. In an instant, a treasure of incalculable value lay gleaming before us. As the rays of the lanterns fell within the pit, there flashed upwards a glow and a glare, from a confused heap of gold and of jewels, that absolutely dazzled our eyes.

I shall not pretend to describe the feelings with which I gazed. Amazement was, of course, predominant. Legrand appeared exhausted with excitement, and spoke very few words. Jupiter's countenance wore, for some minutes, as deadly a pallor as it is possible, in the nature of things, for any negro's visage to assume. He seemed stupified – thunder-stricken. Presently he fell upon his knees in the pit, and, burying his naked arms up to the elbows in gold, let them there remain, as if enjoying the luxury of a bath. At length, with a deep sigh, he exclaimed, as if in a soliloquy, "And dis all cum ob de goole-bug! de putty goole-bug! de poor little goole-bug, what I boosed in dat sabage kind ob style! Aint you shamed ob yourself, nigger? – answer me dat!"

It became necessary, at last, that I should arouse both master and valet to the expediency of removing the treasure. It was growing late, and it behooved us to make exertion, that we might get every thing housed before daylight. It was difficult to say what should be done and much time was spent in deliberation – so confused were the ideas of all. We, finally, lightened the box by removing two thirds of its contents, when we were enabled, with some trouble, to raise it from the hole. The articles taken out were deposited among the brambles, and the dog left to guard them, with strict orders from Jupiter neither, upon any pretence, to stir from the spot, nor to open his mouth until our return. We then hurriedly made for home with the chest; reaching the hut in safety, but after excessive toil, at one o'clock in the morning. Worn out as we were, it was not in human nature to do more immediately. We rested until two, and had supper; starting for the hills immediately afterwards, armed with three stout sacks, which, by good luck, were upon the premises. A little before four we arrived at the pit, divided the remainder of the booty, as equally as might be, among us, and, leaving the holes unfilled, again set out for the hut, at which, for the second time, we deposited our golden burthens, just as the first faint streaks of the dawn gleamed from over the tree-tops in the East.

We were now thoroughly broken down; but the intense excitement of the time denied us repose. After an unquiet slumber of some three or four hours' duration, we arose, as if by preconcert, to make examination of our treasure.

The chest had been full to the brim, and we spent the whole day, and the greater part of the next night, in a scrutiny of its contents. There had been nothing like order or arrangement. Everything had been heaped in promiscuously. Having assorted all with care, we found ourselves possessed of even vaster wealth than we had at first supposed. In coin there was rather more than four hundred and fifty thousand dollars – estimating the value of the pieces, as accurately as we could, by the tables of the period. There was not a particle of silver. All was gold of antique date and of great variety – French, Spanish, and German money, with a few English guineas, and some counters, of which we had never seen specimens before. There were several very large and heavy coins, so worn that we could make nothing of their inscriptions. There was no American money. The value of the jewels we found more difficulty in estimating. There were diamonds – some of them exceedingly large and fine – a hundred and ten in all, and not one of them small; eighteen rubies of remarkable brilliancy; – three hundred and ten emeralds, all very beautiful; and twenty-one sapphires, with an opal. These stones had all been broken from their settings and thrown loose in the chest. The settings themselves, which we picked out from among the other gold, appeared to have been beaten up with hammers as if to prevent identification. Besides all this, there was a vast quantity of solid gold ornaments; – nearly two hundred massive finger and ear rings; – rich chains – thirty of these, if I remember; – eighty-three very large and heavy crucifixes; – five gold censers of great value; – a prodigious golden punch-bowl, ornamented with richly chased vine-leaves and Bacchanalian figures; with two sword-handles exquisitely embossed, and many other smaller articles which I cannot recollect. The weight of these valuables exceeded three hundred and fifty pounds avoirdupois; and in this estimate I have not included one hundred and ninety-seven superb gold watches; three of the number being worth each five hundred dollars, if one. Many of them were very old, and as time keepers valueless; the works having suffered, more or less, from corrosion – but all were richly jewelled and in cases of great worth. We estimated the entire contents of the chest, that night, at a million and a half of dollars; and, upon the subsequent disposal of the trinkets and jewels (a few being retained for our own use), it was found that we had greatly undervalued the treasure.

When, at length, we had concluded our examination, and the intense excitement of the time had, in some measure, subsided, Legrand, who saw that I was dying with impatience for a solution of this most extraordinary riddle, entered into a full detail of all the circumstances connected with it.

"You remember," said he, "the night when I handed you the rough sketch I had made of the *scarabæus*. You recollect also, that I became quite vexed at you for insisting that my drawing resembled a death's-head. When you first made this assertion I thought you were jesting; but afterwards I called to mind the peculiar spots on the back of the insect, and admitted to myself that your remark had some little foundation in fact. Still, the sneer at my graphic powers irritated me – for I am considered a good artist – and, therefore, when you handed me the scrap of parchment, I was about to crumple it up and throw it angrily in the fire."

"The scrap of paper, you mean," said I.

"No; it had much of the appearance of paper, and at first I supposed it to be such, but when I came to draw upon it, I discovered it, at once, to be a piece of very thin parchment. It was quite dirty, you remember. Well, as I was in the very act of crumpling it up, my glance fell upon the sketch at which you had been looking, and you may imagine my astonishment when I perceived, in fact, the figure of a death's-head just where, it seemed to me, I had made the drawing of the beetle. For a moment I was too much amazed to think with accuracy. I knew that my design was very different in detail from this – although there was a certain similarity in general outline. Presently I took a candle, and seating myself at the other end of the room, proceeded to scrutinize the parchment more closely. Upon turning it over, I saw my own sketch upon the reverse, just as I had made it. My first idea, now, was mere surprise at the really remarkable similarity of outline – at the singular coincidence involved in the fact, that unknown to me, there should have been a skull upon the other side of the parchment, immediately beneath my figure of the *scarabæus,* and that this skull, not only in outline, but in size, should so closely resemble my drawing. I say the singularity of this coincidence absolutely stupified me for a time. This is the usual effect of such coincidences. The mind struggles to establish a connection – a sequence of cause and effect – and, being unable to do so, suffers a species of temporary paralysis.

But, when I recovered from this stupor, there dawned upon me gradually a conviction which startled me even far more than the coincidence. I began distinctly, positively, to remember that there had been *no* drawing upon the parchment when I made my sketch of the *scarabæus*. I became perfectly certain of this; for I recollected turning up first one side and then the other, in search of the cleanest spot. Had the skull been then there, of course I could not have failed to notice it. Here was indeed a mystery which I felt it impossible to explain; but, even at that early moment, there seemed to glimmer, faintly, within the most remote and secret chambers of my intellect, a glow-worm-like conception of that truth which last night's adventure brought to so magnificent a demonstration. I arose at once, dismissing all farther reflection until I should be alone.

"When you had gone, and when Jupiter was fast asleep, I betook myself to a more methodical investigation of the affair. In the first place I considered the manner in which the parchment had come into my possession. The spot where we discovered the *scarabæus* was on the coast of the main land, about a mile eastward of the island, and but a short distance above high water mark. Upon my seizing it, it gave me a sharp bite, which caused me to let it drop. Jupiter, with his accustomed caution, before seizing the insect, which had flown towards him, looked about him for a leaf, or something of that nature, by which to take hold of it. It was at this moment that his eyes, and mine also, fell upon the scrap of parchment, which I then supposed to be paper. It was lying half buried in the sand, a corner sticking up. Near the spot where we found it, I observed the remnants of the hull of what appeared to have been a ship's long boat. The wreck seemed to have been there for a very great while; for the resemblance to boat timbers could scarcely be traced.

"Well, Jupiter picked up the parchment, wrapped the beetle in it, and gave it to me. Soon afterwards we turned to go home, and on the way met Lieutenant G——. I showed him the insect, and he begged me to let him take it to the fort. Upon my consenting, he thrust it forthwith into his waistcoat pocket, without the parchment in which it had been wrapped, and which I had continued to hold in my hand during his inspection. Perhaps he dreaded my changing my mind, and thought it best to make sure of the prize at once – you know how enthusiastic he is on all subjects connected with Natural History. At the same time, without being conscious of it, I must have deposited the parchment in my own pocket.

"You remember that when I went to the table, for the purpose of making a sketch of the beetle, I found no paper where it was usually kept. I looked in the drawer, and found none there. I searched my pockets, hoping to find an old letter, when my hand fell upon the parchment. I thus detail the precise mode in which it came into my possession; for the circumstances impressed me with peculiar force.

"No doubt you will think me fanciful – but I had already established a kind of *connection*. I had put together two links of a great chain. There was a boat lying upon a sea-coast, and not far from the boat was a parchment – *not a paper* – with a skull depicted upon it. You will, of course, ask 'where is the connection?' I reply that the skull, or death's-head, is the well-known emblem of the pirate. The flag of the death's-head is hoisted in all engagements.

"I have said that the scrap was parchment, and not paper. Parchment is durable – almost imperishable. Matters of little moment are rarely consigned to parchment; since, for the mere ordinary purposes of drawing or writing, it is not nearly so well adapted as paper. This reflection suggested some meaning – some relevancy – in the death's-head. I did not fail to observe, also, the *form* of the parchment. Although one of its corners had been, by some accident, destroyed, it could be seen that the original form was oblong. It was just such a

THE GOLD-BUG 223

slip, indeed, as might have been chosen for a memorandum – for a record of something to be long remembered and carefully preserved."

"But," I interposed, "you say that the skull was *not* upon the parchment when you made the drawing of the beetle. How then do you trace any connection between the boat and the skull – since this latter, according to your own admission, must have been designed (God only knows how or by whom) at some period subsequent to your sketching the *scarabæus?*"

"Ah, hereupon turns the whole mystery; although the secret, at this point, I had comparatively little difficulty in solving. My steps were sure, and could afford but a single result. I reasoned, for example, thus: When I drew the *scarabæus,* there was no skull apparent upon the parchment. When I had completed the drawing I gave it to you, and observed you narrowly until you returned it. *You,* therefore, did not design the skull, and no one else was present to do it. Then it was not done by human agency. And nevertheless it was done.

"At this stage of my reflections I endeavored to remember, and *did* remember, with entire distinctness, every incident which occurred about the period in question. The weather was chilly (oh rare and happy accident!), and a fire was blazing upon the hearth. I was heated with exercise and sat near the table. You, however, had drawn a chair close to the chimney. Just as I placed the parchment in your hand, and as you were in the act of inspecting it, Wolf, the Newfoundland, entered, and leaped upon your shoulders. With your left hand you caressed him and kept him off, while your right, holding the parchment, was permitted to fall listlessly between your knees, and in close proximity to the fire. At one moment I thought the blaze had caught it, and was about to caution you, but, before I could speak, you had withdrawn it, and were engaged in its examination. When I considered all these particulars,

I doubted not for a moment that *heat* had been the agent in bringing to light, upon the parchment, the skull which I saw designed upon it. You are well aware that chemical preparations exist, and have existed time out of mind, by means of which it is possible to write upon either paper or vellum, so that the characters shall become visible only when subjected to the action of fire. Zaffre, digested in *aqua regia*, and diluted with four times its weight of water, is sometimes employed; a green tint results. The regulus of cobalt, dissolved in spirit of nitre, gives a red. These colors disappear at longer or shorter intervals after the material written upon cools, but again become apparent upon the reapplication of heat.

"I now scrutinized the death's-head with care. Its outer edges—the edges of the drawing nearest the edge of the vellum—were far more *distinct* than the others. It was clear that the action of the caloric had been imperfect or unequal. I immediately kindled a fire, and subjected every portion of the parchment to a glowing heat. At first, the only effect was the strengthening of the faint lines in the skull; but, upon persevering in the experiment, there became visible, at the corner of the slip, diagonally opposite to the spot in which the death's-head was delineated, the figure of what I at first supposed to be a goat. A closer scrutiny, however, satisfied me that it was intended for a kid."

"Ha! ha!" said I, "to be sure I have no right to laugh at you—a million and a half of money is too serious a matter for mirth—but you are not about to establish a third link in your chain—you will not find any especial connection between your pirates and a goat—pirates, you know, have nothing to do with goats; they appertain to the farming interest."

"But I have just said that the figure was *not* that of a goat."

"Well, a kid then—pretty much the same thing."

"Pretty much, but not altogether," said Legrand. "You may have heard of one *Captain* Kidd. I at once looked upon the figure of the animal as a kind of punning or hieroglyphical signature. I say signature; because its position upon the vellum suggested this idea. The death's-head at the corner diagonally opposite, had, in the same manner, the air of a stamp, or seal. But I was sorely put out by the absence of all else – of the body to my imagined instrument – of the text for my context."

"I presume you expected to find a letter between the stamp and the signature."

"Something of that kind. The fact is, I felt irresistibly impressed with a presentiment of some vast good fortune impending. I can scarcely say why. Perhaps, after all, it was rather a desire than an actual belief; – but do you know that Jupiter's silly words, about the bug being of solid gold, had a remarkable effect upon my fancy?

And then the series of accidents and coincidences – these were so *very* extraordinary. Do you observe how mere an accident it was that these events should have occurred upon the *sole* day of all the year in which it has been, or may be, sufficiently cool for fire, and that without the fire, or without the intervention of the dog at the precise moment in which he appeared, I should never have become aware of the death's-head, and so never the possessor of the treasure?"

"But proceed – I am all impatience."

"Well; you have heard, of course, the many stories current – the thousand vague rumors afloat about money buried, somewhere upon the Atlantic coast, by Kidd and his associates. These rumors must have had some foundation in fact. And that the rumors have existed so long and so continuous, could have resulted, it appeared to me, only from the circumstance of the buried treasure still *remaining* entombed. Had Kidd concealed his plunder for a time, and afterwards reclaimed it, the rumors would scarcely have reached us in their present unvarying form. You will observe that the stories told are all about money-seekers, not about

money-finders. Had the pirate recovered his money, there
the affair would have dropped. It seemed to me that some
accident–say the loss of a memorandum indicating its
locality–had deprived him of the means of recovering it, and
that this accident had become known to his followers, who
otherwise might never have heard that treasure had been
concealed at all, and who, busying themselves in vain, because
unguided attempts, to regain it, had given first birth, and then
universal currency, to the reports which are now so common.
Have you ever heard of any important treasure having been
unearthed by the diggers for money along the coast?"

"Never."

"But that Kidd's accumulations were immense, is well
known. I took it for granted, therefore, that the earth still
held them; and you will scarcely be surprised when I tell you
that I felt a hope, nearly amounting to certainty, that the
parchment so strangely found, involved a lost record of the
place of deposit."

"But how did you proceed?"

"I held the vellum again to the fire, after increasing the
heat; but nothing appeared. I now thought it possible that the
coating of dirt might have something to do with the failure; so
I carefully rinsed the parchment, by pouring warm water over
it, and, having done this, I placed it in a tin pan, with the skull
downwards, and put the pan upon a furnace of lighted
charcoal. In a few minutes, the pan having become thoroughly
heated, I removed the slip, and, to my inexpressible joy, found
it spotted, in several places, with what appeared to be figures
arranged in lines. Again I placed it in the pan, and suffered it
to remain another minute. Upon taking it off, the whole was
just as you see it now."

Here Legrand submitted the parchment to my inspection.
The following characters were rudely traced in a red tint,
between the death's-head and the goat:

53‡‡†305))6*;4826)4‡.)4‡);806*;48†8¶60))85;1‡(;:‡*8†83(8
8)5*†;46(;88*96*?;8)*‡(;485);5*†2:*‡(;4956*2(5*−4)8¶8*;4
069285);)6†8)4‡‡;1(‡9;48081;8:8‡1;48†85;4)485†528806*81
(‡9;48;(88;4(‡?34;48)4‡;161;:188;‡?;

"But," said I, returning him the slip, "I am as much in the dark as
ever. Were all the jewels of Golconda awaiting me upon my solution
of this enigma, I am quite sure that I should be unable to earn them."

"And yet," said Legrand, "the solution is by no means so
difficult as you might be led to imagine from the first hasty
inspection of the characters. These characters, as any one
might readily guess, form a cipher – that is to say, they convey a
meaning; but then, from what is known of Kidd, I could not
suppose him capable of constructing any of the more abstruse
cryptographs. I made up my mind, at once, that this was of a
simple species – such, however, as would appear, to the crude
intellect of the sailor, absolutely insoluble without the key."

"And you really solved it?"

"Readily; I have solved others of an abstruseness ten
thousand times greater. Circumstances, and a certain bias of
mind, have led me to take interest in such riddles, and it may
well be doubted whether human ingenuity can construct an
enigma of the kind which human ingenuity may not, by
proper application, resolve. In fact, having once established
connected and legible characters, I scarcely gave a thought to
the mere difficulty of developing their import.

"In the present case – indeed in all cases of secret
writing – the first question regards the *language* of the cipher;
for the principles of solution, so far, especially, as the more
simple ciphers are concerned, depend upon, and are varied by,
the genius of the particular idiom. In general, there is no
alternative but experiment (directed by probabilities) of every
tongue known to him who attempts the solution, until the true
one is attained. But, with the cipher now before us, all

difficulty was removed by the signature. The pun upon the word 'Kidd' is appreciable in no other language than the English. But for this consideration I should have begun my attempts with the Spanish and French, as the tongues in which a secret of this kind would most naturally have been written by a pirate of the Spanish main. As it was, I assumed the cryptograph to be English.

"You observe there are no divisions between the words. Had there been divisions, the task would have been comparatively easy. In such case I should have commenced with a collation and analysis of the shorter words, and, had a word of a single letter occurred, as is most likely, (*a* or *I*, for example,) I should have considered this solution as assured. But, there being no division, my first step was to ascertain the predominant letters, as well as the least frequent. Counting all, I constructed a table thus:

Of the character 8 there are 33.

;	"	26.
4	"	19.
‡)	"	16.
*	"	13.
5	"	12.
6	"	11.
†1	"	8.
0	"	6.
92	"	5.
:3	"	4.
?	"	3.
¶	"	2.
—.	"	1.

"Now, in English, the letter which most frequently occurs is *e*. Afterwards, the succession runs thus: *a o i d h n r s t u y c f g l m w b k p q x z.* *E* predominates so remarkably that an individual sentence of any length is rarely seen, in which it is not the prevailing character.

"Here, then, we have, in the very beginning, the ground-work for something more than a mere guess. The general use which may be made of the table is obvious—but, in this particular cipher, we shall only very partially require its aid. As our predominant character is 8, we will commence by assuming it as the *e* of the natural alphabet. To verify the supposition, let us observe if the 8 be seen often in couples—for *e* is doubled with great frequency in English—in which words, for example, as 'meet,' 'fleet,' 'speed,' 'seen,' 'been,' 'agree,' &c. In the present instance we see it doubled no less than five times, although the cryptograph is brief.

"Let us assume 8, then as *e*. Now, of all *words* in the language, 'the' is the most usual; let us see, therefore, whether there are not repetitions of any three characters, in the same order of collocation, the last of them being 8. If we discover repetitions of such letters, so arranged, they will most probably represent the word 'the.' Upon inspection, we find no less than seven such arrangements, the characters being ;48. We may, therefore, assume that the semicolon represents *t,* 4 represents *h,* and 8 represents *e*—the last being now well confirmed. Thus a great step has been taken.

"But, having established a single word, we are enabled to establish a vastly important point; that is to say, several commencements and terminations of other words. Let us refer, for example, to the last instance by one, in which the combination ;48 occurs—not far from the end of the cipher. We know that the semicolon immediately ensuing is the commencement of a word, and, of the six characters succeeding this 'the,' we are cognizant of no less than five. Let us set these characters down, thus, by the letters we know them to represent, leaving a space for the one unknown—

t eeth.

"Here we are enabled, at once, to discard the 'th,' as forming no portion of the word commencing with the first *t;* since, by experiment of the entire alphabet for a letter adapted to the vacancy, we perceive that no word can be formed of which this *th* can be a part. We are thus narrowed into

t ee,

and, going through the alphabet, if necessary, as before, we arrive at the word 'tree,' as the sole possible reading. We thus gain another letter, *r,* represented by (, with the words 'the tree' in juxtaposition.

"Looking beyond these words, for a short distance, we again see the combination ;48, and employ it by way of *termination* to what immediately precedes. We have thus this arrangement:

the tree ;4(‡?34 the,

or, substituting the natural letters, where known, it reads thus:

the tree thr‡?3h the.

"Now, if, in place of the unknown characters, we leave blank spaces, or substitute dots, we read thus:

the tree thr. . .h the,

when the word *'through'* makes itself evident at once. But this discovery gives us three new letters, *o, u* and *g,* represented by ‡? and 3.

"Looking now, narrowly, through the cipher for combinations of known characters, we find, not very far from the beginning, this arrangement,

83(88, or egree,

which, plainly, is the conclusion of the word 'degree,' and gives another letter, *d,* represented by †.

"Four letters beyond the word 'degree,' we perceive the combination

;46(;88*

"Translating the known characters, and representing the unknown by dots, as before, we read thus:

th.rtee.

an arrangement immediately suggestive of the word 'thirteen,'
and again furnishing us with two new characters, *i* and *n*,
represented by 6 and *.

"Referring, now, to the beginning of the cryptograph, we
find the combination,

53‡‡†.

"Translating, as before, we obtain

.good,

which assures that the first letter is *A*, and that the first two
words are 'A good.'

It is now time that we arrange our key, as far as discovered,
in a tabular form to avoid confusion. It will stand thus:

5	represents	a
†	"	d
8	"	e
3	"	g
4	"	h
6	"	i
*	"	n
‡	"	o
(	"	r
;	"	t

"We have, therefore, no less than ten of the most
important letters represented, and it well be unnecessary to
proceed with the details of the solution. I have said enough to
convince you that ciphers of this nature are readily soluble,
and give you some insight into the *rationale* of their development. But be assured that the specimen before us appertains to
the very simplest species of cryptograph. It now only remains
to give you the full translation of the characters upon the
parchment, as unriddled. Here it is:

*'A good glass in the bishop's hostel in the devil's seat forty-one
degrees and thirteen minutes northeast and by north main branch*

seventh limb east side shoot from the left eye of the death's-head a
bee line from the tree through the shot fifty feet out.' "

"But," said I, "the enigma seems still in as bad a condition
as ever. How it is possible to extort a meaning from all this
jargon about 'devil's seats,' 'death's-heads,' and 'bishop's hotels?' "

"I confess," replied Legrand, "that the matter still wears a
serious aspect, when regarded with a casual glance. My first
endeavor was to divide the sentence into the natural division
intended by the cryptographist."

"You mean, to punctuate it?"

"Something of that kind."

"But how was it possible to effect this?"

"I reflected that it had been a *point* with the writer to run
his words together without division, so as to increase the
difficulty of solution. Now, a not over-acute man, in pursuing
such an object, would be nearly certain to overdo the matter.
When, in the course of his composition, he arrived at a break
in his subject which would naturally require a pause, or a
point, he would be exceedingly apt to run his characters, at
this place, more than usually close together. If you will observe
the MS., in the present instance, you will easily detect five
such cases of unusual crowding. Acting upon this hint, I made
the division thus:

'*A good glass in the Bishop's hostel in the Devil's seat—forty-*
one degrees and thirteen minutes—northeast and by north—main
branch seventh limb east side—shoot from the left eye of the
death's-head—a bee-line from the tree through the shot fifty
feet out.' "

"Even this division," said I, "leaves me still in the dark."

"It left me also in the dark," replied Legrand, "for a few
days; during which I made diligent inquiry, in the neighborhood of Sullivan's Island, for any building which went by the
name of the 'Bishop's Hotel;' for, of course, I dropped the
obsolete word 'hostel.' Gaining no information on the subject,

I was on the point of extending my sphere of search, and proceeding in a more systematic manner, when, one morning, it entered into my head, quite suddenly, that this 'Bishop's Hostel' might have some reference to an old family, of the name of Bessop, which, time out of mind, had held possession of an ancient manor-house, about four miles to the northward of the island. I accordingly went over to the plantation, and re-instituted my inquiries among the older negroes of the place. At length one of the most aged of the women said that she had heard of such a place as *Bessop's Castle,* and thought that she could guide me to it, but that it was not a castle, nor a tavern, but a high rock.

"I offered to pay her well for her trouble, and, after some demur, she consented to accompany me to the spot. We found it without much difficulty, when, dismissing her, I proceeded to examine the place. The 'castle' consisted of an irregular assemblage of cliffs and rocks—one of the latter being quite remarkable for its height as well as for its insulated and artificial appearance. I clambered to its apex, and then felt much at a loss as to what should be next done.

"While I was busied in reflection, my eyes fell upon a narrow ledge in the eastern face of the rock, perhaps a yard below the summit on which I stood. This ledge projected about eighteen inches, and was not more than a foot wide, while a niche in the cliff just above it, gave it a rude resemblance to one of the hollow-backed chairs used by our ancestors. I made no doubt that here was the 'devil's-seat' alluded to in the MS., and now I seemed to grasp the full secret of the riddle.

"The 'good glass,' I knew, could have reference to nothing but a telescope; for the word 'glass' is rarely employed in any other sense by seamen. Now here, I at once saw, was a tele-scope to be used, and a definite point of view, *admitting no variation,* from which to use it. Nor did I hesitate to believe that the phrases, 'forty-one degrees and thirteen minutes,' and 'northeast and by north,' were intended as directions for levelling of the glass. Greatly excited by these discoveries, I hurried home, procured a telescope, and returned to the rock.

"I let myself down to the ledge, and found that it was impossible to retain a seat upon it except in one particular position. This fact confirmed my preconceived idea. I proceeded to use the glass. Of course, the 'forty-one degrees and thirteen minutes' could allude to nothing but elevation above the visible horizon, since the horizontal direction was clearly indicated by the words, 'northeast and by north.' This latter direction I at once established by means of a pocket-compass; then, pointing the glass as nearly at an angle of forty-one degrees of elevation as I could do it by guess, I moved it cautiously up or down, until my attention was arrested by a circular rift or opening in the foliage of a large tree that overtopped its fellows in the distance. In the centre of this rift I perceived a white spot, but could not, at first, distinguish what it was. Adjusting the focus of the telescope, I again looked, and now made it out to be a human skull.

"Upon this discovery I was so sanguine as to consider the enigma solved; for the phrase 'main branch, seventh limb, east side,' could refer only to the position of the skull upon the tree, while 'shoot from the left eye of the death's-head' admitted, also, of but one interpretation, in regard to a search for buried treasure. I perceived that the design was to drop a bullet from the left eye of the skull, and that a bee-line, or, in other words, a straight line, drawn from the nearest point of the trunk through 'the shot,' (or the spot where the bullet fell,) and thence extended to a distance of fifty feet, would indicate a definite point—and beneath this point I thought it at least *possible* that a deposit of value lay concealed."

"All this," I said, "is exceedingly clear, and, although

ingenious, still simple and explicit. When you left the Bishop's Hotel, what then?"

"Why, having carefully taken the bearings of the tree, I turned homewards. The instant that I left 'the devil's seat,' however, the circular rift vanished; nor could I get a glimpse of it afterwards, turn as I would. What seems to me the chief ingenuity in this whole business, is the fact (for repeated experiment has convinced me it *is* a fact) that the circular opening in question is visible from no other attainable point of view than that afforded by the narrow ledge upon the face of the rock.

"In this expedition to the 'Bishop's Hotel' I had been attended by Jupiter, who had, no doubt, observed, for some weeks past, the abstraction of my demeanor, and took especial care not to leave me alone. But, on the next day, getting up very early, I contrived to give him the slip, and went into the hills in search of the tree. After much toil I found it. When I came home at night my valet proposed to give me a flogging. With the rest of the adventure I believe you are as well acquainted as myself."

"I suppose," said I, "you missed the spot, in the first attempt at digging, through Jupiter's stupidity in letting the bug fall through the right instead of through the left eye of the skull."

"Precisely. This mistake made a difference of about two inches and a half in the 'shot'– that is to say, in the position of the peg nearest the tree; and had the treasure been *beneath* 'the shot', the error would have been of little moment; but 'the shot', together with the nearest point of the tree, were merely two points for the establishment of a line of direction; of course the error, however trivial in the beginning, increased as we proceeded with the line, and by the time we had gone fifty feet, threw us quite off the scent. But for my deep-seated impressions that treasure was here somewhere actually buried, we might have had all our labor in vain."

"I presume the fancy of *the skull*—of letting fall a bullet through the skull's eye—was suggested to Kidd by the piratical flag. No doubt he felt a kind of poetical consistency in recovering his money through this ominous insignium."

"Perhaps so; still I cannot help thinking that common-sense had quite as much to do with the matter as poetical consistency. To be visible from the Devil's seat, it was necessary that the object, if small, should be *white;* and there is nothing like your human skull for retaining and even increasing its whiteness under exposure to all vicissitudes of weather."

"But your grandiloquence, and your conduct in swinging the beetle—how excessively odd! I was sure you were mad. And why did you insist upon dropping the bug, instead of a bullet, from the skull?"

"Why, to be frank, I felt somewhat annoyed by your evident suspicions touching my sanity, and so resolved to punish you quietly, in my own way, by a little bit of sober mystification. For this reason I swung the beetle, and for this reason I dropped it from the tree. An observation of yours about its great weight suggested the latter idea."

"Yes, I perceive; and now there is only one point which puzzles me. What are we to make of the skeletons found in the hole?"

"This is a question I am no more able to answer than yourself. There seems, however, only one plausible way of accounting for them—and yet it is dreadful to believe in such atrocity as my suggestion would imply. It is clear that Kidd—if Kidd indeed secreted this treasure, which I doubt not—it is clear that he must have had assistance in the labor. But this labor concluded, he may have thought it expedient to remove all participants in his secret. Perhaps a couple of blows with a mattock were sufficient, while his coadjutors were busy in the pit; perhaps it required a dozen—who shall tell?"

[June 21, 1843]

The Black Cat

For the most wild, yet most homely narrative which I am about to pen, I neither expect nor solicit belief. Mad indeed would I be to expect it, in a case where my very senses reject their own evidence. Yet, mad am I not – and very surely do I not dream. But to-morrow I die, and to-day I would unburthen my soul. My immediate purpose is to place before the world, plainly, succinctly, and without comment, a series of mere household events. In their consequences, these events have terrified – have tortured – have destroyed me. Yet I will not attempt to expound them. To me, they have presented little but Horror – to many they will seem less terrible than *barroques*. Hereafter, perhaps, some intellect may be found which will reduce my phantasm to the common-place – some intellect more calm, more logical, and far less excitable than my own, which will perceive, in the circumstances I detail with awe, nothing more than an ordinary succession of very natural causes and effects.

From my infancy I was noted for the docility and humanity of my disposition. My tenderness of heart was even so conspicuous as to make me the jest of my companions. I was especially fond of animals, and was indulged by my parents with a great variety of pets. With these I spent most of my time, and never was so happy as when feeding and caressing them. This peculiarity of character grew with my growth, and, in my manhood, I derived from it one of my principal sources of pleasure. To those who have cherished an affection for a faithful and sagacious dog, I need hardly be at the trouble of explaining the nature or the intensity of the gratification thus derivable. There is something in the unselfish and self-sacrificing love of a brute, which goes directly to the heart of him who has had frequent occasion to test the paltry friendship and gossamer fidelity of mere *Man*.

I married early, and was happy to find in my wife a disposition not uncongenial with my own. Observing my partiality for domestic pets, she lost no opportunity of procuring those of the most agreeable kind. We had birds, gold-fish, a fine dog, rabbits, a small monkey, and *a cat.*

This latter was a remarkably large and beautiful animal, entirely black, and sagacious to an astonishing degree. In speaking of his intelligence, my wife, who at heart was not a little tinctured with superstition, made frequent allusion to the ancient popular notion, which regarded all black cats as witches in disguise. Not that she was ever *serious* upon this point—and I mention the matter at all for no better reason than that it happens, just now, to be remembered.

Pluto—this was the cat's name—was my favorite pet and playmate. I alone fed him, and he attended me whenever I went about the house. It was even with difficulty that I could prevent him from following me through the streets.

Our friendship lasted, in this manner, for several years, during which my general temperament and character—through the instrumentality of the Fiend Intemperance—had (I blush to confess it) experienced a radical alteration for the worse. I grew, day by day, more moody, more irritable, more regardless of the feelings of others. I suffered myself to use intemperate language to my wife. At length, I even offered her personal violence. My pets, of course, were made to feel the change in my disposition. I not only neglected, but ill-used them. For Pluto, however, I still retained sufficient regard to restrain me from maltreating him, as I made no scruple of maltreating the rabbits, the monkey, of even the dog, when by accident, or through affection, they came in my way. But my disease grew upon me—for what disease is like Alcohol!—and at length even Pluto, who was now becoming old, and consequently somewhat peevish—even Pluto began to experience the effects of my ill temper.

One night, returning home, much intoxicated, from one of my haunts about town, I fancied that the cat avoided my presence. I seized him; when, in his fright at my violence, he inflicted a slight wound upon my hand with his teeth. The fury of the demon instantly possessed me. I knew myself no longer. My original soul seemed, at once, to take its flight from my body; and a more than fiendish malevolence, gin-nurtured, thrilled every fibre of my frame. I took from my waistcoat-pocket a pen-knife, opened it, grasped the poor beast by the throat, and deliberately cut one of its eyes from the socket! I blush, I burn, I shudder, while I pen the damnable atrocity.

When reason returned with the morning—when I had slept off the fumes of the night's debauch—I experienced a sentiment half of horror, half of remorse, for the crime of which I had been guilty; but it was, at best, a feeble and equivocal feeling, and the soul remained untouched. I again plunged into excess, and soon drowned in wine all memory of the deed.

In the meantime the cat slowly recovered. The socket of the lost eye presented, it is true, a frightful appearance, but he no longer appeared to suffer any pain. He went about the house as usual, but, as might be expected, fled in extreme terror at my approach. I had so much of my old heart left, as to be at first grieved by this evident dislike on the part of a creature which had once so loved me. But this feeling soon gave place to irritation. And then came, as if to my final and irrevocable overthrow, the spirit of PERVERSENESS. On this spirit and philosophy takes no account. Phrenology finds no place for it among its organs. Yet I am not more sure that my soul lives, than I am that perverseness is one of the primitive impulses of the human heart—one of the indivisible primary faculties, or sentiments, which give direction to the character of Man. Who has not, a hundred times, found himself committing a vile or a silly action, for no other reason than because he knows he should *not?* Have we not a perpetual inclination, in the teeth of our best judgment, to violate that which is *Law,* merely because we understand it to be such? This spirit of perverseness, I say, came to my final overthrow. It was this unfathomable longing of the soul to *vex itself*–to offer violence to its own nature–to do wrong for the wrong's sake only–that urged me to continue and finally to consummate the injury I had inflicted upon the offending brute. One morning, in cool blood, I slipped a noose about its neck and hung it to the limb of a tree;–hung it with the tears streaming from my eyes, and with the bitterest remorse at my heart;– hung it *because* I knew that it had loved me, and *because* I felt it had given me no reason of offence;–hung it *because* I knew that in so doing I was committing a sin–a deadly sin that would so jeopardize my immortal soul as to place it–if such a thing were possible–even beyond the reach of the infinite mercy of the Most Merciful and Most Terrible God.

On the night of the day on which this cruel deed was done, I was aroused from sleep by the cry of fire. The curtains of my bed were in flames. The whole house was blazing. It was with great difficulty that my wife, a servant, and myself, made our escape from the conflagration. The destruction was complete. My entire worldly wealth was swallowed up, and I resigned myself thenceforward to despair.

I am above the weakness of seeking to establish a sequence of cause and effect, between the disaster and the atrocity. But I am detailing a chain of facts–and wish not to leave even a possible link imperfect. On the day succeeding the fire, I visited the ruins. The walls, with one exception, had fallen in. This exception was found in a compartment wall, not very thick, which stood about the middle of the house, and against which had rested the head of my bed. The plastering had here, in great measure, resisted the action of the fire–a fact which I attributed to its having been recently spread.

About this wall a dense crowd were collected, and many persons seemed to be examining a particular portion of it with very minute and eager attention. The words "strange!" "singular!" and other similar expressions, excited my curiosity. I approached and saw, as if graven in *bas relief* upon the white surface, the figure of a gigantic *cat*. The impression was given with an accuracy truly marvellous. There had been a rope about the animal's neck.

When I first beheld this apparition–for I could scarcely regard it as less–my wonder and my terror were extreme. But at length reflection came to my aid. The cat, I remembered, had been hung in a garden adjacent to the house. Upon the alarm of fire, this garden had been immediately filled by the crowd–by some one of whom the animal must have been cut from the tree and thrown, through an open window, into my chamber. This had probably been done with the view of arousing me from sleep. The falling of other walls had compressed the victim of my cruelty into the substance of the freshly-spread plaster; the lime of which, with the flames, and the *ammonia* from the carcass, had then accomplished the portraiture as I saw it.

Although I thus readily accounted to my reason, if not altogether to my conscience, for the startling fact just detailed, it did not the less fail to make a deep impression upon my fancy. For months I could not rid myself of the phantasm of the cat; and, during this period, there came back into my spirit a half-sentiment that seemed, but was not, remorse. I went so far as to regret the loss of the animal, and to look about me, among the vile haunts which I now habitually frequented, for another pet of the same species, and of somewhat similar appearance, with which to supply its place.

One night as I sat, half stupified, in a den of more than infamy, my attention was suddenly drawn to some black object, reposing upon the head of one of the immense

hogsheads of Gin, or of Rum, which constituted the chief
furniture of the apartment. I had been looking steadily at
the top of this hogshead for some minutes, and what now
caused me surprise was the fact that I had not sooner
perceived the object thereupon. I approached it, and touched
it with my hand. It was a black cat–a very large one–fully
as large as Pluto, and closely resembling him in every respect
but one. Pluto had not a white hair upon any portion of
his body; but this cat had a large, although indefinite
splotch of white, covering nearly the whole region
of the breast.

Upon my touching him, he immediately arose, purred
loudly, rubbed against my hand, and appeared delighted with
my notice. This, then, was the very creature of which I was in
search. I at once offered to purchase it of the landlord; but this
person made no claim to it–knew nothing of it–had never
seen it before.

I continued my caresses, and, when I prepared to go
home, the animal evinced a disposition to accompany me. I
permitted it to do so; occasionally stooping and patting it as I
proceeded. When it reached the house it domesticated itself at
once, and became immediately a great favorite with my wife.

For my own part, I soon found a dislike to it arising within
me. This was just the reverse of what I had anticipated; but–I
know not how or why it was–its evident fondness for myself
rather disgusted and annoyed. By slow degrees, these feelings
of disgust and annoyance rose into the bitterness of hatred. I
avoided the creature; a certain sense of shame, and the
remembrance of my former deed of cruelty, preventing me
from physically abusing it. I did not, for some weeks, strike, or
otherwise violently ill-use it; but gradually–very gradually–
I came to look upon it with unutterable loathing, and to
flee silently from its odious presence, as from the breath
of a pestilence.

What added, no doubt, to my hatred of the beast, was the discovery, on the morning after I brought it home, that, like Pluto, it also had been deprived of one of its eyes. This circumstance, however, only endeared it to my wife, who, as I have already said, possessed, in a high degree, that humanity of feeling which had once been my distinguishing trait, and the source of many of my simplest and purest pleasures.

With my aversion to this cat, however, its partiality for myself seemed to increase. It followed my footsteps with a pertinacity which it would be difficult to make the reader comprehend. Whenever I sat, it would crouch beneath my chair, or spring upon my knees, covering me with its loath-some caresses. If I arose to walk it would get between my feet and thus nearly throw me down, or, fastening its long and sharp claws in my dress, clamber, in this manner, to my breast. At such times, although I longed to destroy it with a blow, I was yet withheld from so doing, partly by a memory of my former crime, but chiefly—let me confess it at once—by absolute *dread* of the beast.

This dread was not exactly a dread of physical evil—and yet I should be at a loss how otherwise to define it. I am almost ashamed to own—yes, ever in this felon's cell, I am almost ashamed to own—that the terror and horror with which the animal inspired me, had been heightened by one of the merest chimæras it would be possible to conceive. My wife had called my attention, more than once, to the character of the mark of white hair, of which I have spoken, and which constituted the sole visible difference between the strange beast and the one I had destroyed. The reader will remember that this mark, although large, had been originally very indefinite; but, by slow degrees—degrees nearly imperceptible, and which for a long time my Reason struggled to reject as fanciful—it had, at length, assumed a rigorous distinctness of outline. It was now the representation of an object that I

shudder to name – and for this, above all, I loathed, and
dreaded, and would have rid myself of the monster *had I
dared* – it was now, I say, the image of a hideous – of a ghastly
thing – of the GALLOWS! – oh, mournful and terrible engine of
Horror and of Crime – of Agony and of Death!

And now was I indeed wretched beyond the wretchedness
of mere Humanity. And *a brute beast* – whose fellow I had
contemptuously destroyed – *a brute beast* to work out for *me* –
for me a man, fashioned in the image of the High God – so
much of insufferable woe! Alas! neither by day nor by night
knew I the blessing of Rest any more! During the former the
creature left me no moment alone; and, in the latter, I started,
hourly, from dreams of unutterable fear, to find the hot breath
of *the thing* upon my face, and its vast weight – in incarnate
Night-Mare that I had no power to shake off – incumbent
eternally upon my *heart*!

Beneath the pressure of torments such as these, the
feeble remnant of the good within me succumbed. Evil
thoughts became my sole intimates – the darkest and most
evil of thoughts. The moodiness of my usual temper increased
to hatred of all things and of all mankind; while, from the
sudden, frequent, and ungovernable outbursts of a fury
to which I now blindly abandoned myself, my uncom-
plaining wife, alas! was the most usual and the most
patient of sufferers.

One day she accompanied me, upon some household
errand, into the cellar of the old building which our poverty
compelled us to inhabit. The cat followed me down the steep
stairs, and, nearly throwing me headlong, exasperated me to
madness. Uplifting an axe, and forgetting, in my wrath, the
childish dread which had hitherto stayed my hand, I aimed a
blow at the animal which, of course, would have proved
instantly fatal had it descended as I wished. But this blow was
arrested by the hand of my wife. Goaded, by the interference,

into a rage more than demoniacal, I withdrew my arm from her grasp and buried the axe in her brain. She fell dead upon the spot, without a groan.

This hideous murder accomplished, I set myself forthwith, and with entire deliberation, to the task of concealing the body. I knew that I could not remove it from the house, either by day or by night, without the risk of being observed by the neighbors. Many projects entered my mind. At one period I thought of cutting the corpse into minute fragments, and destroying them by fire. At another, I resolved to dig a grave for it in the floor of the cellar. Again, I deliberated about casting it in the well in the yard – about packing it in a box, as if merchandize, with the usual arrangements, and so getting a porter to take it from the house. Finally I hit upon what I considered a far better expedient than either of these. I determined to wall it up in the cellar – as the monks of the middle ages are recorded to have walled up their victims.

For a purpose such as this the cellar was admirably adapted. Its walls were loosely constructed, and had lately been plastered throughout with a rough plaster, which the dampness of the atmosphere had prevented from hardening. Moreover, in one of the walls was a projection, caused by a false chimney, or fireplace, that had been filled, or walled up, and made to resemble the rest of the cellar. I made no doubt that I could readily displace the bricks at this point, insert the corpse, and wall the whole up as before, so that no eye could detect any thing suspicious.

And in this calculation I was not deceived. By means of a crowbar I easily dislodged the bricks, and, having carefully deposited the body against the inner wall, I propped it in that position, while, with little trouble, I re-laid the whole structure as it originally stood. Having procured mortar, sand, and hair, with every possible precaution, I prepared a plaster which could not be distinguished from the old, and with this I very carefully went over the new brickwork. When I had finished, I felt satisfied that all was right. The wall did not present the slightest appearance of having been disturbed. The rubbish on the floor was picked up with the minutest care. I looked around triumphantly, and said to myself–"Here at least, then, my labor has not been in vain."

My next step was to look for the beast which had been the cause of so much wretchedness; for I had, at length, firmly resolved to put it to death. Had I been able to meet with it, at the moment, there could have been no doubt of its fate; but it appeared that the crafty animal had been alarmed at the violence of my previous anger, and forbore to present itself in my present mood. It is impossible to describe, or to imagine, the deep, the blissful sense of relief which the absence of the detested creature occasioned in my bosom. It did not make its appearance during the night–and thus for one night at least, since its introduction into the house, I soundly and tranquilly slept; aye, *slept* even with the burden of murder upon my soul!

The second and the third day passed, and still my tormentor came not. Once again I breathed as a freeman. The monster, in terror, had fled the premises forever! I should behold it no more! My happiness was supreme! The guilt of my dark deed disturbed me but little. Some few inquiries had been made, but these had been readily answered. Even a search had been instituted–but of course nothing was to be discovered. I looked upon my future felicity as secured.

Upon the fourth day of my assassination, a party of the police came, very unexpectedly, into the house, and proceeded again to make rigorous investigation of the premises. Secure, however, in the inscrutability of my place of concealment, I felt no embarrassment whatever. The officers bade me accompany them in the search. They left no nook or corner unexplored. At length, for the third or fourth time, they descended into the cellar. I quivered not in a muscle. My heart beat calmly as that of one who slumbers in innocence. I walked the cellar from end to end. I folded my arms upon my bosom, and roamed easily to and fro. The police were thoroughly satisfied and prepared to depart. The glee at my heart was too strong to be restrained. I burned to say if but one word, by way of triumph, and to render doubly sure their assurance of my guiltlessness.

"Gentlemen," I said at last, as the party ascended the steps, "I delight to have allayed your suspicions. I wish you all health, and a little more courtesy. By the bye, gentlemen, this – this is a very well constructed house." [In the rabid desire to say something easily, I scarcely knew what I uttered at all.] –"I may say an *excellently* well constructed house. These walls – are you going, gentlemen? – these walls are solidly put together;" and here, through the mere phrenzy of bravado, I rapped heavily, with a cane which I held in my hand, upon that very portion of the brick-work behind which stood the ghastly corpse of the wife of my bosom.

But may God shield and deliver me from the fangs of the Arch-Fiend! No sooner had the reverberation of my blows sunk into silence, than I was answered by a voice from within the tomb! – by a cry, at first muffled and broken, like the sobbing of a child, and then quickly swelling into one long, loud, and continuous scream, utterly anomalous and inhuman – a howl – a wailing shriek, half of horror and half of triumph, such as might have arisen only out of hell, conjointly from the throats of the damned in their agony and of the demons that exult in the damnation.

Of my own thoughts it is folly to speak. Swooning, I staggered to the opposite wall. For one instant the party upon the stairs remained motionless, through extremity of terror and of awe. In the next, a dozen stout arms were toiling at the wall. It fell bodily. The corpse, already greatly decayed and clotted with gore, stood erect before the eyes of the spectators. Upon its head, with red extended mouth and solitary eye of fire, sat the hideous beast whose craft had seduced me into murder, and whose informing voice had consigned me to the hangman. I had walled the monster up within the tomb!

[August 19, 1843]

E ULALIE – A S ONG

I DWELT ALONE
    In a world of moan,
And my soul was a stagnant tide
Till the fair and gentle Eulalie became my blushing bride –
Till the yellow-haired young Eulalie became my smiling bride.

    Ah, less, less bright
    The stars of the night
Than the eyes of·the radiant girl,
    And never a flake
    That the vapor can make
With the morn-tints of purple and pearl
Can vie with the modest Eulalie's most unregarded curl –
Can compare with the bright-eyed Eulalie's most humble and
        careless curl.

    Now Doubt – now Pain
    Come never again,
For her soul give me sigh for sigh
    While all day long
    Shines bright and strong
Astarté within the sky,
And ever to her dear Eulalie upturns her matron eye –
And ever to her young Eulalie upturns her violet eye.
                    [August 9, 1845; written circa February, 1844]

THE PURLOINED LETTER

Nil sapientia odiosius acumine nimio [Nothing is more hateful to wisdom than too much cleverness].– SENECA.

AT PARIS, JUST after dark one gusty evening in the autumn of 18 –, I was enjoying the twofold luxury of meditation and a meerschaum, in company with my friend C. Auguste Dupin, in his little back library, or book-closet, *au troisième, No. 33, Rue Dunôt, Faubourg St. Germain*. For one hour at least we had maintained a profound silence; while each, to any casual observer, might have seemed intently and exclusively occupied with the curling eddies of smoke that oppressed the atmosphere of the chamber. For myself, however, I was mentally discussing certain topics which had formed matter for conversation between us at an earlier period of the evening; I mean the affair of the Rue Morgue, and the mystery attending the murder of Marie Rogêt. I looked upon it, therefore, as something of a coincidence, when the door of our apartment was thrown open and admitted our old acquaintance, Monsieur G––, the Prefect of the Parisian police.

We gave him a hearty welcome; for there was nearly half as much of the entertaining as of the contemptible about the man, and we had not seen him for several years. We had been sitting in the dark, and Dupin now arose for the purpose of lighting a lamp, but sat down again, without doing so, upon G.'s saying that he had called to consult us, or rather to ask the opinion of my friend, about some official business which had occasioned a great deal of trouble.

"If it is any point requiring reflection," observed Dupin, as he forbore to enkindle the wick, "we shall examine it to better purpose in the dark."

"That is another of your odd notions," said the Prefect, who had a fashion of calling every thing "odd" that was beyond his comprehension, and thus lived amid an absolute legion of "oddities."

"Very true," said Dupin, as he supplied his visiter with a pipe, and rolled towards him a very comfortable chair.

"And what is the difficulty now?" I asked. "Nothing more in the assassination way, I hope?"

"Oh no; nothing of that nature. The fact is, the business is *very* simple indeed, and I make no doubt that we can manage it sufficiently well ourselves; but then I thought Dupin would like to hear the details of it, because it is so excessively *odd*."

"Simple and odd," said Dupin.

"Why, yes; and not exactly that, either. The fact is, we have all been a good deal puzzled because the affair *is* so simple, and yet baffles us altogether."

"Perhaps it is the very simplicity of the thing which puts you at fault," said my friend.

"What nonsense you *do* talk!" replied the Prefect, laughing heartily.

"Perhaps the mystery is a little *too* plain," said Dupin.

"Oh, good heavens! who ever heard of such an idea?"

"A little *too* self-evident."

"Ha! ha! ha! – ha! ha! ha! – ho! ho! ho!" roared out our visiter, profoundly amused, "oh, Dupin, you will be the death of me yet!"

"And what, after all *is* the matter on hand?" I asked.

"Why, I will tell you," replied the Prefect, as he gave a long, steady, and contemplative puff, and settled himself in his chair. "I will tell you in a few words; but, before I begin, let me caution you that this is an affair demanding the greatest secrecy, and that I should most probably lose the position I now hold, were it known that I confided it to any one."

"Proceed," said I.

"Or not," said Dupin.

"Well, then; I have received personal information, from a very high quarter, that a certain document of the last importance, has been purloined from the royal apartments. The individual who purloined it is known; this beyond a doubt; he was seen to take it. It is known, also, that it still remains in his possession."

"How is this known?" asked Dupin.

"It is clearly inferred," replied the Prefect, "from the nature of the document, and from the non-appearance of certain results which would at once arise from its passing *out* of the robber's possession; – that is to say, from his employing it as he must design in the end to employ it."

"Be a little more explicit," I said.

"Well, I may venture so far as to say that the paper gives its holder a certain power in a certain quarter where such power is immensely valuable." The Prefect was fond of the cant of diplomacy.

"Still I do not quite understand," said Dupin.

"No? Well; the disclosure of the document to a third person, who shall be nameless, would bring in question the honor of a personage of most exalted station; and this fact gives the holder of the document an ascendancy over the illustrious personage whose honor and peace are so jeopardized."

"But this ascendancy," I interposed, "would depend upon the robber's knowledge of the loser's knowledge of the robber. Who would dare –"

"The thief," said G., "is the Minister D––, who dares all things, those unbecoming as well as those becoming a man. The method of the theft was not less ingenious than bold. The document in question – a letter, to be frank – had been received by the personage robbed while alone in the royal *boudoir*. During its perusal she was suddenly interrupted by the entrance of the other exalted personage from whom especially it was her wish to conceal it. After a hurried and vain endeavor to thrust it in a drawer, she was forced to place it, open as it was, upon a table. The address, however, was uppermost, and, the contents thus unexposed, the letter escaped notice. At this juncture enters the Minister D ——. His lynx eye immediately perceives the paper, recognises the handwriting of the address, observes the confusion of the personage addressed, and fathoms her secret. After some business transactions, hurried through in his ordinary manner, he produces a letter somewhat similar to the one in question, opens it, pretends to read it, and then places it in close juxtaposition to the other. Again he converses, for some fifteen minutes, upon the public affairs. At length, in taking leave, he takes also from the table the letter to which he had no claim. Its rightful owner saw, but of course, dared not call attention to the act, in the presence of the third personage who stood at her elbow. The minister decamped; leaving his own letter – one of no importance – upon the table."

"Here, then," said Dupin to me, "you have precisely what you demand to make the ascendancy complete – the robber's knowledge of the loser's knowledge of the robber."

"Yes," replied the Prefect; "and the power thus attained has, for some months past, been wielded, for political purposes, to a very dangerous extent. The personage robbed is more thoroughly convinced, every day, of the necessity of reclaiming her letter. But this, of course, cannot be done openly. In fine, driven to despair, she has committed the matter to me."

"Than whom," said Dupin, amid a perfect whirlwind of smoke, "no more sagacious agent could, I suppose, be desired, or even imagined."

"You flatter me," replied the Prefect; "but it is possible that some such opinion may have been entertained."

"It is clear," said I, "as you observe, that the letter is still in possession of the minister; since it is this possession, and not any employment of the letter, which bestows the power. With the employment the power departs."

"True," said G.; "and upon this conviction I proceeded. My first care was to make thorough search of the minister's hotel; and here my chief embarrassment lay in the necessity of searching without his knowledge. Beyond all things, I have been warned of the danger which would result from giving him reason to suspect our design."

"But," said I, "you are quite *au fait* [straightforward] in these investigations. The Parisian police have done this thing often before."

"O yes; and for this reason I did not despair. The habits of the minister gave me, too, a great advantage. He is frequently absent from home all night. His servants are by no means numerous. They sleep at a distance from their master's apartments, and, being chiefly Neapolitans, are readily made drunk. I have keys, as you know, with which I can open any chamber or cabinet in Paris. For three months a night has not passed, during the greater part of which I have not been engaged, personally, in ransacking the D–– Hotel. My honor is interested, and, to mention a great secret, the reward is enormous. So I did not abandon the search until I had become fully satisfied that the thief is a more astute man than myself. I fancy that I have investigated every nook and corner of the premises in which it is possible that the paper can be concealed."

"But is it not possible," I suggested, "that although the letter may be in possession of the minister, as it unquestionably is, he may have concealed it elsewhere than upon his own premises?"

"This is barely possible," said Dupin. "The present peculiar condition of affairs at court, and especially of those intrigues in which D–– is known to be involved, would render the instant availability of the document–its susceptibility of being produced at a moment's notice–a point of nearly equal importance with its possession."

"Its susceptibility of being produced?" said I.

"That is to say, of being *destroyed*," said Dupin.

"True," I observed; "the paper is clearly then upon the premises. As for its being upon the person of the minister, we may consider that as out of the question."

"Entirely," said the Prefect. "He has been twice waylaid, as if by footpads, and his person rigorously searched under my own inspection."

"You might have spared yourself this trouble," said Dupin. "D——, I presume, is not altogether a fool, and, if not, must have anticipated these waylayings, as a matter of course."

"Not *altogether* a fool," said G., "but then he's a poet, which I take to be only one remove from a fool."

"True," said Dupin, after a long and thoughtful whiff from his meerschaum, "although I have been guilty of certain doggrel myself."

"Suppose you detail," said I, "the particulars of your search."

"Why the fact is, we took our time, and we searched *every where*. I have had long experience in these affairs. I took the entire building, room by room; devoting the nights of a whole week to each. We examined, first, the furniture of each apartment. We opened every possible drawer; and I presume you know that, to a properly trained police agent, such a thing as a *secret* drawer is impossible. Any man is a dolt who permits a 'secret' drawer to escape him in a search of this kind. The thing is *so* plain. There is a certain amount of bulk – of space – to be accounted for in every cabinet. Then we have accurate rules. The fiftieth part of a line could not escape us. After the cabinets we took the chairs. The cushions we probed with the fine long needles you have seen me employ. From the tables we removed the tops."

"Why so?"

"Sometimes the top of a table, or other similarly arranged piece of furniture, is removed by the person wishing to conceal an article; then the leg is excavated, the article deposited within the cavity, and the top replaced. The bottoms and tops of bedposts are employed in the same way."

"But could not the cavity be detected by sounding?" I asked.

"By no means, if, when the article is deposited, a sufficient wadding of cotton be placed around it. Besides, in our case, we were obliged to proceed without noise."

"But you could not have removed—you could not have taken to pieces *all* articles of furniture in which it would have been possible to make a deposit in the manner you mention. A letter may be compressed into a thin spiral roll, not differing much in shape or bulk from a large knitting-needle, and in this form it might be inserted into the rung of a chair, for example. You did not take to pieces all chairs?"

"Certainly not; but we did better—we examined the rungs of every chair in the hotel, and, indeed, the jointings of every description of furniture, by the aid of a most powerful microscope. Had there been any traces of recent disturbance we should not have failed to detect it *instanter.* A single grain of gimlet-dust, or saw-dust, for example, would have been as obvious as an apple. Any disorder in the glueing—any unusual gaping in the joints—would have sufficed to insure detection."

"Of course you looked to the mirrors, between the boards and the plates, and you probed the beds and the bed-clothes, as well as the curtains and carpets."

"That of course; and when we had absolutely completed every particle of the furniture in this way, then we examined the house itself. We divided its entire surface into compartments, which we numbered, so that none might be missed; then we scrutinized each individual square inch throughout the premises, including the two houses immediately adjoining, with the microscope, as before."

"The two houses adjoining!" I exclaimed; "you must have had a great deal of trouble."

"We had; but the reward offered is prodigious."

"You include the *grounds* about the houses?"

"All the grounds are paved with brick. They gave us comparatively little trouble. We examined the moss between the bricks, and found it undisturbed."

"And the roofs?"

"We surveyed every inch of the external surface, and probed carefully beneath every tile."

"You looked among D——'s papers, of course, and into the books of the library?"

"Certainly; we opened every package and parcel; we not only opened every book, but we turned over every leaf in each volume, not contenting ourselves with a mere shake, according to the fashion of some of our police officers. We also measured the thickness of every book-*cover,* with the most accurate admeasurement, and applied to them the most jealous scrutiny of the microscope. Had any of the bindings been recently meddled with, it would have been utterly impossible that the fact should have escaped observation. Some five or six volumes, just from the hands of the binder, we carefully probed, longitudinally, with the needles."

"You explored the floors beneath the carpets?"

"Beyond doubt. We removed every carpet, and examined the boards with the microscope."

"And the paper on the walls?"

"Yes."

"You looked into the cellars?"

"We did; and, as time and labour were no objects, we dug up every one of them to the depth of four feet."

"Then," I said, "you have been making a miscalculation, and the letter is *not* upon the premises, as you suppose."

"I fear you are right there," said the Prefect. "And now, Dupin, what would you advise me to do?"

"To make a thorough re-search of the premises."

"That is absolutely needless," replied G–– "I am not more sure that I breathe than I am that the letter is not at the Hotel."

"I have no better advice to give you," said Dupin. "You have, of course, an accurate description of the letter?"

"Oh yes!"–And here the Prefect, producing a memorandum-book, proceeded to read aloud a minute account of the internal, and especially of the external appearance of the missing document. Soon after finishing the perusal of this description, he took his departure, more entirely depressed in spirits than I had ever known the good gentleman before.

In about a month afterwards he paid us another visit, and found us occupied very nearly as before. He took a pipe and a chair and entered into some ordinary conversation. At length I said,–

"Well, but G––, what of the purloined letter? I presume you have at last made up your mind that there is no such thing as overreaching the Minister?"

"Confound him, say I–yes; I made the re-examination, however, as Dupin suggested–but it was all labor lost, as I knew it would be."

"How much was the reward offered, did you say?" asked Dupin.

"Why, a very great deal–a *very* liberal reward–I don't like to say how much, precisely; but one thing I *will* say, that I wouldn't mind giving my individual check for fifty thousand francs to any one who could obtain me that letter. The fact is, it is becoming of more and more importance every day; and the reward has been lately doubled. If it were trebled, however, I could do no more than I have done."

"Why, yes," said Dupin, drawlingly, between the whiffs of his meerschaum, "I really–think, G––, you have not exerted yourself–to the utmost in this matter. You might–do a little more, I think, eh?"

"How?–in what way?"

"Why–puff, puff–you might–puff, puff–employ counsel in the matter, eh?–puff, puff, puff. Do you remember the story they tell of Abernethy?"

"No; hang Abernethy!"

"To be sure! hang him and welcome. But, once upon a time, a certain rich miser conceived the design of spunging upon this Abernethy for a medical opinion. Getting up, for this purpose, an ordinary conversation in a private company, he insinuated his case to the physician, as that of an imaginary individual.

" 'We will suppose,' said the miser, 'that his symptoms are such and such; now, doctor, what would *you* have directed him to take?'

"'Take!' said Abernethy, 'why, take *advice,* to be sure.'"

"But," said the Prefect, a little discomposed, "I am *perfectly* willing to take advice, and to pay for it. I would *really* give fifty thousand francs, every *centime* of it, to any one who would aid me in the matter."

"In that case," replied Dupin, opening a drawer, and producing a check-book, "you may as well fill me up a check for the amount mentioned. When you sign it, I will hand you the letter."

I was astounded. The Prefect appeared absolutely thunder-stricken. For some minutes he remained speechless and motionless, looking incredulously at my friend with open mouth, and eyes that seemed starting from their sockets; then, apparently recovering himself in some measure, he seized a pen, and after several pauses and vacant stares, finally filled up and signed a check for fifty thousand francs, and handed it across the table to Dupin. The latter examined it carefully and deposited it in his pocket-book; then, unlocking an *escritoire,* took thence a letter and gave it to the Prefect. This functionary grasped it in a perfect agony of joy, opened it with a trembling hand, cast a rapid glance at its contents, and then, scrambling and struggling to the door, rushed at length unceremoniously from the room and from the house, without having uttered a solitary syllable since Dupin had requested him to fill up the check.

When he had gone, my friend entered into some explanations.

"The Parisian police," he said, "are exceedingly able in their way. They are persevering, ingenious, cunning, and thoroughly versed in the knowledge which their duties seem chiefly to demand. Thus, when G–– detailed to us his mode of searching the premises at the Hotel D––, I felt entire confidence in his having made a satisfactory investigation– so far as his labors extended."

"So far as his labors extended?" said I.

"Yes," said Dupin. "The measures adopted were not only the best of their kind, but carried out to absolute perfection. Had the letter been deposited within the range of their search, these fellows would, beyond a question, have found it."

I merely laughed–but he seemed quite serious in all that he said.

"The measures, then," he continued, "were good in their kind, and well executed; their defect lay in their being inapplicable to the case, and to the man. A certain set of highly ingenious resources are, with the Prefect, a sort of Procrustean bed, to which he forcibly adapts his designs. But he perpetually errs by being too deep or too shallow, for the matter in hand; and many a schoolboy is a better reasoner than he. I knew one about eight years of age, whose success at guessing in the game of 'even and odd' attracted universal admiration. This game is simple, and is played with marbles, One player holds in his hand a number of these toys, and demands another whether that number is even or odd. If the

guess is right, the guesser wins one; if wrong, he loses one.
The boy to whom I allude won all the marbles of the school.
Of course he had some principle of guessing; and this lay in
mere observation and admeasurement of the astuteness of his
opponents. For example, an arrant simpleton is his opponent,
and, holding up his closed hand, asks, 'are they even or odd?'
Our schoolboy replies, 'odd,' and loses; but upon the second
trial he wins, for he then says to himself, 'the simpleton had
them even upon the first trial, and his amount of cunning is
just sufficient to make him have them odd upon the second, I
will therefore guess odd;'– he guesses odd, and wins. Now, with
a simpleton a degree above the first, he would have reasoned
thus: "This fellow finds that in the first instance I guessed odd,
and, in the second, he will propose to himself, upon the first
impulse, a simple variation from even to odd, as did the first
simpleton; but then a second thought will suggest that this is
too simple a variation, and finally he will decide upon putting
it even as before. I will therefore guess even;'– he guesses even,
and wins. Now this mode of reasoning in the schoolboy, whom
his fellows termed 'lucky,' –what, in its last analysis, is it?"

"It is merely," I said, "an identification of the reasoner's
intellect with that of his opponent."

"It is," said Dupin; "and, upon inquiring of the boy by what
means he effected the *thorough* identification in which his
success consisted, I received answer as follows: 'When I wish
to find out how wise, or how stupid, or how good, or how
wicked is any one, or what are his thoughts at the moment, I
fashion the expression of my face, as accurately as possible, in
accordance with the expression of his, and then wait to see
what thoughts or sentiments arise in my mind or heart, as if to
match or correspond with the expression.' This response of the
schoolboy lies at the bottom of all the spurious profundity
which has been attributed to Rochefoucault, to La Bruyère, to
Machiavelli, and to Campanella."

"And the identification," I said, "of the reasoner's intellect with that of his opponent, depends, if I understand you aright, upon the accuracy with which the opponent's intellect is admeasured."

"For its practical value it depends upon this," replied Dupin; "and the Prefect and his cohort fail so frequently, first, by default of this identification, and, secondly, by ill-admeasurement, or rather through non-admeasurement, of the intellect with which they are engaged. They consider only their *own* ideas of ingenuity; and, in searching for anything hidden, advert only to the modes in which *they* would have hidden it. They are right in this much – that their own ingenuity is a faithful representative of that of *the mass;* but when the cunning of the individual felon is diverse in character from their own, the felon foils them, of course. This always happens when it is above their own, and very usually when it is below. They have no variation of principle in their investigations; at best, when urged by some unusual emergency – by some extraordinary reward – they extend or exaggerate their old modes of *practice,* without touching their principles. What, for example, in this case of D––, has been done to vary the principle of action? What is all this boring, and probing, and sounding, and scrutinizing with the microscope, and dividing the surface of the building into registered square inches – what is it all but an exaggeration of *the application* of the one principle or set of principles of search, which are based upon the one set of notions regarding human ingenuity, to which the Prefect, in the long routine of his duty, has been accustomed? Do you not see he has taken it for granted that *all* men proceed to conceal a letter, – not exactly in a gimlet-hole bored in a chair-leg – but, at least, in *some* out-of-the-way hole or corner suggested by the same tenor of thought which would urge a man to secrete a letter in a gimlet-hole bored in a chair-leg? And do you not see also, that such *recherché* nooks

for concealment are adapted only for ordinary occasions, and
would be adopted only by ordinary intellects; for, in all cases
of concealment, a disposal of the article concealed – a disposal
of it in this *recherché* manner, – is, in the very first instance,
presumed and presumable; and thus its discovery depends, not
at all upon the acumen, but altogether upon the mere care,
patience, and determination of the seekers; and where the case
is of importance – or, what amounts to the same thing in the
policial eyes, when the reward is of magnitude, – the qualities
in question have *never* been known to fail. You will now
understand what I meant in suggesting that, had the purloined
letter been hidden any where within the limits of the Prefect's
examination – in other words, had the principle of its concealment been comprehended within the principles of the Prefect –
its discovery would have been a matter altogether beyond
question. This functionary, however, has been thoroughly
mystified; and the remote source of his defeat lies in the
supposition that the Minister is a fool, because he has acquired
renown as a poet. All fools are poets; this the Prefect *feels;* and
he is merely guilty of a *non distributio medii* [fallacy of the
undistributed middle] in thence inferring that all poets are fools."

   "But is this really the poet?" I asked. "There are two
brothers, I know; and both have attained reputation in letters.
The Minister I believe has written learnedly of the Differential
Calculus. He is a mathematician, and no poet."

   "You are mistaken; I know him well; he is both. As poet
and mathematician, he would reason well; as poet, profoundly;
as mere mathematician, he could not have reasoned at all, and
thus would have been at the mercy of the Prefect."

   "You surprise me," I said, "by these opinions, which have
been contradicted by the voice of the world. You do not mean
to set at naught the well-digested idea of centuries. The
mathematical reason has been long regarded as *the* reason
par excellence."

"*'Il y a à parier,'*" replied Dupin, quoting from Chamfort, "*'que toute idée publique, toute convention reçue, est une sottise, car elle a convenu au plus grand nombre* [It's a good bet that every public idea, every received convention, is foolish; since it appeals to the majority]." The mathematicians, I grant you, have done their best to promulgate the popular error to which you allude, and which is none the less an error for its promulgation as truth. With an art worthy a better cause, for example, they have insinuated the term 'analysis' into application to algebra. The French are the originators of this particular deception; but if a term is of any importance – if words derive any value from applicability – then 'analysis' conveys 'algebra' about as much as, in Latin, *'ambitus'* implies 'ambition,' *'religio'* 'religion,' or *'homines honesti,'* a set of *honorable* men."

"You have a quarrel on hand, I see," said I, "with some of the algebraists of Paris; but proceed."

"I dispute the availability, and thus the value, of that reason which is cultivated in any especial form other than the abstractly logical. I dispute, in particular, the reason educed by mathematical study. The mathematics are the science of form and quantity; mathematical reasoning is merely logic applied to observation upon form and quantity. The great error lies in supposing that even the truths of what is called *pure* algebra, are abstract or general truths. And this error is so egregious that I am confounded at the universality with which it has been received. Mathematical axioms are *not* axioms of general truth. What is true of *relation* – of form and quantity – is often grossly false in regard to morals, for example. In this latter science it is very usually *untrue* that the aggregated parts are equal to the whole. In chemistry also the axiom fails. In the consideration of motive it fails; for two motives, each of a given value, have not, necessarily, a value when united, equal to the sum of their values apart. There are numerous other

mathematical truths which are only truths within the limits of
relation. But the mathematician argues, from his *finite truths,*
through habit, as if they were of an absolutely general
applicability – as the world indeed imagines them to be. Bryant,
in his very learned 'Mythology', mentions an analogous source
of error, when he says that 'although the Pagan fables are not
believed, yet we forget ourselves continually, and make
inferences from them as existing realities.' With the algebraists,
however, who are Pagans themselves, the 'Pagan fables' *are*
believed, and the inferences are made, not so much through
lapse of memory, as through an unaccountable addling of the
brains. In short, I never yet encountered the mere
mathematician who could be trusted out of equal roots, or one
who did not clandestinely hold it as a point of his faith that
x^2+px was absolutely and unconditionally equal to q. Say to
one of these gentlemen, by way of experiment, if you please,
that you believe occasions may occur where x^2+px is *not*
altogether equal to q, and, having made him understand what
you mean, get out of his reach as speedily as convenient, for,
beyond doubt, he will endeavor to knock you down.

"I mean to say," continued Dupin, while I merely laughed
at his last observations, "that if the Minister had been no more
than a mathematician, the Prefect would have been under no
necessity of giving me this check. Had he been no more than a
poet, I think it probable that he would have foiled us all. I
knew him, however, as both mathematician and poet, and my
measures were adapted to his capacity, with reference to the
circumstances by which he was surrounded. I knew him as a
courtier, too, and as a bold *intriguant*. Such a man, I
considered, could not fail to be aware of the ordinary policial
modes of action. He could not have failed to anticipate – and
events have proved that he did not fail to anticipate – the
waylayings to which he was subjected. He must have foreseen,
I reflected, the secret investigations of his premises. His

frequent absences from home at night, which were hailed by the Prefect as certain aids to his success, I regarded only as *ruses*, to afford opportunity for thorough search to the police, and thus the sooner to impress them with the conviction to which G––, in fact, did finally arrive–the conviction that the letter was not upon the premises. I felt, also, that the whole train of thought, which I was at some pains in detailing to you just now, concerning the invariable principle of policial action in searches for articles concealed–I felt that this whole train of thought would necessarily pass through the mind of the Minister. It would imperatively lead him to despise all the ordinary *nooks* of concealment. *He* could not, I reflected, be so weak as not to see that the most intricate and remote recess of his hotel would be as open as his commonest closets to the eyes, to the probes, to the gimlets, and to the microscopes of the Prefect. I saw, in fine, that he would be driven, as a matter of course, to *simplicity,* if not deliberately induced to it as a matter of choice. You will remember, perhaps, how desperately the Prefect laughed when I suggested, upon our first interview, that it was just possible this mystery troubled him so much on account of its being so *very* self-evident."

"Yes," said I, "I remember his merriment well. I really thought he would have fallen into convulsions."

"The material world," continued Dupin, "abounds with very strict analogies to the immaterial; and thus some color of truth has been given to the rhetorical dogma, that metaphor, or simile, may be made to strengthen an argument, as well as to embellish a description. The principle of the *vis inertiæ* [force of inertia], for example, with the amount of *momentum* proportionate with it and consequent upon it, seems to be identical in physics and metaphysics. It is not more true in the former, that a large body is with more difficulty set in motion than a smaller one, and that its subsequent impetus is commensurate with this difficulty, than it is, in the latter, that

intellects of the vaster capacity, while more forcible, more
constant, and more eventful in their movements than those of
inferior grade, are yet the less readily moved, and more embarrassed and full of hesitation in the first few steps of their
progress. Again: have you ever noticed which of the street signs,
over the shop-doors, are the most attractive of attention?"

"I have never given the matter a thought," I said.

"There is a game of puzzles," he resumed, "which is played
upon a map. One party playing requires another to find a
given word – the name of town, river, state or empire – any
word, in short, upon the motley and perplexed surface of the
chart. A novice in the game generally seeks to embarrass his
opponents by giving them the most minutely lettered names;
but the adept selects such words as stretch, in large characters,
from one end of the chart to the other. These, like the over-
largely lettered signs and placards of the street, escape
observation by dint of being excessively obvious; and here the
physical oversight is precisely analogous with the moral
inapprehension by which the intellect suffers to pass
unnoticed those considerations which are too obtrusively and
too palpably self-evident. But this is a point, it appears, somewhat above or beneath the understanding of the Prefect. He
never once thought it probable, or possible, that the Minister
had deposited the letter immediately beneath the nose of the
whole world, by way of best preventing any portion of that
world from perceiving it.

"But the more I reflect upon the daring, dashing, and discriminating ingenuity of D––; upon the fact that the document
must always have been *at hand,* if he intended to use it to good
purpose; and upon the decisive evidence, obtained by the
Prefect, that it was not hidden within the limits of that dignitary's
ordinary search – the more satisfied I became that, to conceal
this letter, the Minister had resorted to the comprehensive and
sagacious expedient of not attempting to conceal it at all.

"Full of these ideas, I prepared myself a pair of green spectacles, and called one fine morning, quite by accident, at the Ministerial hotel. I found D—— at home, yawning, lounging, and dawdling, as usual, and pretending to be in the last extremity of *ennui*. He is, perhaps, the most really energetic human being now alive–but that is only when nobody sees him.

"To be even with him, I complained of my weak eyes, and lamented the necessity of the spectacles, under cover of which I cautiously and thoroughly surveyed the whole apartment, while seemingly intent only upon the conversation of my host.

"I paid especial attention to a large writing-table near which he sat, and upon which lay confusedly, some miscellaneous letters and other papers, with one or two musical instruments and a few books. Here, however, after a long and very deliberate scrutiny, I saw nothing to excite particular suspicion.

"At length my eyes, in going the circuit of the room, fell upon a trumpery fillagree card-rack of pasteboard, that hung dangling by a dirty blue riband, from a little brass knob just beneath the middle of the mantel-piece. In this rack, which had three or four compartments, were five or six visiting cards and a solitary letter. This last was much soiled and crumpled. It was torn nearly in two, across the middle–as if a design, in the first instance, to tear it entirely up as worthless, had been altered, or stayed, in the second. It had a large black seal, bearing the D—— cipher *very* conspicuously, and was addressed, in a diminutive female hand, to D——, the minister, himself. It was thrust carelessly, and even, as it seemed, contemptuously, into one of the uppermost divisions of the rack.

"No sooner had I glanced at this letter, than I concluded it to be that of which I was in search. To be sure, it was, to all appearance, radically different from the one of which the

Prefect had read us so minute a description. Here the seal was large and black, with the D—— cipher; there it was small and red, with the ducal arms of the S—— family. Here, the address, to the Minister, was diminutive and feminine; there the superscription, to a certain royal personage, was markedly bold and decided; the size alone formed a point of correspondence. But, then, the *radicalness* of these differences, which was excessive; the dirt; the soiled and torn condition of the paper, so inconsistent with the *true* methodical habits of D——, and so suggestive of a design to delude the beholder into an idea of the worthlessness of the document; these things, together with the hyperobtrusive situation of this document, full in view of every visiter, and thus exactly in accordance with the conclusions to which I had previously arrived; these things, I say, were strongly corroborative of suspicion, in one who came with the intention to suspect.

"I protracted my visit as long as possible, and, while I maintained a most animated discussion with the Minister, upon a topic which I knew well had never failed to interest and excite him, I kept my attention really riveted upon the letter. In this examination, I committed to memory its external appearance and arrangement in the rack; and also fell, at length, upon a discovery which set at rest whatever trivial doubt I might have entertained. In scrutinizing the edges of the paper, I observed them to be more *chafed* than seemed necessary. They presented the *broken* appearance which is manifested when a stiff paper, having been once folded and pressed with a folder, is refolded in a reversed direction, in the same creases or edges which had formed the original fold. This discovery was sufficient. It was clear to me that the letter had been turned, as a glove, inside out, re-directed, and re-sealed. I bade the Minister good morning, and took my departure at once, leaving a gold snuff-box upon the table.

"The next morning I called for the snuff-box, when we resumed, quite eagerly, the conversation of the preceding day. While thus engaged, however, a loud report, as if of a pistol, was heard immediately beneath the windows of the hotel, and was succeeded by a series of fearful screams, and the shoutings of a terrified mob. D— rushed to a casement, threw it open, and looked out. In the meantime, I stepped to the card-rack, took the letter, put it in my pocket, and replaced it by a *facsimile*, which I had carefully prepared at my lodgings — imitating the D— cipher, very readily, by means of a seal formed of bread.

"The disturbance in the street had been occasioned by the frantic behavior of a man with a musket. He had fired it among a crowd of women and children. It proved, however, to have been without ball, and the fellow was suffered to go his way as a lunatic or a drunkard. When he had gone, D— came from the window, whither I had followed him immediately upon securing the object in view. Soon afterwards I bade him farewell. The pretended lunatic was a man in my own pay."

"But what purpose had you," I asked, "in replacing the letter by a *fac-simile*? Would it not have been better, at the first visit, to have seized it openly, and departed?"

"D—," replied Dupin, "is a desperate man, and a man of nerve. His hotel, too, is not without attendants devoted to his interests. Had I made the wild attempt you suggest, I should never have left the Ministerial presence alive. The good people of Paris would have heard of me no more. But I had an object apart from these considerations. You know my political prepossessions. In this matter, I act as a partisan of the lady concerned. For eighteen months the Minister has had her in his power. She has now him in hers — since, being unaware that the letter is not in his possession, he will proceed with his exactions as if it was. Thus will he inevitably commit himself, at once, to his political destruction. His downfall, too, will not be more precipitate than awkward. It is all very well to talk about the *facilis descensus Averni* [the path down to Hell is an easy one], but in all kinds of climbing, as Catalani said of singing, it is far more easy to get up than to come down. In the present instance I have no sympathy – at least no pity – for him who descends. He is that *monstrum horrendum* [frightful monstrosity], an unprincipled man of genius. I confess, however, that I should like very well to know the precise character of his thoughts, when, being defied by her whom the Prefect terms 'a certain personage,' he is reduced to opening the letter which I left for him in the card-rack."

"How? did you put any thing particular in it?"

"Why – it did not seem altogether right to leave the interior blank – that would have been insulting. To be sure, D—, at Vienna once, did me an evil turn, which I told him, quite good-humoredly, that I should remember. So, as I knew he would feel some curiosity in regard to the identity of the person who had outwitted him, I thought it a pity not to give him a clue. He is well acquainted with my MS., and I just copied into the middle of the blank sheet the words –

> *– –Un dessein si funeste,*
> *S'il n'est digne d'Atrée, est digne de Thyeste.*
> [*–A plan so sinister,*
> *If unworthy of Atreus, is worthy of Thyestes.*]

They are to be found in Crébillon's *Atrée*."

[September, 1844]

THE RAVEN

ONCE UPON A midnight dreary, while I pondered,
   weak and weary,
Over many a quaint and curious volume of forgotten lore—
While I nodded, nearly napping,
   suddenly there came a tapping,
As of some one gently rapping, rapping at my chamber door—
" 'Tis some visiter," I muttered, "tapping at my chamber door—
   Only this and nothing more."

Ah, distinctly I remember it was in the bleak December;
And each separate dying ember wrought its ghost
   upon the floor.
Eagerly I wished the morrow;—vainly I had tried to borrow
From my books surcease of sorrow—
   sorrow for the lost Lenore—
For the rare and radiant maiden
   whom the angels name Lenore—
      Nameless *here* for evermore.

And the silken, sad, uncertain rustling of each purple curtain
Thrilled me—filled me with fantastic terrors never felt before;
So that now, to still the beating of my heart, I stood repeating
" 'Tis some visiter entreating entrance at my chamber door—
Some late visiter entreating entrance at my chamber door;—
   This it is and nothing more."

Presently my soul grew stronger; hesitating then no longer,
"Sir," said I, "or Madam, truly your forgiveness I implore;
But the fact is I was napping, and so gently you came rapping,

And so faintly you came tapping, tapping at my chamber door,
That I scarce was sure I heard you"–
    here I opened wide the door;–
        Darkness there and nothing more.

Deep into that darkness peering, long I stood
    there wondering, fearing,
Doubting, dreaming dreams no mortal ever dared
    to dream before;
But the silence was unbroken, and the darkness gave no token,
And the only word there spoken was the whispered word,
    "Lenore!"
This I whispered, and an echo murmured back the word,
    "Lenore!"
        Merely this and nothing more.

Then into the chamber turning, all my soul
    within me burning,
Soon I heard again a tapping somewhat louder than before.
"Surely," said I, "surely that is something at my window lattice;
Let me see, then, what thereat is, and this mystery explore–
Let my heart be still a moment and this mystery explore;–
        'Tis the wind and nothing more!"

Open here I flung the shutter, when,
    with many a flirt and flutter,
In there stepped a stately Raven of the saintly days of yore;
Not the least obeisance made he; not an instant stopped or
    stayed he;
But, with mien of lord or lady, perched
    above my chamber door–
Perched upon a bust of Pallas just above my chamber door–
        Perched, and sat, and nothing more.

Then this ebony bird beguiling my sad fancy into smiling,
By the grave and stern decorum of the countenance it wore,
"Though thy crest be shorn and shaven, thou," I said,
   "art sure no craven,
Ghastly grim and ancient Raven wandering
   from the Nightly shore—
Tell me what thy lordly name is on the
   Night's Plutonian shore!"
       Quoth the Raven "Nevermore."

Much I marvelled this ungainly fowl to hear
   discourse so plainly,
Though its answer little meaning—little relevancy bore;
For we cannot help agreeing that no sublunary being
Ever yet was blessed with seeing bird
   above his chamber door—
Bird or beast upon the sculptured bust
   above his chamber door,
      With such name as "Nevermore."

But the Raven, sitting lonely on the placid bust, spoke only
That one word, as if his soul in that one word he did outpour.
Nothing farther then he uttered—not a feather
   then he fluttered—
Till I scarcely more than muttered "Other friends
   have flown before—
On the morrow *he* will leave me, as my Hopes
   have flown before."
      Quoth the Raven "Nevermore."

Wondering at the stillness broken by reply so aptly spoken,
"Doubtless," said I, "what it utters is its only stock and store
Caught from some unhappy master whom unmerciful Disaster

Followed fast and followed faster so, when Hope
    he would adjure
Stern Despair returned, instead of the sweet Hope
    he dared adjure –
        That sad answer, "Nevermore!"

But the Raven still beguiling all my sad soul into smiling,
Straight I wheeled a cushioned seat in front of bird,
    and bust and door;
Then, upon the velvet sinking, I betook myself to linking
Fancy unto fancy, thinking what this ominous bird of yore –
What this grim, ungainly, ghastly, gaunt,
    and ominous bird of yore
        Meant in croaking "Nevermore."

This I sat engaged in guessing, but no syllable expressing
To the fowl whose fiery eyes now burned
    into my bosom's core;
This and more I sat divining, with my head at ease reclining
On the cushion's velvet lining that the lamp-light gloated o'er,
But whose velvet-violet lining with the lamp-light gloating o'er,
    She shall press, ah, nevermore!

Then, methought, the air grew denser, perfumed
    from an unseen censer
Swung by angels whose faint foot-falls tinkled
    on the tufted floor.
"Wretch," I cried, "thy God hath lent thee – by these angels
    he hath sent thee
Respite – respite and nepenthe from thy memories of Lenore;
Let me quaff this kind nepenthe and forget this lost Lenore!"
    Quoth the Raven "Nevermore."

"Prophet!" said I, "thing of evil!—prophet still,
    if bird or devil!—
Whether Tempter sent, or whether tempest tossed
    thee here ashore,
Desolate yet all undaunted, on this desert land enchanted—
On this home by Horror haunted—tell me truly, I implore—
Is there—is there balm in Gilead?—tell me—tell me, I implore!"
        Quoth the Raven "Nevermore."

"Prophet!" said I, "thing of evil!—prophet still, if bird or devil!
By that Heaven that bends above us—by that God
    we both adore—
Tell this soul with sorrow laden if, within the distant Aidenn,
It shall clasp a sainted maiden whom the angels name
    Lenore—
Clasp a rare and radiant maiden
    whom the angels name Lenore."
        Quoth the Raven "Nevermore."

"Be that word our sign of parting, bird or fiend!"
    I shrieked, upstarting—
"Get thee back into the tempest and the
    Night's Plutonian shore!
Leave no black plume as a token of that lie
    thy soul hath spoken!
Leave my loneliness unbroken!—quit the bust above my door!
Take thy beak from out my heart, and take thy form
    from off my door!"
        Quoth the Raven "Nevermore."

And the Raven, never flitting, still is sitting, *still* is sitting
On the pallid bust of Pallas just above my chamber door;
And his eyes have all the seeming of a demon
    that is dreaming,

And the lamp-light o'er him streaming throws his shadow
    on the floor;
And my soul from out that shadow that lies floating
    on the floor
        Shall be lifted – nevermore!

                           [February, 1845]

THE IMP OF
THE PERVERSE

IN THE CONSIDERATION of the faculties and impulses – of the *prima mobilia* [first causes] of the human soul, the phrenologists have failed to make room for a propensity which, although obviously existing as a radical, primitive, irreducible sentiment, has been equally overlooked by the moralists who have preceded them. In the pure arrogance of the reason, we have all overlooked it. We have suffered its existence to escape our senses, solely through want of belief – of faith; – whether it be faith in Revelation, or faith in the inner teachings of the spirit. Its idea has not occurred to us, simply because of its seeming supererogation. We saw no *need* for the propensity in question. We could not perceive its necessity. We could not understand, that is to say, we could not have understood, had the notion of this *primum mobile* [first cause] ever obtruded itself – in what manner it might be made to further the objects of humanity, either temporal or eternal. It cannot be denied that all metaphysicianism has been concocted *a priori*. The intellectual or logical man, rather than the understanding or observant man, set himself to imagine designs – to dictate purposes to God. Having thus fathomed, to his satisfaction, the intentions of Jehovah, out of these intentions he reared his innumerable systems of mind. In the matter of phrenology, for example, we first determined, naturally enough, that it was the design of Deity that man should eat. We then assigned to man an organ of alimentiveness, and this organ is the scourge by which Deity compels man to his food. Again, having settled it to be God's will that man should continue his species, we discovered an organ of amativeness, forthwith. And so with combativeness, with ideality, with causality, with constructive-ness, – so, in short, with every organ, whether representing a propensity, a moral sentiment, or a faculty of the pure intellect. And in these arrangements of the *principia* [principles] of human action, the Spurzheimites, whether right or wrong, in part, or upon the whole, have but followed, in principle, the footsteps of their predecessors; deducing and establishing every thing from the preconceived destiny of man, and upon the ground of the *objects* of his Creator.

It would be safer – if classify we must – to classify upon the basis of what man usually or occasionally did, and was always occasionally doing, rather than upon the basis of what we took it for granted the Deity intended him to do. If we cannot comprehend God in his visible works, how then in his inconceivable thoughts, that call the works into being? If we cannot understand him in his objective creatures, how then in his substantive moods and phases of creation?

Induction, *a posteriori*, would have brought phrenology to admit, as an innate and primitive principle of human action, a paradoxical something, which, for want of a better term, we may call Perverseness. In the sense, I intend, it is, in fact, a *mobile* without motive, a motive not *motivirt* [motivated]. Through its promptings we act without comprehensible object; or, if this shall be understood as a contradiction in terms, we may so far modify the proposition as to say, that through its promptings we act, for the reason that we should *not*. In theory, no reason can be more unreasonable; but, in reality, there is none so strong. With certain minds, under certain circumstances, it becomes absolutely irresistible. I am not more sure that I breathe, than that the conviction of the wrong or impolicy of an action is often the one unconquerable *force* which impels us, and alone impels us to its prosecution. Nor will this overwhelming tendency to do wrong for the wrong's sake, admit of analysis, or resolution into ulterior elements. It is a radical, a primitive impulse – elementary. It will be said, I am aware, that when we persist in acts because we feel that we should *not* persist in them, our conduct is but a modification of that which ordinarily springs from the Combativeness of phrenology. But a glance will show the fallacy of this idea. The phrenological combativeness has for its essence, the necessity of self-defence. It is our safeguard against injury. Its principle regards our well-being; and thus the desire to be well must be excited simultaneously with any principle which shall be merely a modification of combativeness, but in the case of that something which I term Perverseness, the desire to be well is not only *not* aroused, but a strongly antagonistical sentiment prevails.

An appeal to one's own heart is, after all, the best reply to the sophistry just noticed. No one who trustingly consults his own soul, will be disposed to deny the entire radicalness of the propensity in question. It is not more incomprehensible than distinct. There lives no man who at some period has not been tormented, for example, by an earnest desire to tantalize a listener by circumlocution. The speaker, in such a case, is aware that he displeases; he has every intention to please; he is usually curt, precise, and clear; the most laconic and luminous language is struggling for utterance upon his tongue; it is only with difficulty that he restrains himself from giving it flow; he dreads and deprecates the anger of him whom he addresses; yet a shadow seems to flit across the brain, and suddenly the thought strikes that, by certain involutions and parentheses, anger may be engendered. That single thought is enough. The impulse increases to a wish, the wish to a desire, the desire to an uncontrollable longing, and the longing, in defiance of all consequences, is indulged.

Again:—We have a task before us which must be speedily performed. We know that it will be ruinous to make delay. The most important crisis of our life calls, trumpet-tongued, for immediate energy and action. We glow, we are consumed with eagerness to commence the work, and our whole souls are on fire with anticipation of the glorious result. It must, it shall be

undertaken to-day, and yet we put it off until to-morrow; and
why? There is no answer, except that we feel *perverse,*
employing the word with no comprehension of the principle.
To-morrow arrives, and with it a more impatient anxiety to do
our duty, but with this very increase of anxiety arrives, also, a
nameless, a positively fearful because unfathomable, craving
for delay. This craving gathers strength as the moments fly. The
last hour for action is at hand. We tremble with the violence
of the conflict within us,–of the definite with the indefinite–
of the substance with the shadow. But, if the contest have
proceeded thus far, it is the shadow which prevails,–we
struggle in vain. The clock strikes, and is the knell of our
welfare, but at the same time, is the chanticleer-note to the
Thing that has so long overawed us. It flies–it disappears–
we are free. The old energy returns. We will labor *now.*
Alas, it is *too late!*

And yet again:–We stand upon the brink of a precipice.
We peer into the abyss–we grow sick and dizzy. Our first
impulse is to shrink from the danger, and yet, unaccountably,
we remain. By slow degrees our sickness, and dizziness, and
horror, become merged in a cloud of unnameable feeling. By
gradations, still more imperceptible, this cloud assumes shape,
as did the vapor from the bottle out of which arose the genius
in the Arabian Nights. But out of this *our* cloud on the
precipice's edge, there grows into palpability, a shape, far more
terrible than any genius, or any demon of a tale, and yet it is
but a *Thought,* although one which chills the very marrow of
our bones with the fierceness of the delight of its horror. It is
merely the idea of what would be our sensations during the
sweeping precipitancy of a fall from such a height. And this
fall–this rushing annihilation–for the very reason that it
involves that one most ghastly and loathsome of all the most
ghastly and loathsome images of death and suffering which
have ever presented themselves to our imagination–*for this*

very cause do we now the most impetuously desire it. And because our reason most strenuously deters us from the brink, *therefore,* do we the more unhesitatingly approach it. There is no passion in nature of so demoniac an impatience as the passion of him, who shuddering upon the edge of a precipice, thus meditates a plunge. To indulge, even for a moment, in any attempt at *thought,* is to be inevitably lost; for reflection but urges us to forbear, and *therefore* it is, I say, that we *cannot.* If there be no friendly arm to check us, or if we fail in a sudden effort to throw ourselves backward from the danger, and so out of its sight, we plunge, and are destroyed.

Examine these and similar actions as we will, we shall find them resulting solely from the spirit of the *Perverse.* We perpetrate them merely because we feel that we should *not.* Beyond or behind this, there is no principle that men, in their fleshly nature, can understand; and were it not occasionally known to operate in furtherance of good, we might deem the anomalous feeling a direct instigation of the Arch-fiend.

I have premised thus much, that I may be able, in some degree, to give an intelligible answer to your queries – that I may explain to you why I am here – that I may assign something like a reason for my wearing these fetters, and tenanting this cell of the condemned. Had I not been thus prolix, you might either have misunderstood me altogether, or, with the rabble, you might have fancied me mad. As it is, you will easily perceive that I am one of the many uncounted victims of the Imp of the Perverse.

It is impossible that any deed could have been wrought with more thorough deliberation. For weeks, for months, I pondered upon the means of the murder. I rejected a thousand schemes, because their accomplishment involved a *chance* of detection. At length, in reading some French memoirs, I found an account of a nearly fatal illness that occurred to Madame Pilau, through the agency of a candle accidentally poisoned.

The idea struck my fancy at once. I knew my victim's habit of reading in bed. I knew, too, that his apartment was narrow and ill-ventilated. But I need not vex you with impertinent details. I need not describe the easy artifices by which I substituted, in his candlestand, a wax-light of my own making, for the one which I there found. The next morning he was dead in his bed, and the verdict was,—"Death by the visitation of God."

Having inherited his estate, all went merrily with me for years. The idea of detection never obtruded itself. Of the remains of the fatal taper, I had myself carefully disposed, nor had I left the shadow of a clue by which it would be possible to convict, or even to suspect me of the crime. It is inconceivable how rich a sentiment of satisfaction arose in my bosom as I reflected upon by *absolute* security. For a very long period of time, I reveled in this sentiment. It afforded me, I believe, more real delight than all the mere worldly advantages accruing from my sin. There arrived at length an epoch, after which this pleasurable feeling took to itself a new tone, and grew, by scarcely perceptible gradations, into a haunting and harassing thought—a thought that harassed because it haunted. I could scarcely get rid of it for an instant. It is quite a common thing to be thus annoyed by the ringing in our ears, or memories, of the burden of an ordinary song, or some unimpressive snatches from an opera. Nor will we be less tormented though the song in itself be good, or the opera air meritorious. In this manner, at last, I would perpetually find myself pondering upon my impunity and security, and very frequently would catch myself repeating, in a low, under-tone, the phrases "I am safe—I am safe."

One day, while sauntering listlessly about the streets, I arrested myself in the act of murmuring, half aloud, these customary syllables. In a fit of petulance at my indiscretion I re-modelled them thus:—"I am safe—I am safe—yes, *if I do not prove fool enough to make open confession.*"

No sooner had I uttered these words, than I felt an icy chill creep to my heart. I had had (long ago, during childhood) some experience in those fits of perversity, whose nature I have been at so much trouble in explaining, and I remembered that in no instance had I successfully resisted their attacks. And now my own casual self-suggestion, that I might possibly prove fool enough to make open confession – confronted me, as if the very ghost of him I had murdered – and beckoned me on to death.

At first, I made strong effort to shake off this nightmare of the soul. I whistled – I laughed aloud – I walked vigorously – faster and still faster. At length I saw – or fancied that I saw – a vast and formless shadow that seemed to dog my footsteps, approaching me from behind, with a cat-like and stealthy pace. It was then that I *ran*. I felt a wild desire to shriek aloud. Every succeeding wave of thought overwhelmed me with new terror, for, alas! I understood too well that to *think*, in my condition, was to be undone. I still quickened my steps. I bounded like a madman through the crowded thoroughfares. But now the populace took alarm, and pursued. Then – then I felt the consummation of my fate. Could I have torn out my tongue, I would have done it – but a rough voice from some member of the crowd now resounded in my ears, and a rougher grasp seized me by the arm. I turned – I gasped for breath. For a moment, I experienced all the pangs of suffocation; I became blind, and deaf, and giddy; and at this instant it was no mortal hand, I knew, that struck me violently with a broad and massive palm upon the back. At that blow the long-imprisoned secret burst forth from my soul.

They say that I spoke with distinct enunciation, but with emphasis and passionate hurry, as if in dread of interruption before concluding the brief but pregnant sentences that consigned me to the hangman and to hell.

Having related all that was necessary for the fullest judicial conviction, I fell prostrate in a swoon.

But why shall I say more? To-day I wear these chains, and am *here.* To-morrow I shall be fetterless! — *but where?*

[*July, 1845*]

The Cask of Amontillado

The thousand injuries of Fortunato I had borne as I best could; but when he ventured upon insult, I vowed revenge. You, who so well know the nature of my soul, will not suppose, however, that I gave utterance to a threat. *At length* I would be avenged; this was a point definitively settled – but the very definitiveness with which it was resolved precluded the idea of risk. I must not only punish, but punish with impunity. A wrong is unredressed when retribution overtakes its redresser. It is equally unredressed when the avenger fails to make himself felt as such to him who has done the wrong.

It must be understood that neither by word nor deed had I given Fortunato cause to doubt my good will. I continued, as was my wont, to smile in his face, and he did not perceive that my smile *now* was at the thought of his immolation.

He had a weak point – this Fortunato – although in other regards he was a man to be respected and even feared. He prided himself upon his connoisseurship in wine. Few Italians have the true virtuoso spirit. For the most part their enthusiasm is adopted to suit the time and opportunity – to practise imposture upon the British and Austrian *millionaires*. In painting and gemmary Fortunato, like his countrymen, was a quack – but in the matter of old wines he was sincere. In this respect I did not differ from him materially; I was skilful in the Italian vintages myself, and bought largely whenever I could.

It was about dusk, one evening during the supreme madness of the carnival season, that I encountered my friend. He accosted me with excessive warmth, for he had been drinking much. The man wore motley. He had on a tight-fitting parti-striped dress, and his head was surmounted by the conical cap and bells. I was so pleased to see him that I thought I should never have done wringing his hand.

I said to him—"My dear Fortunato, you are luckily met. How remarkably well you are looking to-day. But I have received a pipe of what passes for Amontillado, and I have my doubts."

"How?" said he. "Amontillado? A pipe? Impossible! And in the middle of the carnival!"

"I have my doubts," I replied; "and I was silly enough to pay the full Amontillado price without consulting you in the matter. You were not to be found, and I was fearful of losing a bargain."

"Amontillado!"

"I have my doubts."

"Amontillado!"

"And I must satisfy them."

"Amontillado!"

"As you are engaged, I am on my way to Luchresi. If any one has a critical turn, it is he. He will tell me—"

"Luchresi cannot tell Amontillado from Sherry."

"And yet some fools will have it that his taste is a match for your own."

"Come, let us go."

"Whither?"

"To your vaults."

"My friend, no; I will not impose upon your good nature. I perceive you have an engagement. Luchresi—"

"I have no engagement;—come."

"My friend, no. It is not the engagement, but the severe cold with which I perceive you are afflicted. The vaults are insufferably damp. They are encrusted with nitre."

"Let us go, nevertheless. The cold is merely nothing. Amontillado! You have been imposed upon. And as for Luchresi, he cannot distinguish Sherry from Amontillado."

Thus speaking, Fortunato possessed himself of my arm; and putting on a mask of black silk, and drawing a *roquelaire*

closely about my person, I suffered him to hurry me to
my palazzo.

There were no attendants at home; they had absconded to
make merry in honor of the time. I had told them that I
should not return until the morning, and had given them
explicit orders not to stir from the house. These orders
were sufficient, I well knew, to insure their immediate
disappearance, one and all, as soon as my back
was turned.

I took from their sconces two flambeaux, and giving one
to Fortunato, bowed him through several suites of rooms to the
archway that led into the vaults. I passed down a long and
winding staircase, requesting him to be cautious as he
followed. We came at length to the foot of the descent, and
stood together upon the damp ground of the catacombs
of the Montresors.

The gait of my friend was unsteady, and the bells upon his
cap jingled as he strode.

"The pipe," said he.

"It is farther on," said I; "but observe the white web-work
which gleams from these cavern walls."

He turned towards me, and looked into my eyes with two
filmy orbs that distilled the rheum of intoxication.

"Nitre?" he asked, at length.

"Nitre," I replied. "How long have you had that cough?"

"Ugh! ugh! ugh! – ugh! ugh! ugh! – ugh! ugh! ugh! – ugh!
ugh! ugh! – ugh! ugh! ugh!"

My poor friend found it impossible to reply for many
minutes. "It is nothing," he said, at last.

"Come," I said, with decision, "we will go back; your health
is precious. You are rich, respected, admired, beloved; you are
happy, as once I was. You are a man to be missed. For me it is
no matter. We will go back; you will be ill, and I cannot be
responsible. Besides, there is Luchresi –"

"Enough," he said; "the cough is a mere nothing; it will not kill me. I shall not die of a cough."

"True – true," I replied; "and, indeed, I had no intention of alarming you unnecessarily – but you should use all proper caution. A draught of this Medoc will defend us from the damps."

Here I knocked off the neck of a bottle which I drew from a long row of its fellows that lay upon the mould.

"Drink," I said, presenting him the wine.

He raised it to his lips with a leer. He paused and nodded to me familiarly, while his bells jingled.

"I drink," he said, "to the buried that repose around us."

"And I to your long life."

He again took my arm, and we proceeded.

"These vaults," he said, "are extensive."

"The Montresors," I replied, "were a great and numerous family."

"I forget your arms."

"A huge human foot d'or, in a field azure; the foot crushes a serpent rampant whose fangs are imbedded in the heel."

"And the motto?"

"*Nemo me impune lacessit* [No one challenges me with impunity]."

"Good!" he said.

The wine sparkled in his eyes and the bells jingled. My own fancy grew warm with the Medoc. We had passed through long walls of piled skeletons, with casks and puncheons intermingling, into the inmost recesses of the catacombs. I paused again, and this time I made bold to seize Fortunato by an arm above the elbow.

"The nitre!" I said; "see, it increases. It hangs like moss upon the vaults. We are below the river's bed. The drops of moisture trickle among the bones. Come, we will go back ere it is too late. Your cough –"

"It is nothing," he said; "let us go on. But first, another draught of the Medoc."

I broke and reached him a flaçon of De Grâve. He emptied it at a breath. His eyes flashed with a fierce light. He laughed and threw the bottle upwards with a gesticulation I did not understand.

I looked at him in surprise. He repeated the movement–a grotesque one.

"You do not comprehend?" he said.

"Not I," I replied.

"Then you are not of the brotherhood."

"How?"

"You are not of the masons."

"Yes, yes," I said, "yes, yes."

"You? Impossible! A mason?"

"A mason," I replied.

"A sign," he said, "a sign."

"It is this," I answered, producing from beneath the folds of my *roquelaire* a trowel.

"You jest," he exclaimed, recoiling a few paces. "But let us proceed to the Amontillado."

"Be it so," I said, replacing the tool beneath the cloak, and again offering him my arm. He leaned upon it heavily. We continued our route in search of the Amontillado. We passed through a range of low arches, descended, passed on, and descending again, arrived at a deep crypt, in which the foulness of the air caused our flambeaux rather to glow than flame.

At the most remote end of the crypt there appeared another less spacious. Its walls had been lined with human remains, piled to the vault overhead, in the fashion of the great catacombs of Paris. Three sides of this interior crypt were still ornamented in this manner. From the fourth side the bones had been thrown down, and lay promiscuously upon the earth, forming at one point a mound of some size. Within the wall thus exposed by the displacing of the bones, we perceived a still interior crypt or recess, in depth about four feet, in width three, in height six or seven. It seemed to have been constructed for no especial use within itself, but formed merely the interval between two of the colossal supports of the roof of the catacombs, and was backed by one of their circumscribing walls of solid granite.

It was in vain that Fortunato, uplifting his dull torch, endeavored to pry into the depth of the recess. Its termination the feeble light did not enable us to see.

"Proceed," I said; "herein is the Amontillado. As for Luchresi—"

"He is an ignoramus," interrupted my friend, as he stepped unsteadily forward, while I followed immediately at his heels. In an instant he had reached the extremity of the niche, and finding his progress arrested by the rock, stood stupidly bewildered. A moment more and I had fettered him to the granite. In its surface were two iron staples, distant from each other about two feet, horizontally. From one of these depended a short chain, from the other a padlock. Throwing the links about his waist, it was but the work of a few seconds to secure it. He was too much astounded to resist. Withdrawing the key I stepped back from the recess.

"Pass your hand," I said, "over the wall; you cannot help feeling the nitre. Indeed it is *very* damp. Once more let me *implore* you to return. No? Then I must positively leave you. But I must first render you all the little attentions in my power."

"The Amontillado!" ejaculated my friend, not yet recovered from his astonishment.

"True," I replied; "the Amontillado."

As I said these words I busied myself among the pile of bones of which I have before spoken. Throwing them aside,

I soon uncovered a quantity of building stone and mortar. With these materials and with the aid of my trowel, I began vigorously to wall up the entrance of the niche.

I had scarcely laid the first tier of the masonry when I discovered that the intoxication of Fortunato had in great measure worn off. The earliest indication I had of this was a low moaning cry from the depth of the recess. It was *not* the cry of a drunken man. There was then a long and obstinate silence. I laid the second tier, and the third, and the fourth; and then I heard the furious vibration of the chain. The noise lasted for several minutes, during which, that I might hearken to it with the more satisfaction, I ceased my labors and sat down upon the bones. When at last the clanking subsided, I resumed the trowel, and finished without interruption the fifth, the sixth, and the seventh tier. The wall was now nearly upon a level with my breast. I again paused, and holding the flambeaux over the mason-work, threw a few feeble rays upon the figure within.

A succession of loud and shrill screams, bursting suddenly from the throat of the chained form, seemed to thrust me violently back. For a brief moment I hesitated – I trembled. Unsheathing my rapier, I began to grope with it about the recess: but the thought of an instant reassured me. I placed my hand upon the solid fabric of the catacombs, and felt satisfied. I reapproached the wall. I replied to the yells of him who clamored. I re-echoed – I aided – I surpassed them in volume and in strength. I did this, and the clamorer grew still.

It was now midnight, and my task was drawing to a close. I had completed the eighth, the ninth, and the tenth tier. I had finished a portion of the last and the eleventh; there remained but a single stone to be fitted and plastered in. I struggled with its weight; I placed it partially in its destined position. But now there came from out the niche a low laugh that erected the hairs upon my head. It was succeeded by a sad voice, which I

had difficulty in recognising as that of the noble Fortunato.
The voice said –

"Ha! ha! ha! he! he! – a very good joke indeed – an excellent
jest. We will have many a rich laugh about it at the palazzo –
he! he! he! – over our wine – he! he! he!"

"The Amontillado!" I said.

"He! he! he! – he! he! he! – yes, the Amontillado. But is it
not getting late? Will not they be awaiting us at the palazzo,
the Lady Fortunato and the rest? Let us be gone."

"Yes," I said, "let us be gone."

"For the love of God, Montresor!"

"Yes," I said, "for the love of God!"

But to these words I hearkened in vain for a reply. I grew
impatient. I called aloud –

"Fortunato!"

No answer. I called again –

"Fortunato!"

No answer still. I thrust a torch through the remaining
aperture and let it fall within. There came forth in return only
a jingling of the bells. My heart grew sick; it was the dampness
of the catacombs that made it so. I hastened to make an end of
my labor. I forced the last stone into its position; I plastered it
up. Against the new masonry I re-erected the old rampart of
bones. For the half of a century no mortal has disturbed them.
In pace requiescat [May he rest in peace]!

[November, 1846]

Eldorado

Gaily bedight,
  A gallant knight,
In sunshine and in shadow,
  Had journeyed long,
  Singing a song,
In search of Eldorado.

  But he grew old –
  This knight so bold –
And o'er his heart a shadow
  Fell, as he found
  No spot of ground
That looked like Eldorado.

  And, as his strength
  Failed him at length
He met a pilgrim shadow–
  "Shadow," said he,
  "Where can it be –
This land of Eldorado?"

  "Over the Mountains
  Of the Moon,
Down the Valley of the Shadow,
  Ride, boldly ride,"
  The shade replied,–
"If you seek for Eldorado!"

                    [April 21, 1849]

To My Mother

BECAUSE I FEEL that, in the Heavens above,
    The angels, whispering to one another,
Can find, among their burning terms of love,
    None so devotional as that of "Mother,"
Therefore by that sweet name I long have called you—
    You who are more than mother unto me,
And fill my heart of hearts, where Death installed you
    In setting my Virginia's spirit free.
My mother—my own mother, who died early,
    Was but the mother of myself; but you
Are mother to the one I loved so dearly,
    And thus are dearer than the mother I knew
By that infinity with which my wife
    Was dearer to my soul than its soul-life.

[July 7, 1849]

Annabel Lee

It was many and many a year ago,
    In a kingdom by the sea,
That a maiden there lived whom you may know
    By the name of Annabel Lee; –
And this maiden she lived with no other thought
    Than to love and be loved by me.

I was a child and *she* was a child,
    In this kingdom by the sea;
But we loved with a love that was more than love –
    I and my Annabel Lee –
With a love that the wingëd seraphs of Heaven
    Coveted her and me.

And this was the reason that, long ago,
    In this kingdom by the sea,
A wind blew out of a cloud, chilling
    My beautiful Annabel Lee;
So that her high-born kinsmen came
    And bore her away from me,
To shut her up in a sepulchre,
    In this kingdom by the sea.

The angels, not half so happy in Heaven,
    Went envying her and me –
Yes! – that was the reason (as all men know,
    In this kingdom by the sea)
That the wind came out of the cloud by night,
    Chilling and killing my Annabel Lee.

But our love it was stronger by far than the love
    Of those who were older than we –
    Of many far wiser than we –
And neither the angels in Heaven above,
    Nor the demons down under the sea,
Can ever dissever my soul from the soul
    Of the beautiful Annabel Lee: –

For the moon never beams, without bringing me dreams
    Of the beautiful Annabel Lee;
And the stars never rise, but I feel the bright eyes
    Of the beautiful Annabel Lee: –
And so, all the night-tide, I lie down by the side
Of my darling – my darling – my life and my bride,
    In her sepulchre there by the sea –
    In her tomb by the sounding sea.

[October 9, 1849]

THE BELLS

1.

HEAR THE SLEDGES with the bells —
   Silver bells!
What a world of merriment their melody foretells!
   How they tinkle, tinkle, tinkle,
     In the icy air of night!
   While the stars that oversprinkle
   All the Heavens, seem to twinkle
     With a crystalline delight;
   Keeping time, time, time,
     In a sort of Runic rhyme,
To the tintinabulation that so musically wells
From the bells, bells, bells, bells,
     Bells, bells, bells —
     From the jingling and the tinkling of the bells.

2.

   Hear the mellow wedding bells —
   Golden bells!
What a world of happiness their harmony foretells!
   Through the balmy air of night
   How they ring out their delight! —
     From the molten-golden notes
     And all in tune,
   What a liquid ditty floats
   To the turtle-dove that listens while she gloats
     On the moon!
   Oh, from out the sounding cells
What a gush of euphony voluminously wells!
     How it swells!
     How it dwells

On the Future! – how it tells
Of the rapture that impels
To the swinging and the ringing
Of the bells, bells, bells! –
Of the bells, bells, bells, bells,
Bells, bells, bells –
To the rhyming and the chiming of the bells!

3.

Hear the loud alarum bells –
Brazen bells!
What a tale of terror, now, their turbulency tells!
In the startled ear of Night
How they scream out their affright!
Too much horrified to speak,
They can only shriek, shriek,
Out of tune,
In a clamorous appealing to the mercy of the fire –
In a mad expostulation with the deaf and frantic fire,
Leaping higher, higher, higher,
With a desperate desire
And a resolute endeavor
Now – now to sit, or never,
By the side of the pale-faced moon.
Oh, the bells, bells, bells!
What a tale their terror tells
Of despair!
How they clang and clash and roar!
What a horror they outpour
On the bosom of the palpitating air!
Yet, the ear, it fully knows,
By the twanging
And the clanging,
How the danger ebbs and flows: –

Yes, the ear distinctly tells,
  In the jangling
  And the wrangling,
 How the danger sinks and swells,
By the sinking or the swelling in the anger of the bells –
  Of the bells –
  Of the bells, bells, bells, bells,
  Bells, bells, bells –
   In the clamor and the clangor of the bells.

4.

 Hear the tolling of the bells –
  Iron bells!
What a world of solemn thought their monody compels!
  In the silence of the night
  How we shiver with affright
At the melancholy menace of the tone!
  For every sound that floats
  From the rust within their throats
   Is a groan.
  And the people – ah, the people
  They that dwell up in the steeple
   All alone,
  And who, tolling, tolling, tolling,
   In that muffled monotone,
  Feel a glory in so rolling
   On the human heart a stone –
They are neither man nor woman –
They are neither brute nor human,
  They are Ghouls: –
And their king it is who tolls: –
And he rolls, rolls, rolls,
  Rolls
  A Pæan from the bells!

And his merry bosom swells
With the Pæan of the bells!
And he dances and he yells;
Keeping time, time, time,
In a sort of Runic rhyme,
        To the Pæan of the bells—
        Of the bells:—
Keeping time, time, time,
In a sort of Runic rhyme,
        To the throbbing of the bells—
Of the bells, bells, bells—
        To the sobbing of the bells:—
Keeping time, time, time,
        As he knells, knells, knells,
In a happy Runic rhyme,
        To the rolling of the bells—
Of the bells, bells, bells:—
        To the tolling of the bells—
Of the bells, bells, bells, bells,
        Bells, bells, bells—
To the moaning and the groaning of the bells.

[November, 1849]

. . .

ESSAYS

Edgar Allan Poe

BY

GEORGE BERNARD SHAW

THERE WAS A time when America, the Land of the Free, and the birthplace of Washington, seemed a natural fatherland for Edgar Allan Poe. Nowadays the thing has become inconceivable: no young man can read Poe's works without asking incredulously what the devil he is doing in *that* galley. America has been found out; and Poe has not; that is the situation. How did he live there, this finest of fine artists, this born aristocrat of letters? Alas! he did not live there: he died there, and was duly explained away as a drunkard and a failure, though it remains an open question whether he really drank as much in his whole lifetime as a modern successful American drinks, without comment, in six months.

If the Judgment Day were fixed for the centenary of Poe's birth, there are among the dead only two men born since the Declaration of Independence whose plea for mercy could avert a prompt sentence of damnation on the entire nation; and it is extremely doubtful whether those two could be persuaded to pervert external justice by uttering it. The two are, of course, Poe and Whitman; and there is between them the remarkable difference that Whitman is still credibly an American, whereas even the Americans themselves, though rather short of men of genius, omit Poe's name from their Pantheon, either from a sense that it is hopeless for them to claim so foreign a figure, or from simple Monroeism. One asks, has the America of Poe's day passed away, or did it ever exist?

Probably it never existed. It was an illusion, like the respectable Whig Victorian England of Macaulay. Karl Marx stripped the whitewash from that sepulchre; and we have ever

since been struggling with a conviction of social sin which
makes every country in which industrial capitalism is rampant
a hell to us. For let no American fear that America, on that
hypothetic Judgment Day, would perish alone. America would
be damned in very good European company, and would feel
proud and happy, and contemptuous of the saved. She would
not even plead the influence of the mother from whom she
has inherited all her worst vices. If the American stands today
in scandalous preeminence as an anarchist and a ruffian, a liar
and a braggart, an idolater and a sensualist, that is only
because he has thrown off the disguises of Catholicism and
feudalism which still give Europe an air of decency, and sins
openly, impudently, and consciously, instead of furtively,
hypocritically, and muddle-headedly, as we do. Not until he
acquires European manners does the American anarchist
become the gentleman who assures you that people cannot be
made moral by Act of Parliament (the truth being that it is
only by Acts of Parliament that men in large communities can
be made moral, even when they want to); or the American
ruffian hand over his revolver and bowie knife to be used for
him by a policeman or soldier; or the American liar and
braggart adopt the tone of the newspaper, the pulpit, and the
platform; or the American idolater write authorized
biographies of millionaires; or the American sensualist secure
the patronage of all the Muses for his pornography.

Howbeit, Poe remains homeless. There is nothing at all
like him in America: nothing, at all events, visible across the
Atlantic. At that distance we can see Whistler plainly enough,
and Mark Twain. But Whistler was very American in some
ways: so American that nobody but another American could
possibly have written his adventures and gloried in them
without reserve. Mark Twain, resembling Dickens in his
combination of public spirit and irresistible literary power
with a congenital incapacity for lying and bragging, and a

congenital hatred of waste and cruelty, remains American by
the local color of his stories. There is a further difference. Both
Mark Twain and Whistler are as Philistine as Dickens and
Thackeray. The appalling thing about Dickens, the greatest of
the Victorians, is that in his novels there is nothing personal
to live for except eating, drinking, and pretending to be
happily married. For him the great synthetic ideals do not
exist, any more than the great preludes and toccatas of Bach,
the symphonies of Beethoven, the paintings of Giotto and
Mantegna, Velasquez and Rembrandt. Instead of being heir to
all the ages, he came into a comparatively small and smutty
literary property bequeathed by Smollett and Fielding. His
criticism of Fechter's Hamlet, and his use of a speech of
Macbeth's to illustrate the character of Mrs. Macstinger, shew
how little Shakespeare meant to him. Thackeray is even worse:
the notions of painting he picked up at Heatherley's school
were further from the mark than Dickens' ignorance; he is
equally in the dark as to music; and though he did not, when
he wished to be enormously pleasant and jolly, begin, like
Dickens, to describe the gorgings and guzzlings which make
Christmas our annual national disgrace, that is rather because
he never does want to be enormously pleasant and jolly than
because he has any higher notions of personal enjoyment. The
truth is that neither Dickens nor Thackeray would be tolerable
were it not that life is an end in itself and a means to nothing
but its own perfection; consequently any man who describes
life vividly will entertain us, however uncultivated the life he
describes may be. Mark Twain has lived long enough to
become a much better philosopher than either Dickens or
Thackeray: for instance, when he immortalized General
Funston by scalping him, he did it scientifically, knowing
exactly what he meant right down to the foundation in the
natural history of human character. Also, he got from the
Mississippi something that Dickens could not get from

Chatham and Pentonville. But he wrote A Yankee at the Court of King Arthur just as Dickens wrote A Child's History of England. For the ideal of Catholic chivalry he had nothing but derision; and he exhibited it, not in conflict with reality, as Cervantes did, but in conflict with the prejudices of a Philistine compared to whom Sancho Panza is an Admirable Crichton, an Abelard, even a Plato. Also, he described Lohengrin as "a shivaree" though he liked the wedding chorus; and this shews that Mark, like Dickens, was not properly educated; for Wagner would have been just the man for him if he had been trained to understand and use music as Mr. Rockefeller was trained to understand and use money. America did not teach him the language of the great ideals, just as England did not teach it to Dickens and Thackeray. Consequently, though nobody can suspect Dickens or Mark Twain of lacking the qualities and impulses that are the soul of such grotesque makeshift bodies as Church and State, Chivalry, Classicism, Art, Gentility, and the Holy Roman Empire; and nobody blames them for seeing that these bodies were mostly so decomposed as to have become intolerable nuisances, you have only to compare them with Carlyle and Ruskin, or with Euripides and Aristophanes, to see how, for want of a language of art and a body of philosophy, they were so much more interested in the fun and pathos of personal adventure than in the comedy and tragedy of human destiny.

Whistler was a Philistine, too. Outside the corner of art in which he was a virtuoso and a propagandist, he was a Man of Derision. Important as his propaganda was, and admired as his work was, no society could assimilate him. He could not even induce a British jury to award him substantial damages against a rich critic who had "done him out of his job"; and this is certainly the climax of social failure in England.

Edgar Allan Poe was not in the least a Philistine. He wrote always as if his native Boston was Athens, his Charlottesville

University Plato's Academy, and his cottage the crown of the heights of Fiesole. He was the greatest journalistic critic of his time, placing good European work at sight when the European critics were waiting for somebody to tell them what to say. His poetry is so exquisitely refined that posterity will refuse to believe that it belongs to the same civilization as the glory of Mrs. Julia Ward Howe's lilies or the honest doggerel of Whittier. Tennyson, who was nothing if not a virtuoso, never produced a success that will bear reading after Poe's failures. Poe constantly and inevitably produced magic where his greatest contemporaries produced only beauty. Tennyson's popular pieces, The May Queen and The Charge of the Six Hundred, cannot stand hackneying: they become positively nauseous after a time. The Raven, The Bells, and Annabel Lee are as fascinating at the thousandth repetition as at the first.

Poe's supremacy in this respect has cost him his reputation. This is a phenomenon which occurs when an artist achieves such perfection as to place himself *hors concours*. The greatest painter England ever produced is Hogarth, a miraculous draughtsman and an exquisite and poetic colorist. But he is never mentioned by critics. They talk copiously about Romney, the Gibson of his day; freely about Reynolds; nervously about the great Gainsborough; and not at all about Rowlandson and Hogarth, missing the inextinguishable grace of Rowlandson because they assume that all caricatures of this period are ugly, and avoiding Hogarth instinctively as critically unmanageable. In the same way, we have given up mentioning Poe: that is why the Americans forgot him when they posted up the names of their great in their Pantheon. Yet his is the first–almost the only name that the real connoisseur looks for.

But Poe, for all his virtuosity, is always a poet, and never a mere virtuoso. Poe put forward his Eureka, the formulation of his philosophy, as the most important thing he had done. His

poems always have the universe as their background. So have
the figures in his stories. Even in his tales of humor, which we
shake our heads at as mistakes, they have this elemental
quality. Toby Dammit himself, though his very name turns up
the nose of the cultured critic, is more impressive and his end
more tragic than the serious inventions of most story-tellers.
The short-sighted gentleman who married his grandmother is
no common butt of a common purveyor of the facetious: the
grandmother has the elegance and free mind of Ninon de
l'Enclos, the grandson the *tenue* of a marquis. This story was
sent by Poe to Horne, whose Orion he had reviewed as poetry
ought to be reviewed, with a request that it might be sold to an
English magazine. The English magazine regretted that the
deplorable immorality of the story made it for ever impossible
in England!

In his stories of mystery and imagination Poe created a
world-record for the English language: perhaps for all the
languages. The story of the Lady Ligeia is not merely one of
the wonders of literature: it is unparalleled and unapproached.
There is really nothing to be said about it: we others simply
take off our hats and let Mr. Poe go first. It is interesting to
compare Poe's stories with William Morris'. Both are not
merely stories: they are complete works of art, like prayer
carpets; and they are, in Poe's phrase, stories of imagination.
They are masterpieces of style: what people call Macaulay's
style is by comparison a mere method. But they are more
different than it seems possible for two art works in the same
kind to be. Morris will have nothing to do with mystery.
"Ghost stories," he used to say, "have all the same explanation:
the people are telling lies." His Sigurd has the beauty of
mystery as it has every other sort of beauty, being, as it is,
incomparably the greatest English epic; but his stories are in
the open from end to end, whilst in Poe's stories the sun
never shines.

Poe's limitation was his aloofness from the common
people. Grotesques, negroes, madmen with delirium tremens,
even gorillas, take the place of ordinary peasants and courtiers,
citizens and soldiers, in his theatre. His houses are haunted
houses, his woods enchanted woods; and he makes them so
real that reality itself cannot sustain the comparison. His
kingdom is not of this world.

Above all, Poe is great because he is independent of cheap
attractions, independent of sex, of patriotism, of fighting, of
sentimentality, snobbery, gluttony, and all the rest of the vulgar
stock-in-trade of his profession. This is what gives him his
superb distinction. One vulgarized thing, the pathos of dying
children, he touched in Annabel Lee, and devulgarized it at
once. He could not even amuse himself with detective stories
without purifying the atmosphere of them until they became
more edifying than most of Hymns, Ancient and Modern. His
verse sometimes alarms and puzzles the reader by fainting
with its own beauty; but the beauty is never the beauty of the
flesh. You never say to him as you have to say uneasily to so
many modern artists: "Yes, my friend, but these are things that
men and women should *live* and not write about. Literature is
not a keyhole for people with starved affections to peep
through at the banquets of the body." It never became one in
Poe's hands. Life cannot give you what he gives you except
through fine art; and it was his instinctive observance of this
distinction, and the fact that it did not beggar him, as it would
beggar most writers, that makes him the most legitimate, the
most classical, of modern writers.

It also explains why America does not care much for him,
and why he has hardly been mentioned in England these
many years. America and England are wallowing in the
sensuality which their immense increase of riches has placed
within their reach. I do not blame them: sensuality is a very
necessary and healthy and educative element in life.

Unfortunately, it is ill distributed; and our reading masses are
looking on at it and thinking about it and longing for it, and
having precarious little holiday treats of it, instead of sharing it
temperately and continuously, and ceasing to be preoccupied
with it. When the distribution is better adjusted and the
preoccupation ceases, there will be a noble reaction in favor of
the great writers like Poe, who begin just where the world, the
flesh, and the devil leave off.

George Bernard Shaw (1856–1950), a British playwright and critic, was one
of the leading literary figures of London society at the turn of the century. A
prolific writer of both popular and satirical plays, Shaw was awarded the
Nobel Prize for Literature for his work, including *Arms and the Man*,
Candida, and *Pygmalion*.

Edgar Allan Poe

BY

WILLIAM CARLOS WILLIAMS

POE WAS NOT "a fault of nature," "a find for French eyes," ripe but unaccountable, as through our woollyheadedness we've sought to designate him, but a genius intimately shaped by his locality and time. It is to save our faces that we've given him a crazy reputation, a writer from whose classic accuracies we have not known how else to escape.

The false emphasis was helped by his Parisian vogue and tonal influence on Baudelaire, but the French mind was deeper hit than that. Poe's work strikes by its scrupulous originality, *not* "originality" in the bastard sense, but in its legitimate sense of solidity which goes back to the ground, a conviction that he *can judge* within himself. These things the French were *ready* to perceive and quick to use to their advantage: a new point from which to readjust the trigonometric measurements of literary form.

It is the New World, or to leave that for the better term, it is a *new locality* that is in Poe assertive; it is America, the first great burst through to expression of a re-awakened genius of *place*. . . . The local causes shaping [his] genius were two in character: the necessity for a fresh beginning, backed by a native vigor of extraordinary proportions,—with the corollary, that all "colonial imitation" must be swept aside. This was the conscious force which rose in Poe as innumerable timeless insights resulting, by his genius, in firm statements on the character of form, profusely illustrated by his practices; and, *second* the immediate effect of the locality upon the first, upon his nascent impulses, upon his original thrusts; tormenting the depths into a surface of bizarre designs by which he's known and which are *not at all* the major point in question.

Yet BOTH influences were determined by the locality, which, in the usual fashion, finds its mind swayed by the results of its stupidity rather than by a self-interest bred of greater wisdom. As with all else in America, the value of Poe's genius to OURSELVES must be *uncovered* from our droppings, or at least uncovered from the "protection" which it must have raised about itself to have survived in any form among us–where everything is quickly trampled.

Poe "saw the end"; unhappily he saw his own despair at the same time, yet he continued to attack, with amazing genius seeking to discover, and discovering, points of firmness by which to STAND and grasp, against the slipping way they had of holding on in his locality. Either the New World must be mine as I will have it, or it is a worthless bog. There can be no concession. His attack was *from the center out*. Either I exist or I do not exist and no amount of pap which I happen to be lapping can dull me to the loss. It was a doctrine, anti-American. Here everything was makeshift, everything was colossal, in profusion. The frightened hogs or scared birds feeding on the corn– It left, in 1840, the same mood as ever dominant among us. Take what you can get. What you lack, copy. It was a population puffed with braggadocio, whom Poe so beautifully summarizes in many of his prose tales. . . .

Lowell, Bryant, etc., concerned poetry with literature, Poe concerned it with the soul; hence their differing conceptions of the use of language. With Poe, words were not hung by usage with associations, the pleasing wraiths of former masteries, this is the sentimental trap-door to beginnings. With Poe words were figures; an old language truly, but one from which he carried over only the most elemental qualities to his new purpose; which was, to find a way to tell his soul. Sometimes he used words so playfully his sentences seem to fly away from sense, the destructive! with the conserving abandon, foreshadowed, of a Gertrude Stein. The particles of language must be clear as sand. (See *Diddling*.) [V, 210–13]

This was an impossible conception for the gluey imagination of his day. Constantly he labored to detach SOMETHING from the inchoate mass– That's it:

His concern, the apex of his immaculate attack, was to detach a "method" from the smear of common usage–it is the work of nine tenths of his criticism. He struck to lay low the "*niaiseries*" of form and content with which his world abounded. It was a machine-gun fire; even in the slaughter of banality he rises to a merciless distinction. (See *Rufus Dawes*.) [XI, 131] He sought by stress upon construction to hold the loose-strung mass off even at the cost of an icy coldness of appearance; it was the first need of his time, an escape from the formless mass he hated. It is the very sense of a beginning, as *it is the impulse which drove him to the character of all his tales*; to get from sentiment to form, a backstroke from the swarming "population."

He has a habit, borrowed perhaps from algebra, of balancing his sentences in the middle, or of reversing them in the later clauses, a sense of play, as with objects, or numerals which he *has* in the original, disassociated, that is, from other literary habit; separate words which he feels and turns about as if he fitted them to his design with *some* sense of their individual quality: "those who belong properly to books, and to whom books, perhaps, do not quite so properly belong."

The strong sense of a beginning in Poe is in *no one* else before him. What he says, being thoroughly local in origin, has some chance of being universal in application, a thing they never dared conceive. . . . The difficulty is in holding the mind down to the point of seeing the *beginning* difference between Poe and the rest. One cannot expect to see as wide a gap between him and the others as exists between the Greek and the Chinese. It is only in the conception of a *possibility*

that he is most distinguished. His greatness is in that he
turned his back and faced inland, to originality, with the
identical gesture of a Boone.

And for *that* reason he is unrecognized. Americans have
never recognized themselves. How can they? It is impossible
until someone invents the ORIGINAL terms. As long as we are
content to be called by somebody else's terms, we are
incapable of being anything but our own dupes. . . . it is
precisely here that lies Hawthorne's lack of importance to our
literature when he is compared with Poe; what Hawthorne
loses by his willing closeness to the life of his locality in its
vague humors; his lifelike copying of the New England
melancholy; his reposeful closeness to the town pump—
Poe *gains* by abhorring; flying to the ends of the earth
for "original" material—

By such a simple, logical twist does Poe succeed in being
the more American, heeding more the local necessities, the
harder structural imperatives—by standing off to SEE instead of
forcing himself too close. Whereas Hawthorne, in his tales, by
doing what everyone else in France, England, Germany was
doing *for his own milieu*, is no more than copying their
method with another setting; does not ORIGINATE; has not a
beginning literature at heart that must establish its own
rules, own framework,—Poe has realized by adopting a more
elevated mien.

This feeling in Poe's tales, that is, the hidden, under,
unapparent part, gives him the firmness of INSIGHT into the
conditions upon which our literature must rest, always the
same, a local one, surely, but not of sentiment or mood, as not
of trees and Indians, but of original fibre, the normal
toughness which fragility of mood presupposes, if it will be
expressive of anything— It is the expression of Poe's clearness of insight into the true difficulty, and his soundness
of judgment.

To understand what Poe is driving at in his tales, one should read first NOT the popular, perfect – *Gold-Bug*, *Murders in the Rue Morgue*, etc., which by their brilliancy detract from the observation of his deeper intent, but the less striking tales – in fact all, but especially those where his humor is less certain, his mood lighter, less tightly bound by the incident, where numerous illuminating *faults* are allowed to become expressive, *The Business Man*, *The Man That Was Used Up*, *Loss of Breath*, *BonBon*, *Diddling*, *The Angel of the Odd* – and others of his lesser Tales.

It should be noted how often certain things take place – how often there is death but not that only; it is the body broken apart, dismembered, as in *Loss of Breath* – [II, 151–67]

Then, as in *Hop-Frog, The System of Dr. Tarr and Professor Fether* and the *Murders in the Rue Morgue* – the recurrent image of the ape. Is it his disgust with his immediate associates and his own fears, which cause this frequent use of the figure to create the emotion of extreme terror? –"Your majesty cannot conceive of the *effect* produced, at a masquerade, by eight chained orang-outangs, imagined to be real ones by the most of the company; and rushing in with savage cries, among the crowd of delicately and gorgeously habited men and women. The contrast is inimitable." [VI, 223]

Note, in *Silence – a Fable*: "sorrow and weariness and disgust with mankind and a longing for solitude." [II, 222]

Many colloquial words could be detached from Poe's usage if it were worth while, to show how the language he practices varies from English, but such an exercise would be of little value – *hipped, crack*, etc. – it does not touch bottom.

The Tales continue the theories of the criticism, carrying out what they propose:

1. In choice of material, abstract. 2. In method, a logical construction that clips away, in great part, the "scenery" near at hand in order to let the real business of composition *show*.

3. A primitive awkwardness of diction, lack of polish, colloquialism that is, unexpectedly, especially in the dialogues, much in the vein of Mark Twain.

One feels that in the actual composition of his tales there must have been for him, as they embody it in fact, a fascination other than the topical one. The impulse that made him write them, that made him enjoy writing them – cannot have been the puerile one of amazement, but a deeper, logical enjoyment, in keeping with his own seriousness: it is that of PROVING even the most preposterous of his inventions plausible – that BY HIS METHOD he makes them WORK. They go: they *prove* him potent, they confirm his thought. And by the very extreme of their play, by so much the more do they hold up the actuality of that which he conceives. . . .

Of his method in the Tales, the significance and the secret is: authentic particles, a thousand of which spring to the mind for quotation, taken apart and reknit with a view to emphasize, enforce and make evident, the *method*. Their quality of skill in observation, their heat, local verity, being *overshadowed* only by the detached, the abstract, the cold philosophy of their joining together; a method springing so freshly from the local conditions which determine it, by their emphasis of firm crudity and lack of coordinated structure, as to be worthy of most painstaking study – The whole period, America 1840, could be rebuilt, psychologically (phrenologically) from Poe's "method."

William Carlos Williams (1883–1963) was an American poet, essayist, and novelist, as well as a physician who maintained a life-long practice in his New Jersey hometown. He won the Pulitzer Prize in 1962 for his collection of poems entitled *Pictures from Breughel.*